Aleck Hunter and Erik Kirschbaum

SWIM + BIKE + RUN

Triathlon – the Sporting trinity

London

GEORGE ALLEN & UNWIN

Boston   Sydney

George Allen & Unwin (Publishers) Ltd,
40 Museum Street, London WC1A 1LU, UK

George Allen & Unwin (Publishers) Ltd,
Park Lane, Hemel Hempstead, Herts HP2 4TE, UK

Allen & Unwin Inc.,
9 Winchester Terrace, Winchester, Mass 01890, USA

George Allen & Unwin Australia Pty Ltd.
8 Napier Street, North Sydney, NSW 2060, Australia

First published 1985

ISBN 0–04–796–107–4

Set in 11 on 13 point Palatino by Computape (Pickering) Ltd
and printed in Great Britain by Hazell Watson and Viney, Aylesbury, Bucks.

Contents

Introduction

There is it seems a razor-thin line in our society between what is considered fabulous and what is considered foolhardy, between what is perceived as madness and what is perceived as brilliance. What is the difference?

Some people think of triathletes as insane to push their bodies to such limits. Some people think it's fabulous that athletes and nonathletes alike are shedding their industrial world neckties and obesity to return their bodies to a more natural state. What is it that is so alluring about the triathlon? Why are so many people, people who in their lives have never so much as run for a bus, suddenly running and swimming and biking countless miles?

Contemplate, for a moment, the view of a seagull passing by at the start of a triathlon. There they are, assembled at a beach somewhere down below, shivering already even before these nearly naked humans have even put a single foot into the water. They stand around down there, with bright orange rubber skin on their heads, and funny-looking bubbles on their eyes. And then suddenly they run into the ocean, dashing ahead not unlike suicidal lemmings.

They run not only blindly, but enthusiastically to what could be their death. They swim rapidly out to sea. They were not made to swim; they have no gills, they have no fins. But there they go, foolishly trying to do something they aren't naturally equipped to do. Higher culture, huh?

An hour or so later, they begin to stumble awkwardly out of the water, some falling back down the minute they stand up out of the water. Their hands shake uncontrollably. They can't see straight. Some ask where their bikes are even though they are standing right in front of them and looking straight at them.

Some pedal for five hours into punishing headwinds, and up jagged mountain tops. Some need 10 hours. This is no leisure cycling. They are grunting. And they are moaning. And, as incredible as it seems to the seagull, they say they love it.

Then they have to run. Their bodies are already ready for bed. But they have to run, and not just around the block. Two, three, four, five or even six hours they must run. In pain. They are of course elated when it's over. But they are even happier to have done it. They have spent a day hovering on this fine line between madness and excellence. It's the struggle they enjoy, the fight to survive. There is something potent in there, something intoxicating indeed.

I am indebted most to my co-author Aleck Hunter who inspired the whole project. He persuaded me to cross the Atlantic and then provided me with five star accommodation so that we could work in harmony. Without him, this book would never have been completed. Dr Luise Parsons kindly checked the medical information and I am also grateful for the ideas, criticism and direction of our able editor, Derek Wyatt.

Last, but not least, a big thanks to the countless triathletes who shared their tips, advice and problems, who whether they realised it or not, were writing many of the pages within.
E.K.

The publishers wish to thank Ken Pyne for the amusing cartoons and Richard Francis (All Action Photographic), Adrian Murrell (All Sport) and Veronica Trew for the photographs. Especial thanks are due to Prentice-Hall Inc for permission to reproduce the swimming diagrams taken from James E. Counsilman's *The Science of Swimming*.

PART I

The Triathlon – A Balanced Sport

Chapter 1

Opening Up

'There's nothing else like it,' laughed seventy year-old Bob Robinson after crossing the finishing line at a triathlon race one summer's day in 1984. 'There's something just mystical about this sport.'

There is indeed nothing else quite like the triathlon; it is the ultimate fitness sport. Somehow, too, it has captured the imagination of a restless populace in the United States, and within a few years it has created an entirely new type of athlete. It has become the most exciting mass participant sport in existence, outshining even the 'fun runs' for its enthusiastic participants.

And, fortunately, as with the transported success of the mass marathon, that magic quality has also captivated European athletes as well. No one, it seems, who has given the triathlon a try, has not plunged further into it.

'It's a fantastic sport,' says Chip Rimmer of Reading. 'I thoroughly enjoy it. I just can't seem to get enough of it. It's absolutely the best possible sport I could imagine.'

One of the most attractive aspects of the triathlon is its thorough conditioning of the entire body. All the major muscle groups of the body are challenged in the triathlon, from the head down through the arms and back to the legs. What is more, the triathlon offers seemingly limitless room for improvement. Triathletes often find that not just seconds or minutes drop off their times, as in the case with runners or recreational bowlers who reach plateaux that seem impossible to improve on, but quarters, halves, and even full hours melt away from their performance times in an almost unbelievably short time. Even marathon runners who have drifted into the world of the triathlon find that their marathon performances are being improved – not damaged – by supplementing, even substituting parts of their running training with swimming or cycling work-outs. Sebastian Coe, for one, used cycling to maintain his

fitness level. Alberto Salazar and Rob DeCastella, two of the world's fastest marathoners, swim regularly.

There are dozens of possible reasons for the triathlon's becoming so popular so quickly. But the principal one is that people around the world have found swimming, bicycling and running to be the ideal combination of aerobic exercise, training, toning and conditioning the body better than anything else.

The triathlon lets people search for, and discover their limits. The sport not only demands fitness, it gives it as well. It develops the entire body, leaves no one muscle group in atrophy. It also develops the heart, the lungs, and the entire cardiovascular system, strengthening the vital organs like no other training can. Triathlons are also relatively injury-free, precisely because the work load is so widely distributed. It can even improve your sex life because in addition to

improving the condition of your heart and lungs the awareness of your senses improves the fitter you become.

But perhaps the most enticing aspect of the sport is that anyone can take part. Born as the triathlon was, in the United States, with its lack of class distinctions or social taboos, the sport can be enjoyed by anyone from stevedores labourers to brain surgeons. It is, happily, a sport for everyone.

It is a sport for the former school athlete who is looking for new arenas of fitness, new challenges and camaraderie. It is a sport also for the non-sports person, the person who has never in his or her life participated in any sport, but who is now in search of well-rounded fitness.

'There was a triathlon in Mansfield, a short course with a 400 yard swim, and there were lots of Mrs Joe Bloggses there,' notes Sarah Springman, a 28 year old PhD student from Cambridge University. 'They were thoroughly enjoying themselves. They were laughing and smiling more than they had in the previous month. They felt a tremendous sense of satisfaction to have finished. And they weren't Mrs Joe Bloggs anymore. A lot of women have liberated themselves through the running movement, and a lot more will hopefully be liberated through the triathlon.'

The sport is also a new and greater challenge for athletes who have had success, or narrowly missed success, in other sports. They are searching for new challenges, new triumphs, and perhaps even finding out what their ultimate limits are. Top, mediocre, and even poor athletes from a wide range of sporting backgrounds are switching to the sport. There are even former Olympic athletes, coming from sports that have absolutely nothing to do with swimming, biking, or running.

Top marathoners, deep sea divers, hockey players, former basketball stars, and cricketers are all giving the triathlon a try – and liking what they find. So are motor-cycle salesmen, pilots, policemen and policewomen, dentists, doctors and ski instructors, writers, models and pool attendants, housewives, midwives and fire-fighters, psychologists, newsagents, hat clerks and shipping clerks, all of whom have discovered the triathlon.

From a mere idea in the early 1970s to a sport with more than a half million active participants in half a decade has there ever been a sport that has grown so fast? In 1984 the sport came so close to being named an Olympic event that it seems assured of being included in the near future.

A further contributing factor in the success of the triathlon may be the very newness of the sport. Triathlons are not bound or restricted by rules and traditions. There are no obtrusive governing bodies. There is no rule book, no zealous organisations seeking to complicate the sport. The only rules, in fact, say that you, alone, have to swim, cycle and run the distances without aid. Period. And there is even something elementally delightful too, most observers concur, about watching triathletes bare their bottoms in public after the swim. The triathlon, then, is an invention of the twentieth century, that obeys the rules of the twentieth century. At last, Britain has a post-Victorian sport for the masses.

A further confirmation of the break with tradition is that triathlons are open equally for men and women. There is no sort of sex barrier, nor has there ever been. Even the notion that women might be excluded, or in certain instances handicapped, sounds somehow laughable. Similarly there is also no age barrier, nor limits, as Bob Robinson at seventy so clearly demonstrates each time he trots smiling across a finish line.

Apart from the initial Hawaii Ironman Competition in 1978, when only fifteen men took part (no women applied for entry) there has not been a triathlon where women have been forbidden from participating. Indeed, if anything, there exists the occasional triathlon which excludes men. Fortunately there are only a handful of such women-only triathlons, for the sport has proven to be such an equalizer of the sexes that women are enjoying phenomenal success against the men, including winning an occasional triathlon outright. On January 15, 1984, Jacqueline Shaw, of Calgary in Canada won the Maui Triathlon in Kaanapali, Hawaii, defeating a field of 58 mostly male competitors. Jann Girard, of Austin, Texas, has won three triathlons against large fields of men, including an Ironman distance triathlon in Texas, and the Western Kentucky (half Ironman distance), and a third half Ironman distance triathlon.

Unlike the struggles women long-distance runners have had to contend with, women triathletes have been regarded from the outset with no trace of discrimination at all and they are demonstrating to more than a few men that women are as capable – and in some cases *more* capable – of performing outstanding feats over long endurance distances. At the 1984 Nice World Championship the first women finishers, Colleen Cannon and Julie Moss, finished sixteenth and seventeenth respectively, in front of nearly 400 men.

The triathlon is the antithesis of other sports. Where most sports evolve from a small to a larger scale over decades, if not centuries, the triathlon began with a boom – the 1978 Ironman in Hawaii with its immortalised distances of 2.4 miles swimming, 112 cycling, and 26.2 running – and has spread around the world to smaller events. It is not unlike the 'Big Bang' theory.

Chapter 2

A new sport

The birth of any new sport will always be accompanied by a certain amount of legend. The triathlon is no exception. Legend tells us that there was, once upon a time, a US naval officer by the name of John Collins. He was, the story goes, having a few beers with a few colleagues one day when the discussion turned to who was the fittest athlete of them all: a swimmer, a biker or a runner.

In the discussion, the swimmer claimed to be the fittest. Years and years of aerobic training in the pool is the best possible base. The biker also claimed to be the fittest. Thousands of miles not only builds up endurance capabilities, but lungs are enlarged and tolerance to pain is enhanced as well. Naturally the runner claimed he, too, was the fittest. It was an endless argument, thought, at first, to be a virtually insolvable dispute.

But why was it unsolvable? asked Commander Collins. Hawaii already had three classic distance events. Why not string the three ultimate endurance challenges together and see which athlete could win the ultimate endurance race: the 2.4 miles Waikiki Rough Water swim, the 112 mile Around Oahu bike race, and the Honolulu Marathon.

'I remember the first night John Collins told us about this idea of an Ironman contest,' recalls Peggy Trask, a member of the same Masters swimming club that Collins belongs to. 'He came up with it at the club's Fall banquet in October 1977. Everyone was rolling on the floor laughing, but Collins said "I've got 11 people willing to try it".'

Fifteen college students, military personnel, and a few professional people lined up one drizzling morning, 18 February 1978. At 7.19 am they plunged into the surf off Waikiki. History, as they say, had been made.

Nearly twelve hours later, Gordon Haller, a 27 year old naval officer, crossed the finish line first. His prize was an odd-looking trophy made of iron pipes, which Collins had brazed together himself. The race has changed since then, but not the trophy.

Fourteen of the original fifteen starters completed the race. The following year, fifteen again took part, including the event's first woman competitor, Lyn Lemaire, of Boston, who finished in 12:55:38, beating many of the men. Thirty-five year old Tom Warren won the event in 11:15:56. In 1979 the race was covered by *Sports Illustrated*. Although it may not have an enormous circulation, it is read by influential people. Someone from ABC television saw the article and plenty of athletes read it as well for, in the 1980 race, 108 people lined up to try their luck at the event, which by then had officially become known as the 'Ironman'. (The race became the 'International Triathlon' in 1981, but the race director, Valerie Silk, was besieged with letters from outraged triathletes, who wanted the name to remain Ironman. She acquiesced.)

An ABC television crew had been sent to Hawaii to take some footage of the event, to see how it looked on film. Stormy weather forced the organisers of the race (by this point Commander Collins had relinquished the organisational headaches to a Honolulu chain of fitness centres) to move the swim from Waikiki to a calmer spot in Ala Moana Park. It was still rough water, so rough that no boats could navigate the high seas, but the adverse conditions only served to heighten the drama. The film footage, when shown on television, was spectacular.

The year 1980 was also the year in which Dave Scott, a 26 year old Master swim coach from Davis, California first took part in the race. 'I first heard about the race in '78', he recalls. 'I was over in Oahu doing a Rough Water swim and had read about the Ironman in *Sports Illustrated*. At the time, I thought, my gosh, that's inconceivable. I thought it sounded pretty bizarre. I hadn't done any cycling at all, and only a little running on my own. A friend sort of conned me into it.'

Scott had swum the 500-metre and 1500-metre races in college, and had played water polo as well. He had never really met tremendous success, however, until he tried the triathlon. He began biking seriously, and running seriously too, upping his weekly mileage from 30 to 60 miles. He won the 1980 Ironman, his first, in 9:24. It was 1:51 faster than the previous course best.

ABC was astounded as well. The Ironman coverage was ranked as that station's 'most popular program of the year'. Suddenly, everyone seemed to want to do the Ironman, wanted to swim miles, bike hundreds of miles, and run marathons. It touched off a craze such as the USA had not seen since the hula-hoop.

Balding men, overweight housewives, doctors, students, factory workers, diabetics and polio victims suddenly began queuing up for entry blanks.

No fewer than 326 – triple the number of the previous year – were on the starting line for the 1981 race. The one notable absence was Scott, who had injured his knee running hard in training.

By this point, the race had grown too large for the densely populated island of Oahu, so the race director, Valerie Silk, decided to move it to the sparsely populated 'Big Island' or 'Hawaii' itself.

The 1981 race proved to be the watershed year for the sport in the United States. Overnight, it changed from a sport on the fringe of the establishment to a major spectacle. It also marked the birth of a martyr. And martyrs are not easily forgotten.

The marathon of course had a celebrated history long before it had become a sport run by the masses. It had legend, that of Pheidippides, the Greek warrior who supposedly ran the 23½ miles between the village of Marathon and Athens, with the news, 'Rejoice, We Conquer'. He then collapsed, the legend goes, and died.

The marathon race also had its martyr, the Italian runner Dorando Pietri. When the marathon was revived for the first modern Olympics in Greece in 1896, the course length was 23.5 miles. When the 1908 Olympics were held in London, Queen Alexandria had the course route extended by 2.7 miles so that her children could watch the start from their window in Windsor Castle and watch the finish directly in front of the Queen's box as well. Pietri had won the 23.5 mile race many times before. He was comfortably in the lead also at 23.5 miles on that fateful day in 1908 and was still leading after 26 miles, but by this point he was in trouble. His energy stores had been spent. As he entered the stadium with less than 200 yards separating him from the gold medal, he began to stumble. He collapsed repeatedly, and was still more than 100 yards from the finish line when the second place runner, Johnny Hayes of the United States, entered the stadium. The drama was a non-pareil. Pietri began frantically to crawl towards the finish line. A zealous police officer picked the Italian off the ground, and he managed to stagger across the finish line just ahead of Hayes. The crowd went berserk.

But Pietri was denied the gold medal, being disqualified for receiving the aid. Hayes was awarded the gold medal, and the Queen, perhaps embarrassed at the extra torturing distance she had added, awarded the recuperating Pietri a special award, a gold cup. But it was not Johnny Hayes whom those who saw that spectacle remembered. It was Dorando Pietri. All at once the 26.2 mile distance became immortalised as the standard distance. The marathon had finally found its martyr.

The triathlon did not have to wait 2,300 years for its martyr. It took just six. A mere 20 yards from victory at the 1982 Ironman, Julie Moss collapsed. Like Pheidippides and Pietri before her, she had pushed herself to a point beyond where the body can obey a mind determined and set on an unalterable course. There is something intangible about this uncanny drive, this thirst that is satiated only by completion of superhuman deeds and which leads to near self-mutilation and yet, at the same time, captivates the imagination of observers and participants alike.

Thanks to television, this contemporary martyr was not only recorded on film but her collapse and heroic crawl to the finish line were beamed into living rooms around the world. The sight of a woman, with faeces running down her leg, valiantly crawling towards the finish line, in a state of such utter exhaustion that the body refused to go any further, proved to be great television.' And it proved to be a great event too for the triathlon for after that the triathlon boom almost literally exploded.

Julie Moss herself, a 22 year old student, became a celebrity throughout the country, and throughout the world. Triathlons began springing up all over the USA. A few were the same distance as Hawaii, but most were considerably shorter, most often under half the distances of Hawaii. Few were organised without minor, and sometimes major, hitches. But even mis-directed, or lost, racers, racers who received no water, or triathletes whose shoes were misplaced, never seemed to be discouraged enough to give up the sport. The growing pains were considerable; but most who started the sport stuck with it. Despite the gremlins that haunted the first races and race directors alike, the triathlon continued to expand.

Runners, particularly bored runners, began flocking into the sport. At one time an estimated 70 per cent of all triathletes were originally runners. Many of the same people who jumped on to the fitness craze of the 1970s in the United States leaped into the triathlon. Many others, who had never done anything athletic in their lives, were suddenly swept up by enthusiasm for the triathlon.

Veronica Baker, of Nottingham, was living in San Jose, California for three years while her husband worked for a computer programmer there. She had never participated in a single athletic endeavour in her life, and yet when she first saw a triathlon, she was hooked. She did a Bonne Bell triathlon, exclusively for women, and fell permanently in love with the sport.

'It was tremendous,' she recalled. 'I loved it. I absolutely loved it. The spirit was great. I just wish there were as many women doing triathlons in England as there are in the U.S.'

All sorts of other athletes began pouring into the sport as well. Olympic bike racers, Olympic speed skaters like Eric and Beth Heiden, Olympic swimmers, Olympic bi-athletes (cross-country skiing and shooting). By 1984 there were an estimated 500,000 active triathletes, participating in 2,000 events in the United States alone.

Running magazines began devoting considerable space to the triathlon, as did cycling and swimming magazines. Magazines devoted exclusively to the triathlon also began appearing in 1982 and 1983. Within a few months of their birth, the magazines actually began turning a profit, unheard of in the American publishing industry where three or five years is regarded as the normal period of deficit apprenticeship.

Books on the subject began to appear and triathlon training camps turned up all over the country. 'Triathlon Conditioning' was the title of a course offered at the California State University at Northridge.

All sorts of variations on the triathlon began to evolve as well. An 'Escape from Alcatraz Island' triathlon, from the rock island a mile out in the middle of San Francisco Bay which was once reputably the world's most escape-proof prison, was one such endeavour which was followed by mountain climbing triathlons, indoor triathlons (in a pool, on an indoor track and indoor cycling machines) triathlons with swims in lakes, oceans and even swimming pools. Triathlons have been staged with distances as short as a 50 yard run, 25 yard swim, and 400 yard bike ride. On the other hand some ultra long distance triathlons were strung out over three days, with a 5 mile swim, a 224 mile bike ride, and a 54 mile run.

The state of Minnesota, which is approximately 400 miles from north to south, has 12,000 lakes within its borders. Every summer the state stages a border to border triathlon run over a weekend. Solo triathlete, Chris Chambers, staged a triathlon of his own when he swam 10 miles, biked 216 miles and ran 104 miles across Death Valley in California, where ground temperature reached 180 degrees. He did it all in less than three days.

The birth of the United States triathlon series in 1982 added further momentum to the snowballing popularity of the sport. By staging triathlons across the country with uniform distances of 2,000 metre swims, 40 kilometre bike rides, and 15 kilometre runs, distances which the organisers felt could be completed by any reasonably fit athlete, they hoped to attract even more people to the sport.

The races proved to be a success beyond the hopes and aspirations of everyone involved. The first year had five races, primarily in West Coast cities. By 1983, twelve cities across the country had races, from St Petersburg (Florida) to Seattle, to Chicago and New York City, and in San Diego. More than 6,000 people took part. The following year, 1984, the races were shortened to a 1,500 metre swim, 40 kilometre bike ride and a 10 kilometre run so that even more could take part.

The Ironman did not suffer from this, instead it continued to grow at a fast pace. In October 1982 a second race was held following the February 1982 race, because many European and East Coast triathletes had complained that a February race left them at a considerable disadvantage. Rather than wait a year and a half, therefore, it was decided to stage a second 1982 race. 700 people applied for the first 1982 race. It took the last two finishers 24 hours, but 542 out of the 580 who started finished. By June of 1982, 850 had applied for the October 1982 race. In 1983 there were also 850. For the 1984 race, 1153 started, which the organisers said would be the uppermost limit that the course could logistically handle.

The excitement of the triathlon has not been lost on the rest of the world. The first triathlon in Europe was in Holland, in 1981, and the first major triathlon was in November 1982, in Nice. Dubbed the 'World Championship', 56 triathletes took part, twenty of whom were from Britain. A handful of French, German, and Dutch triathletes competed as well, but the Americans stole the show.

Originally, the American television network CBS – a rival of ABC – wanted a triathlon staged in Monaco, Italy and France – the swim, the cycle and running portion in each of the three countries, but the death of Princess Grace forced postponement of the event.

'It just didn't work out in Monaco,' explained Shona Baker, one of the organisers of the original race that put Europe on the triathlon map. 'There were all sorts of complications, and it turned out that the people in Nice wanted to do it very much. We wanted to make it the classiest triathlon in the world, and that's been the goal in the back of our minds since we started.'

Of the 56 people who plunged into the 57°F. water of the Mediterranean that November, ten had to be pulled out during the swim suffering from varying stages of hypothermia. For most of the Europeans competing, it was a first triathlon. Few, if any had more than six months to prepare for it, and yet they were going to attempt the two-mile swim, 80-mile bike race, and 26.2-mile run. Not surprisingly, the attrition rate was high. Less than half of those who started actually finished.

'We didn't know that to expect,' remembers the race director Jeremy Palmer-Tomkinson. 'But if you could have seen the humanity, the spirit, the expressions on the faces that first year . . . . I'd never seen anything like it. But we all knew we'd seen something special. We saw the people who did it, the visibly hypothermic cases of people not even able to hold on to a cup of tea. We saw the personal side. We saw a sport grow in Europe. We saw it explode.'

By 1983 there were 221 who entered, and the Europeans fared much better against the Americans. Stephen Russell, of Kent, was the first European finisher, placed 12th. Mike Harris was not far behind in 13th place. West Germany's Klaus Klaeren was 17th.

By 1984, 417 started, competing for £35,000 in prize money, and the Europeans turned in an even more impressive performance, placing 11 in the top 20. Eight of these were from West Germany, two from Britain, and one from Holland. Unspectacular as the European's debut into the sport may have been in 1982, its growth in Europe has been nothing short of phenomenal.

Triathlon associations have been set up in England, Holland, West Germany, Ireland, Switzerland, Austria, Sweden, Denmark, Italy, Belgium, Norway,

Luxembourg, France, Spain, Czechoslovakia, Finland and Austria, and also in New Zealand and Brazil. Triathlon clubs, newsletters, and training camps have all sprung up within a few years of the sport's arrival in Europe, eclipsing even the relatively rapid growth in the United States. Thousands of Europeans have begun swimming, biking and running. National Championships are held annually in England, Holland, West Germany and Denmark.

In 1984 a European Union was formed, and established a Short, a Long and a Relay Team championship distance courses to be held in different countries on a rotating basis. In the summer of 1985 they established the permanent distances of a short-distance triathlon championship (900-metre swim, 45-kilometre bike, 10-kilometre run), the middle-distance championship (1.9-kilometre swim 90-kilometre bike, and 21-kilometre run), and long-distance championship distances (3.8-kilometre swim, 180-kilometre bike, and 42-kilometre run). In the summer of 1985 West Germany hosts the short-distance championship, Denmark the middle-distance and Holland the long-distance championship. Ireland once again hosts the Relay championship.

Australia and New Zealand have also been experiencing the triathlon boom. At one race in Australia in March 1984, real estate worth $75,000 was awarded to the first man and first woman across the finish line. The fledgling Australian Triathlon Association already has 1,200 members.

Several South Africans have also enjoyed great success in the triathlon. Thirty year old Moira Hornby of South Africa has finished 15th, and in 1984 fifth in the Ironman. David McCarney, also of South Africa, finished eighth at the 1984 Nice race.

In Great Britain, the triathlon movement was first spearheaded by Mike Ellis, one of the original participants at Nice in 1982. Ellis staged a short triathlon, in preparation for the Nice race, in Reading, believed to be the first triathlon in England. In the winter of 1982–3, the British Triathlon Association was formed. Although beset by many of the problems that plague a fledgling organisation, the BTA survived to grow to more than 600 members within 24 months. It staged championship races at the short-course and long-course distances, and had helped to sponsor national champions to take part in races in Nice, and in the United States.

At the original race in Nice in 1982, Danny Nightingale, a former Olympic Gold Medalist in the Pentathlon, was the top British and European finisher, placing ninth overall behind the Americans. Jim Woods, Britain's top finisher in the biathlon at the 1984 winter Olympics in Sarajevo (12th overall), has been a consistent top 10 finisher at many triathlons in England.

In early 1984, a group of Americans tried to get the triathlon accepted by the International Olympic Committee for at least demonstration sport status for the

1988 Olympics. Despite the IOC's conservative leanings in such matters, the motion was nearly approved. A sport has to be participated in in at least 50 nations, by men and women, to be considered. Despite the rejection on this occasion, it appears likely that the triathlon will someday be included in the summer Olympic programme.

Chapter 3

A balanced sport

From the nuclear event of the Ironman competitions sprang the thousands of shorter-course triathlons that became established first across the United States and Canada, and then across the world. Alongside came the magazines, books, triathlon clubs, professional leagues, and even new chains of triathlon sporting goods stores springing up at a growth rate that even McDonald's might envy. As more and more people learn of the sport, more and more join its ranks.

An unexpected aspect of the triathlon is that it is a sport in which schools and school-aged athletes only seldom compete. When they do, they are at a distinct disadvantage. 37 year old Steve Trew, and 38 year old Alan Bell consistently beat most competitors a decade or more their junior. The triathlon is, indeed a sport where youth does not necessarily help, and can, in fact, be a disadvantage. The top triathletes seem mostly to be between the ages of 27 and 32, although the upper limit seems to go higher each year. Bell, for example, is consistently placed second and third in his races. 'I've found that it's great to be able to compete with your own age group as well as compete with the whole field overall,' notes Barry Turner, a 43 year old dentist from Essex. 'And I must admit, perhaps beating some people much younger than you are is very exciting. It's a fresh challenge.'

What helps these 'middle-aged' athletes is that cardiovascular fitness and oxygen uptake are so important in endurance activities. There is less emphasis on speed, and more on endurance and stamina. It takes years, not weeks, to develop strong cardiovascular systems, so that these older triathletes are competing very successfully with many who are not much more than half their age.

Endurance events do not seem to hurt older people as much as anaerobic, and while age does not seem to make quite as much of a difference in individual endurance activities, like swimming, cycling and running, experience and being organised, two qualities which tend to be more common among older athletes, more than compensates triathletes over thirty.

For the triathlon has returned to the human body what other sports, including running, may have taken away from it. Triathlons are the optimal combination of physical activities. Unlike simply running, or just swimming or bicycling by itself, triathlons challenge and work all major muscle groups of the body, not leaving any single area undeveloped. Take a close look at some of the world's top runners. Their upper bodies and faces appear scrawny, almost emaciated. Then look at a triathlete. The physique is well defined. There is usually superb muscle tone from the head down to the feet. Even triathletes who only mildly pursue the sport develop well-defined bodies within a matter of months. Where the runner may look emaciated, the triathlete looks healthy. Where the biker has disproportionately bulging thighs, the triathlete shows well-defined and balanced muscle throughout. Even if the swimmer has outstanding shoulders and triceps, the legs may be startlingly weak.

But there is more to good health than simply a healthy appearance. And while the running boom has appreciably improved the health of thousands of people, it has also extracted from thousands a heavy toll. To become good at running, you need a thin, light-weight body, a good tolerance of boredom, and the desire to run 50 or 60 or 70 miles each week. That brings a great deal of stress on to your system; and not surprisingly, more than a few runners end up with serious injuries, or deflated interests.

Triathletes, on the other hand, are rarely injured. Because the sport is so balanced, because no one system is, as Dr Edwin Boys puts it, 'hammered' in triathlon work-outs or in a race, any person of any shape or size, or mental disposition, can participate in a triathlon. Injuries, indeed, are all but non-existent.

The benefits do not stop there, however. Civilised men and women living in the industrialised world, have grown extraordinarily ignorant of what their bodies need and do not need. We consume too many of the wrong foods, and far too few of the right ones. We are committing, whether we realise it or not, slow suicide by eating too much, drinking too much and exercising too little. One California physician says that, based on the autopsies he has carried out, two out of three deaths are premature.

Before the western world became industrialised, heart disease, which is the single greatest killer in the West, was hardly the problem it is today. Why? Because people walked where they went, worked countless hours in the fields, carried water, and worked hard physically. That is partly why we still eat three meals each day although the average civilised citizen needs perhaps only half that.

A balanced sport

'The average American young man has a middle-aged body,' said Thomas K. Cureton, a professor at the University of Illinois Physical Fitness Laboratory. 'He can't run the length of a city block, he can't climb a flight of stairs without getting breathless. In his twenties, he has the capacity that man is expected to have in his forties. The average middle-aged man in this country is close to death. He is only one emotional shock or one sudden exertion away from a serious heart attack.'

While climbing the 280 steps inside the *Königsschloss* in southern Bavaria recently a thirty year old man turned to his friends, and gasped. 'No wonder they used to die so young.' Ironically, the climbing of the stairs in the pre-elevator days probably extended far more lives than it cut short.

Why? The heart is primarily made up of muscle. When you exercise, you are first and foremost working your heart muscle. By periodically raising your heart-rate via exercise, you strengthen the heart. Clarence DeMar was a champion long-distance runner who died in 1958. He had run for nearly fifty years, including more than a hundred marathons. His autopsy was enlightening. Despite his seventy years of age, he had strong coronary arteries, two or three times the normal size, and his heart was considerbly larger than is normal.

As you train, and your heart and lungs become more efficient, you will find your resting heart-rate lowering, one of the first signs of fitness. Even people with high blood pressure, and other industrial-society coronary ailments, can anticipate a healthier cardiovascular system. Pulse rates of triathletes often fall below 60 beats per minute and, in some cases, below 50 or even 40 beats per minute while resting. Compare these levels with the average 72 beats per minute a saving of up to thirty hundred thousand a day, this is probably the best single sign of fitness.

In fact the cardiovascular endurance is the single most important indicator of overall health. While training, the lung capacity increases, our endurance increases, our oxygen intake capacity increases, our muscle strength increases and our ability to dissipate heat increases as well. The fitter we become, the quicker our pulse rates and blood pressures return to normal, and the more efficient we become, the less oxygen we need.

'Endurance exercises not only protect against heart disease but contribute to a growing list of broadly based benefits,' Dr Ferdy Massimino, a 32 year old physician and triathlete has said. 'It promotes strong and healthy bones, particularly as we grow older. It provides an outlet to help control both physical and emotional stress. The release of the chemical endorphins from the brain contributes to a feeling of enhanced well-being, and is responsible for the addictive potential of endurance activity. It offers a realistic way to lose weight, and keep it off. It has even been reported that a regular programme of exercise can improve your intellectual capacity and productivity.'

What is remarkable about the sport is how quickly the overweight, pudgy body becomes a trim, taut collection of muscles. Because training for a triathlon requires several times as many calories as training for, say a marathon, weight loss is often rapid, and permanent. Yet despite the extra training, and the extra calorie demands, the triathlete's body does not suffer the same bone-pounding trauma by which the runner is often afflicted.

People of all shapes and sizes – particularly those with no athletic background or experience – have been jumping into pools for daily mile swims, cycling 100 miles per week, running 25 miles or more each week, and singing the praises of the sport. Mark Allen, who has won the Nice World Championship three years in a row, need not look warily over his shoulder just yet, for these, competition is a secondary consideration. They are losing weight – with almost laughable ease – and, even more importantly, they are keeping it off.

Much depends, of course, on the initial condition of the person involved before beginning triathlons. But on the average, with a regular routine of, say 5–10 hours of training each week – 45–90 minutes each day – surprising results can be extracted.

'It's better than sitting at home in front of the telly,' says Kathy Harvey, a 31 year old swimming instructor who has been swimming for the past three years. 'I'll tell you, I feel younger since I started this triathlon. It gives me a spark. I feel a lot more energetic. And I've lost about half a stone too.'

Training for an hour or more each day can burn a lot of calories. Depending on the intensity of the work-out, a triathlete can burn up to 840 calories per hour. Compared to swimming, biking and running, only lumberjacks and rowers burn a comparable number of calories per hour (see graph on p. 141).

Whereas an hour of running each day will leave the runner's legs exhausted, but the rest of the body largely unexercised, the triathlete will discover that the arms are fully capable of pulling his or her body through the water for another half an hour or more. And should you want to climb on your bike for a 90-minute ride, even after running for an hour, you will find, to your initial amazement, that the muscles being called into action (primarily the quadraceps and the rump) have not been as thoroughly taxed on the run as you may have assumed. The triathlon finds these untapped muscles, works them and leaves the body pleasantly satisfied.

To burn 2,000 extra calories each day, which is what 2–3 hours of training will do, can turn even the most obese into a fitter healthier person in a matter of months. For the benefits of what has come to be known as 'cross-over training' are impressive and intriguing. The total of exercising in three events is greater than, not equal to, the sums of the parts.

'Even though I ran before I tried the triathlon, I work in an office and only running never seemed to do the trick, I was still fat,' one woman from Milton

Keynes confided. 'Once I began training for all three events, the weight started coming right off.'

The triathlon in fact provides a most sensible means of weight loss and weight control. Crash diets more often than not lead to reciprocal raids on refrigerators, for when the body loses weight through diet, it is allowing fat cells to shrink. The body is not stupid. It has fat cells for an important reason, to protect against famine. Why should people care so much about their body all of a sudden? They may have abused it for years, but it still functions.

There is a fundamentally satisfying quality about the triathlon that is not well understood, nor easy to define. It has much to do, however, with our inherent need to and deep-seated joy of, struggle, our lust for hard work, and hardship, and the feelings of accomplishment that come after effort. Nothing that comes easily ever seems as satisfying as something that at first appears unattainable. Struggle is the spice of life. How often do people look back at the Great Depression with relish in their eyes? What about the spirit of wartime? It seems contradictory but most who survive the struggle have fond memories of it. Hardship brings out the best in humans, it awakens their senses like nothing else. This is a primary reason why the triathlon is the ultimate sport.

After his first triathlon in April 1984, Terry Mason, who is 38, who had not trained at all for it apart from a few miles of running, thought to himself afterwards, 'Never again!' His legs were exhausted, his arms drained, and his energy reserves completely spent. 'I did it purely out of curiosity,' he said. 'I thought it looked interesting. It was difficult. It was challenging, the diversity and all. But I thought to myself, "Never again"!'

But, sure enough, Mason was there at the starting line for the start of the next triathlon. 'Can't stop now,' he said. 'It's too much fun.'

Chapter 4

Getting started

The simplicity of the triathlon is part of its beauty. The beginner needs only a swimming suit, a pair of running shoes and shorts, and a bicycle, but it is not necessary to go out and buy the most expensive Italian bike to have an initial shot at the sport.

'The first race I ever did I had baskets on my bike,' relates Colleen Cannon, who a few years later won the Nice World Championships. 'I was going to school and a friend asked me if I wanted to go up to do this race with him. I really didn't know what to expect, but I said "sure, why not?" I really liked it though. It was appealing, and I've sort of gone nuts about it, as you can probably tell.'

At the first London triathlon in August 1984, many competitors rode on bikes that would do any commuter proud. Mudguards, lamps, bells, and even bikes equipped with FM radios were seen on the course.

To start out, fancy equipment is the least important consideration, but determining your interest in the sport is. The chances are good that you'll enjoy the sport so much, you will soon be speaking the language of an authorised 'bikie' or trained swimmer or marathon runner. The transformation that many once non-sports people undergo when they try the triathlon has been astounding. Since the magnetic appeal of the sport has not been lost on its estimated million or so participants, it is not likely to be lost even on the unfit beginner.

If there is a short-distance triathlon being staged somewhere in your area, try and contact the organiser of the race. He or she will more than likely be glad to advise you on whether or not you would be capable of completing the distances involved. Generally, if you have already been running, swimming or biking or are a reasonably fit individual, a short-course triathlon of approximately a 500-metre (or less) swim, a 15-mile bike ride (or less) and a 4-mile run (or less), would be well within the range of many beginners, with just a few weeks special training.

"ARE YOU SURE YOU'VE HAD ENOUGH PRACTICE FOR THIS?"

If you are out of shape, and have taken part in no exercise for many years, it would be better after a medical check to try the three sports on separate days over short-distances. It is vital to condition youself carefully and slowly according to your body's requirements.

'Listen to your body'

For the beginner the swim is the most crucial, and potentially the most dangerous. Fortunately, in virtually every triathlon the swim comes first, thus ensuring that all competitors are fresh for the demands and dangers, of swimming. It is vital that beginners practice (by building up) swimming at least the distance involved in the actual race, preferably non-stop, and optimally with some supervision and instruction. The crawl stroke will propel you through the water faster, but if you are uneasy at first about having your head underwater, the breaststroke is a suitable stroke for trying out the sport. As you improve, you may later want to switch over and learn the crawl stroke for in addition to its greater speed potential, the crawl stroke spares the legs for the latter stages of a triathlon.

Other than being able to swim the distance involved, a first triathlon for anyone is certainly a feat that can be accomplished.

If there are no short-course races available in your vicinity, there is no reason why you cannot stage a solo practice triathlon on your own. Simply jump into a local pool or lake (with someone watching, or better, accompanying you in a row boat or kayak), and swim a steady 400 yards. Then hop on your bike, any bike, and ride for up to one hour, and then, immediately, run for around half an hour.

There is no need to try and set a world record in the process, nor is it necessary to strip in public for your transitions (as many triathletes do in races to save time). What is important is to gauge how much you enjoy the triple work-out. Naturally, the first few minutes on the bike are difficult after the swim, as are the first few

minutes on the run, but if, at the finish, a feeling of pleasure greets you, that wonderful tranquillity of all your body having been taxed, of discovering that the limitations of your body are greater than the mind had led you to believe, then you will have discovered why this sport has captivated nearly everyone it has touched. All you need to worry about now are the uncontrollable urges to swim, bike and run your way to unemployment.

Thirty-seven year old Brian Spicer of London, had run, over four years, half a dozen marathons just outside the three hours – his closest to a sub-three-hour marathon was in Paris, 3:02. 'I read about this London triathlon in a running magazine, and I thought I'd give it a try,' he remembers.

Although he had had no previous swimming experience, he gradually built up to a mile in the eight weeks before the race, swimming perhaps three or four times each week. He rode four 20-mile bike rides, two 30-milers, and one 35-mile bike ride – the distance the race would entail. He continued running his usual 35 miles each week, and had no trouble finishing the race, which consisted of a one-mile swim, the 35-mile bike ride, and an 8-mile run. 'It was tremendous,' he said afterwards. 'I loved it. I can't wait for the next one.'

There are triathlons of all sizes, custom-tailored for the entire spectrum of triathletes. For the beginner, there are literally dozens of races open. In 1983 there were less than 20 triathlons in Great Britain. By 1984, just a year later, there were more than 50. In the United States, there were 400 triathlons in 1983; by 1984, there were more than 2,000 races to choose from.

The short-course, sometimes referred to as the 'sprint' triathlon, provides an ideal baptism. Some mini-course triathlons are as short as 50-yards swimming, 100-yards running, and a 400-yard bike ride. A short-course triathlon is usually classified as any race up to 1,000 metres swimming, up to 25-mile bike ride, and up to 10-kilometres (6.2 miles) run.

The atmosphere at the short-course races is usually electrifying. There are people from all sorts of backgrounds, in all sorts of levels of fitness, mingling together and competing together in search of one overriding goal: having a good time.

The United States Triathlon Series, (USTS) a short-distance series of races spread across the summer in the United States, was designed precisely to introduce the sport to more people. They are run over short courses of 1,500-metres swim (just under a mile), a 40-kilometre bike ride (25 miles), and a 10-kilometre run. Anyone with a little training can complete the races, and indeed a good percentage of the participants will have only just begun the sport. In West Germany a series of triathlons *für Jedermann* (for everyone) have been run in Cologne and in Bavaria, with more than 2,000 people taking part.

Clearly, the triathlon is for anyone and everyone. There are long events, which challenge the fittest of athletes to days of gruelling endurance. There are middle-distance events which challenge speed and endurance, and there are short-distance triathlons, which challenge both sprinters and beginners alike.

There are relay triathlons, such as the London to Paris relay triathlon, with its 102-mile run (London to Dover), 22-mile swim, (Dover to Calais), and 186-mile bike ride (Calais to Paris) run over three days. The London Triathlon is also a highly successful middle-distance race, with more than 400 athletes taking part.

There are flat courses to race on, and mountainous courses. There are relay triathlons and indoor triathlons. There are triathlons run across North America, across borders, and across deserts. There are all-women triathlons, and children-only triathlons.

There are no restrictions, apart from the category races, as to who can enter a triathlon. Diabetics have successfully completed the Ironman in Hawaii. Recovered heart-attack patients, grandfathers, great-grandmothers, recovered alcoholics, retired policemen, obese and anorexics, surgeons and school children, unemployed, and over-employed people have all taken part.

Although the greatest number of triathletes are former runners, some 50 per cent converted bikers and swimmers are also swelling the ranks of the triathlon. Whether or not we realise it, the triathlon is in many respects a return to our more primeval life or a sub-conscious return to our childhood. As children we ran, we swam, we rode our bikes. Little did we realise that we were in fact training for the triathlon then. And likewise, little do many of us realise now that part of the tremendous enjoyment we experience in the sport may indeed derive from this very subtlety.

In their wonderful innocence, children have no overriding concerns, except perhaps where the next ice cream will come from. Nuclear war, deadlines, taxes and fire insurance register in the child's mind with about as much interest as spinach, liver and lima beans. It is no wonder then that adults, for years, perhaps even decades, burdened by the headaches of industrial society, have submerged themselves wholeheartedly into sport. There are no deadlines, no nuclear wars, no taxes, and no fire insurance to worry about while swimming, biking or running. It is for many a return to that cherished innocence, that delightful age of childhood.

Clearly, it is as diverse a sport as there is. And the triathletes themselves are as diverse a group of people as one can hope to find anywhere.

PART II

Swimming, Biking and Running

Chapter 5

Preparing for your first triathlon

Whether or not you enjoy swimming, biking or running as individual sports, it is almost certain that you will thoroughly enjoy the triathlon. Once you have tried bringing the three sports together you will probably become mesmorised by it.

'If only I didn't have this addiction to triathlons,' laughs Julie Moss, only half seriously. 'Aside from my job and family,' says Mike Harris, a top 32 year old British triathlete from Morpeth, 'the triathlon has become my life.' He was not exaggerating.

Dean Harper, a leading California triathlete, has given up a promising career as an attorney to pursue triathlon training full-time. He has sacrificed a financially rewarding future in order to toil eight hours a day for a few hundred dollars in prize money. But, he says, he is happy.

Not everyone, of course, becomes so overcome by the sport that their whole life revolves around it, but there are thousands, in North and South America, Europe, South Africa and Australia who have pursued the sport for fun, and have found precisely that.

There are four basic distances of triathlons: The sprint (or short-distance), the middle-distance, and the long-distance, and the ultra (or Ironman) distance.

	Swim	*Bike*	*Run*
Sprint	up to 1,000 metres	up to 20 miles	up to 10 km
Middle	1 km–3 km	20–50 miles	10 km–20 km
Long	3 km–3.8 km	50–100 miles	20 km–40 km
Ultra	3.8 km	112 miles	42.2 km

Although it makes little sense to attempt an ultra distance triathlon before trying the sport out in shorter-distance races, many people do so. Fortunately, now that there are many shorter races available, most triathletes will have a year's experience before trying the ultra.

'There's no reason why you can't try an ultra within your first year in the sport,' says Julie Moss. Although her dramatic struggle to finish the 1981 Ironman had captured the world's imagination, and she had played a lot of sport, she had never swum, biked or run seriously before her first triathlon. 'It just depends on what kind of shape you're in, and how much work you've put in beforehand. But your goal with an ultra has to be just to finish. You can't really think about winning, or placing or anything. You just should pace yourself sensibly to finish the race as healthy as possible. After you have one under your belt, then you can start thinking about moving up in the field.'

The most important first step is to determine what sort of shape you are in. Can you run a mile-and-a-half in under 12 minutes? Can you bike 25 miles non-stop in under an hour-and-a-half? Can you swim 400 metres without difficulty? If so, then you are probably in decent enough condition at least to finish a short-distance race. If you have been active as a swimmer, biker or runner, you may already be essentially fit enough for a short triathlon. Practice in your two new sports is of course advisable.

If, on the other hand, you are in relatively poor condition, then you should concentrate on achieving those goals before seriously considering doing a triathlon. But don't despair. Anyone, with a little bit of effort, can achieve a level of fitness where they can complete the distances. The time it takes is inversely proportional to how badly out of shape you are. If you have maintained a reasonable level of fitness, you might be ready for a first shorter triathlon within a month. If you are out of shape, but were at one time or another a runner, or a biker, or a swimmer, then you might find your condition coming back rapidly and that a month or so would also be a reasonable amount of preparation for a short triathlon.

If you are completely out of shape, and have never in your life tried anything athletic, you should give yourself a reasonable period (three to six months) to build up to the demands of even a short race. If you are a fast learner, and can, within a few weeks, swim 1,000 metres, then you might start looking for a race right away.

Physiologists are beginning to unlock some of the secrets of successful endurance performance. One of the most profound discoveries in recent years has been the distinguishing between what are known as 'fast-twitch' muscle fibres, and 'slow-twitch' muscle fibres. Athletes who have a high concentration of fast-twitch muscle fibres are usually better adapted to shorter-distance events, where a lot of speed and power are required. Athletes who have a high concentration of slow-twitch muscle fibres, up to 80–90 per cent slow-twitch fibres in some cases,

28

have a tendency to excel in longer-distance events, where stamina and endurance are important.

Some triathletes who do exceptionally well in short-distance races are often disappointed when they attempt longer ones. Despite augmented training, they are simply not capable of maintaining their effort for more than a few hours at the most.

Other triathletes who fare poorly in shorter races, who find they do not even begin to catch people until the very end of a race, quite often find the longer distance races better suited to their abilities. Dave Scott has had only moderate success at shorter distance races, whereas he is virtually unbeatable at ultra distances. Scott Molina, on the other hand, wins short-distance races consistently. The heat and the length of an ultra race are just not suited to his talents.

The short-distance triathlon

Anyone is capable of doing a short-distance triathlon, which are usually run over courses of less than 1,000 metres swimming, less than 20 miles on the bike, and less than a 10-kilometre run. A majority of today's triathletes are wisely beginning with the short-distance triathlon, for it is an excellent race to start with, particularly for the non-swimmers, because it reveals what the races are like, what the transitions consist of, what it is like to swim in open water, what it is like to feel like a sardine at the start and to change in a hurry, how it feels to run after biking, and how your body responds to the varied demands. But most importantly perhaps, a first short triathlon offers a good indicator of where your weaknesses may be.

Every triathlete, from Joe Bloggs to Dave Scott, has a weakness. If you plan or dream about doing a long or ultra triathlon, and you discover that 1000-metres swimming in open water is too difficult at this stage, you know what you need to develop. Triathletes who have the most success are those who spot their weaknesses, and work on them. It is not as much fun at first to train on your weak event, but, as you improve, and your weak sport becomes your strength (as is often the case), the joy that that brings is enormous.

Short-distance triathlons are fun as well. The pressure is low. It is relatively easy for most people to finish within a few hours, and yet it offers a feeling of accomplishment. At every short-distance race I have attended, people have buzzed with excitement before, during and after the race. Training ideas and tips are shared by people anxious to improve, plans for future races are eagerly made, total strangers become friends, and a festival atmosphere is created.

Although it is advisable to be able to swim, bike and run the distances involved on three separate days before the race, even that is not mandatory. So long as you maintain a steady pace, well within your aerobic capacity, finishing a short-distance race is anything but impossible.

Which leads to another important aspect: your mental suitability. Are you capable of pushing yourself through the stages of 'bonk' as bikers call it, or 'the wall', which is how runners refer to the point in an event where your energy stores are depleted? That is one of the most important parts of the triathlon: having the mental toughness to persevere.

'It's all very well being the fittest on the earth,' as Sarah Springman, who works as a consulting engineer, describes it, 'but if you haven't got the mental strength as well you'll never succeed in the triathlon. You can train your body ad infinitum, but you have to train your mind as well.'

If you are in relatively poor shape, even after a month of training, you will find even the short-distance race a test of your will: can you finish? Even the short races take from two to four hours for some people to finish, roughly equal to the energy output for a marathon. A certain amount of mental determination is important therefore, not only in a race but also in training. The amount you train is often reflected in how well you race; the more you can motivate yourself to work-out, the better you are likely to perform. 'Basically, it's the training,' said Martin Dyer after winning a race in Milton Keynes last summer. 'The more you train, the better you do.'

The middle-distance triathlon

When distances are increased to 1-3-kilometre swims, 20–50-mile bikes, and 10-20-kilometre runs, the possibilities of overcoming a bad start, or for that matter, losing a big lead are increased. The fatigue factor, and successfully running on 'empty' are also more important in the middle-distance races. You must travel at a fast pace to have any chance of finishing well up in the field but: too fast and you burn out too soon; too slow and you finish the race just warmed up. Speed is still important but endurance is playing a bigger role.

Many triathletes believe that the middle-distance races are the ideal distances – not too gruelling, yet challenging. Training is certainly necessary to complete a middle-distance race, yet there is no need to train for hours each day to be competitive in most races. In fact many triathletes have said that, on as little as three hours training per week, they have been able to finish middle-distance triathlons without major difficulty. 'It's fine if you can spend fantastic hours training,' notes Dr Edwin Boys, an anaesthetist from Suffolk, 'but I don't think most people can afford to do that. I rarely train more than four or five hours each week, and in the winter, it's far less than that. But I do enjoy the triathlon, and haven't had any trouble finishing one yet.'

Mike Harris, Britain's Short Course National Champion in 1984, consistently trains 25 hours each week. At one point in his career, Dave Scott trained 50 hours each week. Partly because he decided he wanted to do more with his time, and partly because he has reached such a plateau of performance, his weekly training has decreased to 32–40 hours per week.

But even if you are only able to afford 6–10 hours consistently each week you can, after a while, expect to do reasonably well. I have never spent more than 20 hours in any single week working out, and rarely is my total number weekly above 10 hours, yet I have still managed to win two short-distance races and one middle-distance race. You need not be intimidated by the fact that you cannot devote your life to the sport. But you can still experience some success.

Middle-distance races can be undertaken frequently. Unlike the long or ultra races, which require long build-up and recovery phase, the middle-distance races can be done almost fortnightly throughout the season. This is generalising of course, and four races in two months is quite a burden. However, assuming the courses are not excessively gruelling (e.g. there are few unmerciful hills, and the heat is not too brutal), then there is no reason why the fit athlete cannot take part in races nearly as frequently as fortnightly. If your energy level begins to drop, or you find you are not recovering fast enough, that is a sign that it might be too demanding on your body to compete so often. If your body tells you not to race, then don't. But the point is, middle-distance races do not exact as great a toll on the body; but the longer events do.

The long-distance triathlon

These are races which require from 5–10 hours to complete. That is, naturally, a long time for your heart to be pounding away at 140–160 beats per minute. The long-distance triathlon is, as its title implies, a long race. And a long day. Suddenly, the complications that the shorter-distance racers need not concern themselves with, become worries. For instance, consuming food is vital. Knowing when to eat, how much to eat, what to eat, and perhaps just as importantly, what *not* to eat, are all part of the game. The long-distance race is never an all-out burst of energy, it is a steady slow burn, a muscle-draining, mind-challenging day. In a sense, it resembles a chess match. When do you make your moves, which morsels of energy do you hold on to, which do you expend, when should you drink?

The long-distance race is not really for beginners, especially if they are unprepared for it. But once you have finished short or middle-distance races in good condition, then the long and the ultra can be tackled with a greater sense of understanding and confidence.

Even though long-distance races are indisputably exhausting, they offer some of the more poignant moments of the triathlon. Here finally is a field where the endurance specialists, who were never considered fast when running, swimming or biking short distances, and were perhaps failures in soccer or basketball or cricket, find their sweet revenge.

Whereas those with fast-twitch muscles fade long before the race is over, those with plenty of slow-twitch muscles seem effortlessly to float on by, sailing on, it often appears, as if there would never be a need to stop. This triathlon is for the endurance specialist, who, even running a marathon, found the pace too fast, and the distance too short.

Dave Scott enjoys the longer triathlons. He likes watching the competition melt, he says. In the longer races, he believes, you see what a person is really made out of. Blinding speed and natural talent are no longer crucial as determination and will-power.

Because longer distance triathlons require a considerable amount of preparation, they can perhaps be appreciated a bit more. If you spend a month training 10–14 hours each week getting ready for a long-distance race, certainly race day will mean considerably more than just another half marathon. And similarly, after a long triathlon, you need a longer period of recovery than usual. Several triathletes say that they don't really feel their tanks are full again for another month after a long race.

The final advantage of the long race over the ultra is that the long-distance is manageable. You can ride your bike with the throttle out somewhat. You can push the swim somewhat, and you can let everything loose on the run. Unlike the ultra where so much of the race is conserving what you've got, the long-distance race though it certainly cannot be run all out, can be more of a race than a pure test of stamina.

The ultra distance triathlon

'Your first ultra is hell, pure hell,' says Colleen Cannon, the women's winner at the 1984 Nice triathlon. 'It's the pits. You hate it, and it's murder. Believe me it is really murder. But the next one is much easier. You know what to expect, how to get ready for it, like resting and eating, and you just have a better idea of what's coming. But the first one is pure hell, it really is.'

If you're still interested in trying an ultra, then read on. But if not, and if you never have any desire whatsoever to try an ultra, then fear not. You are perhaps more sane, and will certainly experience less pain.

Ultra distance races last anywhere from nine hours if you happen to be brilliant, but more like twelve to fifteen hours, or even twenty hours. If you are looking for an ultimate challenge, this certainly qualifies. For the entire week leading up to the race, particularly if it is your first ultra, you think about it in a strange way, as though you are about to take a flight to the moon. Some people call it the Mount Everest of athletics. Others call it the most satisfying thing they have ever done. Still others call it the most painful thing they have ever done. It is not easy. It is not easy, for example, to train that much (10–25 hours per week seems to be the minimum) and it is certainly not easy for your body to run a marathon *after* you have hit the wall.

'The nature of the race,' offers Julie Moss, 'is that you've got to do what you've got to do at the time. I've learned that you've got to flow with the race. It's such a long day, you can only do each leg as best as you can, and not defeat yourself. Most people beat themselves instead of getting beat. The winner is usually the survivor.'

'I was so pleased when the race was over,' said Sarah Springman, shortly after finishing her first ultra at Hawaii in 1984. She finished 11th woman overall, in a time of 11:22, which would have won the first Ironman race outright. 'If I can do the Ironman, I feel I can attempt almost any triathlon.'

She found that the greatest obstacles were dehydration and depletion of energy. She ate as many bananas as she could manage throughout the bike ride and the run, and somehow managed to run the second half of the marathon three minutes faster than the first half.

'The sun seemed to be mercilessly hot. Onlookers with garden hoses were a godsend. I had to play mind games to reduce the run to 26 individual races from aid station to aid station. At moments like those I wished I'd never heard of the triathlon, let alone the Ironman! I was so happy to have done it, but I think one can only face so many Ironman races. They are really tough.'

Springman felt that one of the keys to the Ironman is preparing for it, not just in the training during the months before, but in the week leading up to the race. A week before the race she began tapering down her work-outs, swimming just a little each day to stay tuned. On the day before the race, aside from eating six meals, she lay on her bed and did nothing else.

Julie Moss finds it crucial as well to eat a lot and also to relax. 'You should eat extra amounts in the days leading up to the race. Instead of just one big pig-out the night before the race, you need to eat constantly the day before the race. Eat five or six times a day. And you shouldn't spend the day running around. Just take it easy, put your feet up, and relax. Get to bed early, and try to get some sleep.'

Moss says that she could have won that 1982 Ironman race, when she collapsed mere yards short of the victory. 'If I had known then what I know now I would have won the race,' she says. 'I would have walked, instead of trying to run the whole race. At Hawaii almost everyone has to walk at some point. There are only a few people who can run the whole 26 miles. I tried to do that the first year, and that's why I had problems.' 'My first Ironman was my best, time-wise,' she adds. 'I don't know how I pulled it off. I really don't. It was a lot of fun though.'

Chapter 6

Swimming: Getting better in the water

A few years ago I was soliciting advice about swimming. Much to my surprise, a number of friends kept suggesting the name of a pudgy, overweight un-athletic-looking colleague named Hans. Hans had been, they said, a good swimmer in high school.

Maybe so, I thought, but at 22, his days of athletic prowess looked a decade and 35 extra pounds behind him. Nonetheless I was so anxious to take my one mile swim time below the magic 30-minute barrier, that I invited him for a swim one day, confident that I could keep up with, if not thoroughly thrash him, this chain smoker.

He was like a fish. He lapped me six times, and finished his mile before I had even reached 1,000 metres; and he was doing 100-metre butterfly intervals while waiting for me to finish the 1600 metres. By the time I had splashed the mile in at 32 minutes he had swum nearly a mile-and-a-half. I was ready for a shower. He was just warming up.

'It's all in the technique,' he said. He reminded me that he had said the same thing on the way to the pool, that swimming is eighty per cent technique, but I had not wanted to hear such nonsense. Swimming, like running and biking, I believed, was largely a matter of strength. Was I ever wrong!

'Good swimmers have good technique. Great swimmers have great technique. Their strokes are nearly flawless,' he continued. This time I was listening. 'Their bodies just glide through the water. Their arms move smoothly, and there's no unnecessary movements at all. They don't pull any extra water along with them. Swimming is eighty per cent technique, ten per cent strength and ten per cent mental. You have to be able to stand hours looking at underwater tiles.'

Swimming is, indeed largely a matter of technique. It cannot be over-emphasised how vital good form is when swimming. For the newcomer to

35

swimming, as most triathletes are, it is crucial to master the mechanics at the outset.

There are some outstanding books on the subject. One, *The Science of Swimming*, by 'Doc' James Counsilman, is reverently referred to by top swimmers as 'the bible' of swimming. Another excellent book, by the two European authors, Kurt Wilke and Madson, is *Das Training des jungendlichen Schwimmers*, (The Training of the Young Swimmers).

For the non-swimmer, someone who has never swum more than a few laps of a pool or a few yards in the sea, the triathlon can prove to be a titanic struggle. Unlike the beginning runner, or biker, the beginning swimmer is faced with an alien environment. Underwater. The normal factors of conciousness, balance and understanding disappear. There are no birds chirping. There are no flowers to smell. There are no trees. The swimmer is suspended in an atmosphere of water, soundless beyond the din of moving water, and aromaless beyond chlorinated water. The five senses are either lost, or to a degree impaired. Sound and smell are, for all essential purposes, lost. Vision is greatly impaired. Touch and taste are also largely useless in water.

For the neophyte, for the person who does not even enjoy having his head under the covers, let alone underwater, it can be a harrowing experience indeed to be largely submerged in an airless environment. Even for the practised swimmer, being semi-submerged in an open body of water, where pool lane lines and walls disappear, is nerve wracking.

'For women I think the most frightening thing about triathlons is swimming in open water,' says 31 year old Kathy Harvey, out of her experience as a swimming instructor in London. 'Swimming in a pool is no problem. But swimming in the sea . . . . I'm just not as comfortable, you know what I mean? For fellas, it's probably not as bad, but for us, it's frightening not knowing what's in there'.

Even developing confidence in the water in a swimming pool is not an easy task for some. Kevin Gill, a 37 year old aerobics instructor, took three months to swim a half-mile non-stop. 'Everyone said it's got to be the front crawl. It's the fastest stroke. So I thought, okay, I've got to do it. They tried to teach me how to breath face down in the water. I just couldn't do it. I just didn't feel comfortable, so I had to give it up and go back to the breast stroke.'

After a few humiliating swims, including the London triathlon in which he finished the penultimate swimmer, completing the mile course in just under an hour, Gill decided to take another look at the crawl. He and a friend started training with a swimming club in the evenings, and were given their own lane to work in. They also received occasional instruction and advice from coaches and other swimmers in the club. The bonuses of watching good swimmers in action, above and below water, added to the experience.

'I began to feel much more confident in the water,' Gill continued. 'I wasn't afraid of it nearly as much, and as far as keeping my head under water . . . . I just didn't even have to think about it anymore. I really used to hate the swimming. The temptation to stop and have a rest in the pool was really great, but I gradually learned to overcome that temptation and keep going. But sometimes about halfway down the pool, I would really panic. There have been a few occasions where I just had to stop in the middle of the length and wade to the side, get out and go have breakfast. I really wouldn't want to go back to the pool, and the only reason I persevered was because I wanted to try the triathlon. I wouldn't have believed anyone if they had told me I would be able to swim a half a mile three months later. Not a chance.'

Beginning swimmers often admit that many of their problems could have been avoided had they learned the stroke properly at the outset. 'The best thing I did was to find a coach who knew what he was doing and had some patience,' says Gill. 'There are people who can help. It's just a question of asking about.'

'I couldn't swim at all when I started,' confesses Howard Jones ironically, who, spent years in the Royal Navy. 'I thought I could, but I really couldn't. I pretty much had to start from scratch. But I've had some good coaching and that's made a world of difference. I really feel confident in the water now. No troubles whatsoever.'

Once you have acquired a certain amount of confidence in the water, and can, without undue anxiety, swim the crawl with your head submerged most of the time, you may want to begin thinking about a crucial element in smooth swimming: making the body as resistance-free as possible.

There are two main forces which determine the speed with which the swimmer

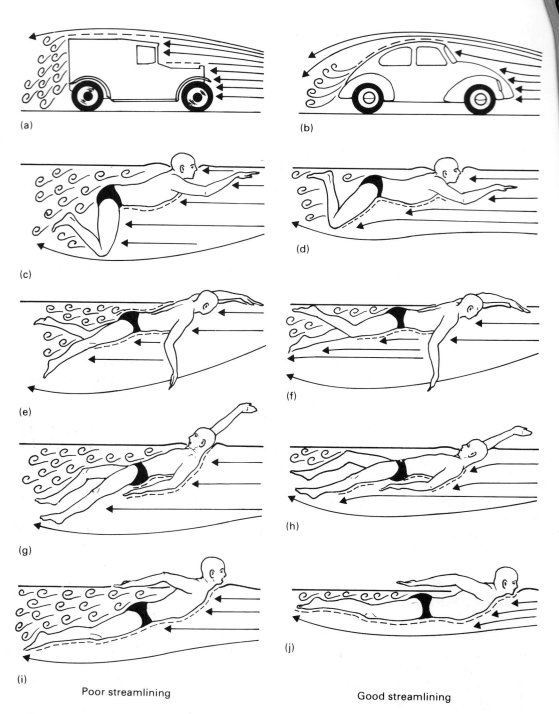

Poor streamlining   Good streamlining

Fig. 1

38

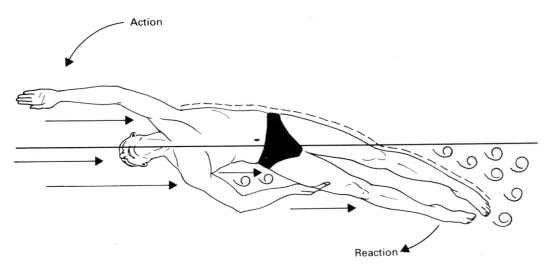

Fig. 2 *Lateral movement*

travels. One force, resistance, or drag holds back (Fig. 1). The other force creates forward motion, or propulsion. To swim faster, you must either decrease resistance, or increase propulsion. Or both. Complex technical sport though swimming is, it can be reduced to these two fundamental forces.

With the beginning swimmer, large improvements can be made by decreasing resistance. Even if you feel you are a fair swimmer already, you are probably creating far more drag than necessary. There are dozens of sources of this resistance. Some are obvious, such as long hair or baggy swimming trunks. Others are highly subtle, such as a slight wiggle in the hips, for example (Fig 2) which not only pulls the body out of line and creates more resistance around the hips but more important as far as drag is concerned, the water molecules are pulled in a side direction. This water in tow is adding even more resistance, much the way an invisible scarf would do.

An initial goal, then, for the neophyte is to reduce drag as much as possible. It is not as easy however, as it sounds. Because the swimmer, encapsulated in this watery world with reduced vision, cannot see poor form as easily as a runner in front of a plate-glass window, it takes him years, even decades to become a great swimmer. A few months in a local pool on a regular basis will unquestionably result in some noteworthy gains. However, it should be pointed out at the outset that it does take a long time, and that many miles need to be swum in a pool before it is possible to swim a mile in under 25 minutes.

To swim a mile in under 30 minutes nevertheless is another matter. With a

1. Rotate the head on its axis instead of lifting and lowering it (notice the mouth is in the concavity in back of the bow wave).

3. Instead of pushing upward the force should be applied in a more backward direction (notice elbow bend).

2. Instead of pushing downward, the force should be applied in a more backward direction (notice elbow high position).

1. Lifting and lowering head to breathe

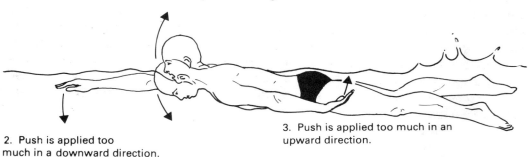

3. Push is applied too much in an upward direction.

2. Push is applied too much in a downward direction.

Fig. 3

streamlined stroke, perhaps a bit of coaching or criticism from a competent observer and a few months training, it is within the capabilities of most people to swim 1600 metres in approximately 30 minutes. Gains after that will be difficult, because the faster you swim, the more resistance you encounter. The law of squares applies here: to swim twice as fast means that there will be four times as much water resistance, which will require 16 times as much energy. Because water is obviously so much more dense than air, bikers and runners are sometimes baffled by the at-times haltered improvement in their swimming times. They reach a plateau, and then many frustrating months go by without any further gain.

40

And then again, suddenly, the times start dropping again. Within a few months I was able to swim a sub-30 minute mile; but it took me six more months to get below 29 minutes, and then after a year and a half had gone by with essentially no improvement, I was suddenly able to swim a mile in under 25 minutes.

It is worth interjecting a word here on the aims of the swimmer, because it is important to be realistic. If you have never swum anything but the dog paddle, you should not expect to set a new world's record for the mile this year. On the other hand, if you are already a fairly able swimmer, and are prepared to spend three to eight hours per week training in the pool or lake or sea, you will, with intelligent training, improve.

Gradually working up to the point of being able to swim 800 metres (a half-mile) is a first goal for a beginner. 'Learning how to swim was definitely the hardest part for me' explains Steve Search, an insurance worker of Seven Kings, Essex. 'The first time I tried to swim I got exhausted after two lengths. I used to think, "how am I ever going to be able to swim a mile?" I didn't think I'd ever be able to do it. I really admired those guys who could swim a mile. I thought they really must be super fit.

'I just kept setting myself goals like being able to swim a certain number of lengths non-stop. The first target was 10 lengths (250 yards) non-stop. It took me three weeks of going to the pool five times a week to get to that point, and then once I got that, I aimed for 15 lengths non-stop, and gradually built up to a mile. It was hard. I'd come out of the pool feeling shattered. It sounds crazy now because 15 lengths is nothing anymore. It was a challenge then, but it almost seems easy now. It was a great day when I reached a mile non-stop. I went out and celebrated. It wasn't very fast, probably 50 minutes, but I thought it wasn't so bad. Swimming a mile could be done.'

For triathletes who initially can swim a mile in 35–40 minutes, there is good news. With some effort, you can more than likely bring your time below 30 minutes within a few months. And even on longer triathlons with swims of a mile to two miles or more, even the top swimmers will not be able to swim more than 30 per cent (if that much) faster than you. If you are a good runner and cyclist, the few minutes lost in the water can usually be recovered on the bike and the run portions of the race unless you are in one with the top triathletes. For top triathletes will be able to swim a 21 minute mile, cycle 22 miles per hour, and run 6 minute miles. In many triathlons, however, the swim portions are relatively short in terms of overall time. Top swimmers can only gain a few minutes, therefore, on average swimmers in a one-mile swim. But a top cyclist can take half an hour or more away from an average biker on an 80 mile bike course. And on the run, a 2:20 marathoner will gain a lot of time from a 3:30 marathoner. The 30 minute mile, the two miles per hour pace, then, is an important plateau for the swimmer to aim for.

This sequence of drawings shows the swimmer performing a conventional six beat crawl stroke with a continuous arm action.

1. As the right hand enters the water at shoulder width with the palm facing downward, the pulling arm has accomplished half of its pull. Air is being exhaled from the mouth and nose in a steady trickle, indicating a rhythmical breathing pattern.

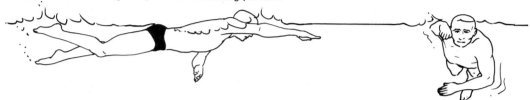

2. The downward momentum developed by the hand during the recovery causes the right hand to sink downward for its catch. The pulling arm continues its pull backward with the palm still facing backward.

3. The right hand continues to move downward slowly as the pulling hand starts to come back toward the centre line of the body.

4. The arm depressor muscles now start to contract actively and depress the right arm downward.

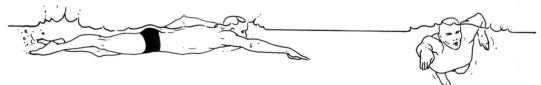

5. The left arm has almost completed its pull and the swimmer is now applying force with both hands. The force of the right hand is not as yet directed backward sufficiently to contribute any forward propulsion to the body.

Fig. 4

6. As the left arm finishes its pull the left leg thrusts downward vigorously. This action cancels out the effect that the upward action of the arms has upon depressing the swimmer's hips.

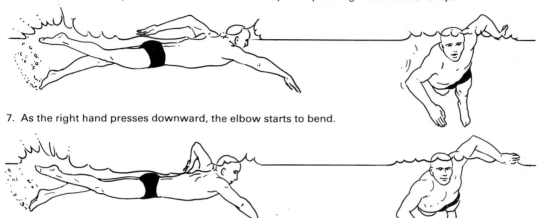

7. As the right hand presses downward, the elbow starts to bend.

8. The elbow-up position of both the recovery arm and the pulling arm is apparent.

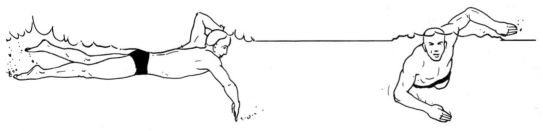

9. The pulling hand has accomplished half of its pull and the hand starts to rotate on its longitudinal axis. The amount of air being exhaled begins to increase.

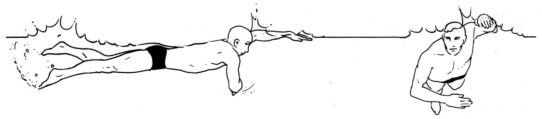

10. The pulling hand has accomplished half of its pull and the head starts to rotate on its longitudinal axis. The amount of air being exhaled begins to increase.

11. The head continues to turn to the side as the chin appears to follow the action of the elbow as it goes backward. The pulling hand starts to round out and come back toward the centre line of the body.

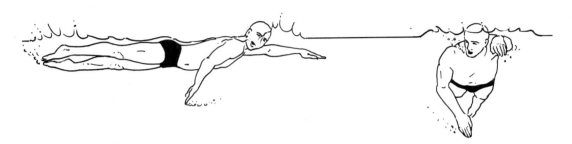

12. The swimmer's mouth is opened further as the volume of air exhaled is increased.

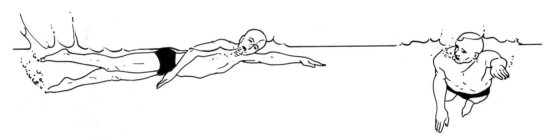

13. The pulling hand is no longer facing directly backward, but is held at an angle of about 45°. The thumb-out position at this point is noticeable in many good swimmers, but is neither detrimental nor beneficial.

14. The downward thrust of the right leg starts as the right arm finishes its pull. The mouth finally breaks the surface of the water and the inhalation is about to begin.

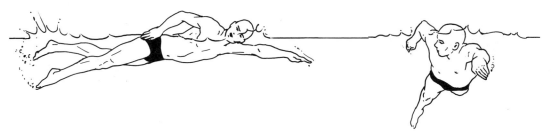

15. Immediately before the hand breaks the surface of the water, it is turned so the palm faces inward toward the body. The swimmer opens his eyes and starts his inhalation.

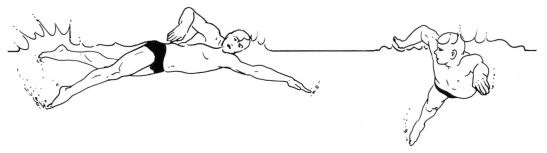

16. The downward thrust of the right leg ends as the swimmer starts his right arm forward. The inhalation is almost completed.

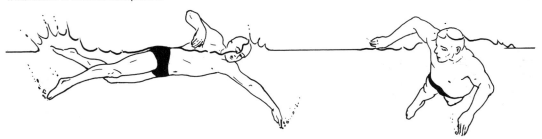

17. The head starts to rotate back toward the centre line of the body as the recovering arm swings forward.

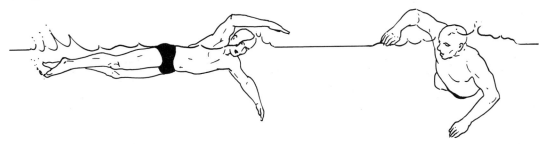

18. The swimmer starts to exhale as the face is almost completely submerged. The left arm is about to enter the water and complete the stroke cycle.

The Crawl Stroke (Fig. 4, 1–18)

It is crucial to avoid resistance as much as possible. It is astounding how drag is responsible for slowing the swimmer. Plenty of swimmers can swim 1600 metres in less than 17 minutes, but the world record for the 1500 metre swim, the longest Olympic swimming distance, is 14 minutes and 57 seconds. That is *fast*. Some people cannot run a mile that fast, and certainly, it takes an effort to walk a mile in under 15 minutes. Aside from oxygen intake capacity, talent and training, swimming at that speed is largely attributable to flawless form in which resistance has been kept to a minimum.

A good coach or knowledgeable swimmer is therefore the logical solution. He or she can see the flaws and excess resistance which you cannot see. The stroke, for example, needs constant monitoring and checking, even when a swimmer has developed a good form.

First of all, it is important for the swimmer using the crawl stroke to realise not only how to perform the correct mechanics of the stroke, so that they are registered into the mind but, just as importantly, why. Some swimmers have such natural ability that they can jump into the water and simply zip along without apparently thinking about what they are doing. They have what experts call a 'feel for the water', and it is a quality that some people are born with. The rest of us have to practise, think, and practise, and think some more. It is akin to learning a foreign language: children are naturals, adults, on the contrary, have to struggle with the grammatical rules, trying to find logical patterns where none may exist.

Swimming is, incidentally, an ideal sport for children. On the one hand, there is no pounding of joints, on the other hand, there is the advantage that a year or so of heavy training will greatly strengthen and enlarge the adolescent's heart – excellent exercise for youths who are still growing. A competitive swimmer's heart has to be large in order to deliver the huge volume of blood needed by the muscles. Some 15 year old swimmers, in fact, have hearts as large as top class 30 year old marathoners. Swimming also taxes all the main muscle groups of the body, but does not leave any one area devastated.

The body position in the free-style stroke should be as streamlined and as flat as possible. The head should optimally be thrust ahead of the body at a slightly tilted angle, so that the water is at the level of the hairline, an inch or two above the eyebrows. Imagine a Jumbo jet aircraft sitting on a runway, its nose the forward-most point of the body. It is streamlined. It is aerodynamically sound to aid speed and conserve energy. This is the same positon, unnatural though it may seem at first, when you try to adopt it. Prone. Sleek. And efficient.

It is important however, not to push the head too high out of the water (see Fig. 3). That is the natural tendency, particularly in open bodies of water, for we are land-based animals and are happier when we can see and breathe. But keep the head as flat as and as synchronised as possible with the rest of the body. For if the head is raised unnecessarily high, the trunk will sink lower into the water, which will then create more drag. Keep Newton's Third Law of Physics in mind: for every action there is a reaction.

Much of the reaction, of course, is hidden from the swimmer, who cannot see or feel when his own body is misaligned, particularly underwater where the normal senses are not at home, coupled with the fact that there is no visual reinforcement of the receptor readings.

You should be using your energy to propel the body through the water, not on top of it. (Fig. 3) Rotating the head on a hypothetical axis in order to breathe, instead of lifting it up and down in the water, will save immeasurable amounts of energy and also, of course, prevent the subsequent sinking reaction somewhere else. The air is the same at the surface of the water as it is six inches above it, so it is best to try to breathe as closely to the surface of the water as possible. There is a trough in the water, just behind and to each side of the head. It is possible to breathe in this trough, which is actually well below the surface of the water in front of your head. If you have ever noticed the wave in front of a ship, you will also have noted that the water level directly behind the bow is several inches lower. Imagine your head therefore as the bow of a ship, so that, by breathing on either side, you will not have to lift your head as high out of the water nor work as hard as the swimmer who insists on lifting his head in front to breathe and whose momentum is then lost. The closer to the surface you can breathe, the better.

The occasional wave, whether in a pool or ocean, will undoubtedly catch the swimmer unawares and the inevitable mouthful of water will be the result. This is not the end of the world. Irritating and discouraging though it can be, it is only water, and will not kill you. It will not even sink you. In fact, if you do not swallow an occasional mouthful of water, you are probably not breathing close enough to the surface of the water anyway. Even the best swimmers will admit that there is no way to avoid the occasional mouthful.

'Taking in water used to worry me,' admits Kevin Gill. 'But it doesn't anymore. I used to swallow a lot of it, and it would really distract me. I over-compensated and stuck my head far too far out of the water. I noticed on videos of races that I was bringing my head up far too high, much higher than the other swimmers. That really helped me, seeing how poor my technique was. Now when water gets into my mouth, I usually spit it right back out before the next breath.'

Exhaling
There have been different, and conflicting, ideas on exhaling during the stroke. Some Eastern European coaches have taught swimmers to hold the breath in the

47

lungs as long as possible, in order to add a fraction of buoyancy, and then to blow out rapidly just before inhaling. Other coaches avoid this method because the jerky motion it tends to create outweighs any slight gains in buoyancy. It is better they say, particularly over long-distance swims, to remain as smooth and efficient as possible.

The extra buoyancy is negligible when contrasted with the extra energy expended when the smoothness of the stroke is sacrificed for the quick blow out of air. Thus, a steady stream of air bubbles pushed out through the lips, and nose if you wish, is preferable. The swimmer may want to blow slightly harder after the mouth has broken the surface of the water in order to blow away any water that may be dripping off of the face and into the mouth. Many swimmers also form an oval with their mouth, their lips extending out a quarter of an inch or so (much like a fish mouth) to block any water dripping down over the mouth.

After taking in the air as close to the surface of the water as possible, you should roll your head back into the water, trying to keep it close to its longitudinal axis. Once back in the water, the mouth begins to release a steady trickle of air and a stroke later the process is repeated.

Some top triathletes, many of whom are former swimmers – Dave Scott is the most prominent – advocate what is known as 'bi-lateral' breathing. That is to say, they breathe every third stroke, instead of every second, so that the side they breathe on alternates with each breath. For excellent swimmers this stroke is fine. But as one of England's authorities on swimming, Roger Parsons, points out, remaining within your aerobic limits is vital, and, as he explains, most

triathletes are just unable to get enough oxygen when they breathe only every third stroke.

A triathlete can ill-afford to go into oxygen debt on the swim, otherwise the energy stored within the body is burned much faster and at a highly inefficient rate, and there will then be problems during the run section and perhaps even during the bike section as well. Staying aerobic is vital. For most swimmers this means breathing every other stroke, although as you become proficient in the water, you may want to experiment with bi-lateral breathing in training. Even if you can only do it every second or third length, it is useful practice because you are balancing your stroke as well as challenging your aerobic capacities.

'It's hard at first, no doubt about it,' relates Maureen Fitzgerald. 'I kept on swallowing water, and feeling like I was going to drown. I didn't think I'd ever be able to do it, but it's amazing how soon you pick it up if you just stick with it.'

For longer distance races, however, even James Counsilman advises swimmers to breathe every second stroke. In any event, of course, it is a good idea to be able to breathe on both sides. Apart from balancing your stroke, being able to breathe on either side can prove important in a race where the ocean spray is blowing in your face, or if the waves keep knocking you on the one side you breathe on. In many triathlons there are complaints about the buoys being placed on the side opposite to that on which some of the swimmers breathe – if you can breathe on both sides this problem obviously disappears.

The Kick

Clearly the most important part of the crawl is the arm stroke because nearly all of the propulsive force comes from the arms. This is in stark contrast to what many people mistakenly believe, which is that the propulsion comes equally from the legs. In fact, the legs contribute essentially nothing to forward speed. Their major function is to stabilise the body, much like a rudder, and to prevent the tail end of the body from sinking too deeply into the water, and thereby creating drag.

James Counsilman has demonsrated emphatically through a series of impressive experiments that at almost every speed, the kick, no matter how hard or soft, contributes nothing to forward speed. 'The arm stroke in the crawl is the main source of propulsion,' he concludes. 'And in the case of most swimmers, the only source of propulsion.'

This idea was understandably radical when Counsilman first proposed it in the early 1950s, but most coaches today concur. Counsilman's experiments show how only at very slow speeds does the kick add anything to forward speed.

'If I were to teach swimming,' says Randy Williams, who holds many long-distance swimming records in the United States, 'I would not teach any kicking.

Long-distance swimmers rarely kick. It sounds surprising, I know, but kicking tires you out more than it helps.'

The forward momentum comes then almost entirely from the arms. This is another reason why the triathlon is such an outstanding event. The arms are taxed in the swim, but the legs, especially if you digest the advice of successful long-distance swimmers and minimise the effort expended by the legs, can be spared any great strain until the bike ride starts. As the arms play a decreasing role as the day unfolds, the legs play an ever increasing role. Cyclists need the arms somewhat, particularly on the hills. But by the time the run starts, the arms are fairly exhausted. The legs, conversely, play a minimal role in the swim, an increasingly important role on the bike, and are of course the principal workers on the run.

"YOU'RE KICKING TOO HARD!"

Triathletes, however, seem not to have understood this fundamental message. At the 1984 World Championships in Nice, many of the 420 starters were kicking furiously from the start. Not surprisingly many began to fade within a few hundred metres of the starting line, and others began to have trouble only a half-mile into the two-mile swim.

'I couldn't believe how hard the people were kicking,' said Josie May, the former National Ladies Triathlon Champion from Nelson, Lancashire. 'You don't need to kick hard at all. Especially in salt water like that. You float so well that you can almost forget about your legs altogether.' May was kicking two beats for every four or six strokes, essentially allowing her legs to float behind her. 'I didn't feel the need to kick.' What sort of kick, then, does one use?

Many long-distance swimmers, and coaches, recommend a two beat kick for any swim more than a half-mile (800 metres) in distance. That is, just two kicks per arm-cycle. Many beginning swimmers kick six or more beats per arm-cycle, far too many say the experts. Two kicks requires two thirds less energy, a lot of which can thus be liberated for use by the arms. Two light beats is sufficient for most swimmers. It might at first seem as if your legs are sinking but you will quickly sense just how powerless your legs are in the crawl stroke.

What is important, in any event, is the timing of the kick. It should be timed so that as the right arm finishes its pull and begins its recovery, the right leg should kick to keep the body balanced. By kicking as the arm begins its out-of-the water phase, you can compensate for the extra weight being placed on that side of the body as the right arm leaves the water. The same applies for the left side. Some swimmers even use what is called a 'cross-over' two-beat kick. You may be doing a variation of the cross-over kick already without even realising it. By crossing over slightly the leg opposite to the side you breathe on, you are balancing the slight shift of weight as you breathe.

The longer the race, the less emphasis should be placed on the kick, according to Counsilman. There are two primary reasons: one, because the long-distance swimmer travels at a slower speed than the sprinter or the middle-distance swimmer, the body rides slightly lower in the water, and thus does not need as hard a kick as the sprinter does (to maintain a higher position in the water) Second, the heart can supply only a certain amount of blood to the active muscles. If blood must be directed to the legs, that is blood (with its valuable oxygen content) which is not available for use by the arms.

'There is less blood available to the muscles which pull the arms through the water, with the result that they fatigue more easily,' writes Counsilman. 'I have long advocated a reduced emphasis on the kick, particularly in distance swimming. In recent years, world records have been set in the distance events by swimmers with reduced kicks, some of whom kicked as few as two beats per cycle.'

On the other hand swimmers can kick too little. Individual experimentation seems to be the present course, partly because there are such tremendous individual variations in buoyancy and arm strength. Competent coaches should also be able to offer advice. If the legs are ignored too much and the hips begin to drop too low in the water, the entire stroke will suffer because of the added drag, among other things. The primary role of the kick, remember, is not to propel, but to stabilise.

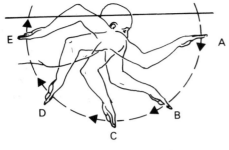

1. The dropped-elbow pull

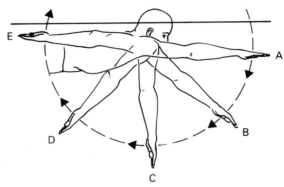

2. The straight arm pull

3. The correct pull

Fig. 5

The Pull: (Fig. 5)

The armstroke can be divided into two distinct phases: the pull, and the recovery. Inexperienced or poor swimmers tend to make mistakes with both parts of the stroke. Some of the more common errors are over-reaching, bending the elbows or wrists on the pull, and having too wide a recovery; breathing at the wrong time, holding the head too high out of the water, lunging at different speeds through the water, and plunging your arms too deeply into the water, thereby wasting energy in pushing down and up.

Correcting faulty swimming technique is far more difficult than correcting flawed running or biking technique. The swimmer largely submerged in his watery world, cannot see or feel with the same clarity. Even top swimmers who need minor alterations to their stroke mechanics, are often surprised to learn of the flaws in their strokes. What they think they are doing, and what they are really doing are often surprisingly different. I usually try to make it a habit, every time I get to know a good swimmer reasonably well, to ask him or her to criticise my

stroke. Some provide excellent tips, and can really spot those crucial errors that from time to time develop. Juliet Smith, a County swimmer from Clacton-on-sea, once told me that I was flipping my left hand as I started the recovery, but that my right hand was fine. 'What?' I thought to myself, but sure enough, I tried concentrating on what my left wrist was doing and caught the offending hand in the act. It had been robbing me of energy needlessly, minor though it was, and more than likely was affecting something on the right side of my body as well. The potential for developing such habits is enormous in both experienced swimmers and beginners alike. Observation is essential and the open-minded swimmer who absorbs criticism without becoming unduly sensitive will improve. The ultra-sensitive swimmer who rejects suggestions will find himself or herself not fulfilling their potential, and short of coaches as well.

Fortunately, there are usually good swimmers in most pools at one time of the day or another, and in most cases they are more than happy to advise the novice. There are also swim clubs which, depending on the area, will more than likely provide assistance for the newcomer to the sport. It just takes a little asking. It is not unlike asking someone out for the first time. You dread it, fear it, anticipate hostile rejection, and then are amazed when the entire process is an enjoyable one.

Perhaps the most common mistake that afflicts beginning swimmers is the dropped elbow on the pull. It is important to keep the elbow firm and moving back underneath your body, even with your hand and wrist (see Fig. 5).

If you allow your elbow to drop, to give way to the pressure of the water as is the natural reaction at first, you will lose most of your forward propulsion. If you are moving slowly through the water, you may well be guilty of this error. It is of course easier to drop the elbow and allow it to travel backwards in advance on the hand. Certainly, your hand will move through the water with considerably less effort, but you will lose most of your pulling surface (i.e. your inner forearm) if you pull it backwards in advance of your hand.

Most of the forward thrust in the pull comes from a point beneath the water surface about 6–12 inches after the 'catch' is made to just before the thigh. To let the arm in this area wobble is to allow the stroke to deteriorate. Viewed from underneath, the arm stroke of a good swimmer forms an 'S' shape, or an inverted question mark (see diagram).

Over-reaching is another frequent mistake. It is important not to over-extend the arm in front when dropping it into the water, for this over-extension can cause the head and shoulders to be pulled off centre as well as create other imbalances on the body. For the extra millimetres gained by reaching as far forward as possible, the damage to the streamlining of the body is more detrimental to the speed and efficiency of the stroke. Naturally you will want to extend your lead arm as far forward as possible, but not to a point where the shoulders and head are affected. If you find you are not swimming as fast as you think you are capable of, this could be the source of the trouble.

Wide recoveries are another flaw that swimmers should watch for. Besides endangering swimmers in adjacent lanes in a crowded pool, or rivals in a close race, wide recoveries waste energy, disperse somewhat the forward motion as the arm sweeps out and back in, and they can also throw the body out of alignment. The more flexible you are, the more compact your recovery can be, the higher you can raise your arms out of the water, and the less your body will have to roll in compensation for the wide recovery. (A body roll of about 30° is about average.) If you are occasionally slapping the hand, wrist, arm or (worse) head of swimmers in neighbouring lanes, then the chances are that you (and not, as you think, they) have a recovery which is too wide. Try stretching exercises, reaching back to touch your hands behind your back, for example; but if you continue to suffer, take heart. Even Dave Scott admits that he has a 'horrible recovery', with a wide sweeping motion which, he says, every coach tells him needs work. Even so he still swims a mile in under 20 minutes.

As the recovery begins, the palm should be facing backwards and tilted slightly upwards. The wrist should remain relaxed. As the hand swings forward past the shoulder, it is in line with the elbow. From this point the hand passes the elbow, and the palm should gradually have been turning to face the water. As gravity accelerates the hand back towards the water, the swimmer should be cautioned not to rush the arm movement as well, for too hurried an entry into the water creates more resistance, makes it difficult to pull properly with the other arm, and potentially throws the body out of alignment. Thus a natural drop of the (relaxed) arm into the water is the ideal.

At the completed recovery, the palm should be face down at the start and the elbow slightly bent as the hand enters the water. The hand should enter just ahead of the rest of the arm. Many swimmers at this moment believe that they should push down at first, then backwards; this is known as the incorrect and inefficient 'straight-arm pull', and it only wastes energy. The body will float at a certain level, no matter how fat or thin you are. There is no way to elevate your body in the water, and in long-distance swims (longer than 200 metres) it is foolhardy to attempt it. It is like trying to lift yourself off the ground by bootstraps. If you push down in the water before pulling back, you will rise slightly higher in the water for a split second. But you will not stay there, you will sink back down to your original level almost instantaneously and continue to sink as your body, like a swinging pendulum, settles on the right depth. Thus, the net gain for lifting yourself higher in the water by pushing down is zero; you have wasted energy trying to create a force other than forward, and you have sunk deeper than when you started, causing even more drag.

The advantages of buoyancy tend to be exaggerated. World records have been set by extremely buoyant people who could float on their backs all day, and world records have been set by swimmers who were incapable of floating in any position. Lack of buoyancy in one particular swimmer is often the result of more muscle mass, which may help the less buoyant (though stronger) swimmer to travel faster. Without a doubt, swimmers who 'float' higher in the water displace less water when they swim (though technically more air is displaced). It follows logically that, with less water resistance, they should be able to swim faster or use less energy moving through the water. Although this is indeed the case, there is no way of making yourself more buoyant. Certain Eastern Europe swimming coaches have experimented with 'pumping' extra oxygen into the body to increase buoyancy, but none of this has yet proved successful.

'Channel Stroke'

A variation of the crawl stroke which many triathletes are using with success and satisfaction is a form of the so-called 'channel stroke' also known as the 'catch up' or 'glide' stroke. Some authorities criticise this, arguing that it set swimming back fifty years after its introduction in the early 1930s. For champion swimmers, the glide stroke might indeed limit ultimate potential, sacrificing utmost fluency for a slightly jerky forward motion. For the triathlete, however, who will never even dream of swimming a sub-20 minute mile, the catch-up or glide stroke can be most helpful. Never before in my life had I been able to swim more than three laps (150 metres), but when a friend introduced me to this stroke, I was amazed because suddenly, I could swim 1000 metres without a break.

The main idea incorporated into the stroke is that the recovering arm rests for a second or two before pulling backwards. Once your lead arm drops into the water, you simply allow it to sink for a second or so, until it reaches a depth of about 12–18 inches, and then you pull back hard directly under the body. The seemingly insignificant period of rest enables the arm to recuperate from the hard pull; but the rest, brief though it is, is precious.

It is again vital to keep the wrists firm and the elbow bent at a 90-degree angle on the pull. Follow through as usual out beyond the thigh, and lead the out-of-water recovery with the elbow first, the hand following as if you were pulling something out of your hip pocket.

The stroke was first popularised after the 1932 Olympics, when the Japanese swimmers dominated many swimming events by using a form of this catch-up stroke. Although many swimming coaches reject the stroke today, arguing that the lack of continuous speed slows the overall speed of the swimmer, the glide stroke has proven a boon for more than a few heretofore slow-swimming triathletes.

'I'm positive it's helped me,' says 30 year old Wilfried Reichel of Cologne. 'The second or two that your arm is relaxed is important for recovery.'

REMEMBER THAT NO TWO PEOPLE ARE THE SAME. EXPERIMENT TO FIND 'WHAT'S BEST FOR YOU'.

Training

There are distinct advantages, as runners and bikers and non-swimmers quickly discover, about training in a swimming pool; on the other hand, there are distinct disadvantages as well. Physically, the body can absorb a lot of swimming. Psychologically, the mind cannot. The pounding that runners are endangered by is virtually non-existent in swimming, and the odds against injuring yourself swimming are astronomical. You almost have to want to get hurt to hurt yourself swimming.

It is no mere coincidence that Alberto Salazar and other top runners have taken to pool training, particularly with interval work, to enhance their aerobic capacities without jolting the joints of the body. Many injured runners have taken to the pool as a surrogate activity during the period of recuperation. Some have found the pool to be a long-neglected friend; some find it a bane. Many runners trapped in bitterly cold climates, switch from the frozen roads to the watery lanes during the coldest winter months, and experience no fall-off in their performances the following spring. Other runners prefer getting fat during the winter months rather than wet.

Triathletes, of course, have no such option. To complete or compete successfully in a triathlon, you have to become proficient in the water. Because swimming relies so heavily on technique, it is paramount not only to develop a suitable form, it is equally important to polish, refine, and maintain it. Says Peter Moysey, who at 22 has already won more triathlons than most people will win in a lifetime, 'I find that even if I go just two days without a swim my stroke starts falling apart.'

Maintaining a stroke can only be done through practice and, unless you have your own pool, or a lake or sea to swim in, the chlorinated pool is a place you should get acquainted with and learn to like. Some top triathletes spend between 10–20 hours per week in the pool. This is, of course, extreme, but to become a relatively proficient swimmer, you should reckon on spending at least two or three hours there per week.

Training ideas for the non-swimmer
For the non-swimmer the most important thing to consider is proper form. If you do not have an efficient stroke already, it is well worth seeking assistance from competent swimmers on the mechanics. Although some triathletes, like Dr Edmund Boys claim to have taught themselves how to swim, it is a sport that does not lend itself to do-it-yourself thinking.

Swimming is potentially one of the easiest sports to learn, but to do it properly requires patience, determination, concentration and hard work. In some respects, the non-swimmer is at an advantage over the person who already swims but with poor stroke mechanics. Once poor form is imprinted on the mind or on the body, it is difficult to 'unlearn' it, to root out and correct it.

A reasonable goal which a non-swimmer can aim for in the first few weeks of swimming, once he or she has the proper form, is to swim continuously for ten minutes. You can easily build up from that point, adding two-minute intervals or more, up to a 30-minute continuous swim. When you attempt a 30-minute swim, your pace should be even throughout, and you should of course remain within your aerobic capacity for the entire half-hour, as though you may want to push yourself for the last minute or so.

Swimming a mile (1600 metres or 1760 yards) non-stop is the eventual goal for the beginner. If you can swim a mile non-stop, you are ready for almost any triathlon, although if the swim is much longer, it is worth trying to swim the distance involved in at least one training session. With a relaxed easy form most individuals should be able to swim a mile within a few months of their entry into the sport. Improvements will come rapidly once the technique is down, but it is crucial, once again, to have the stroke monitored by experienced observers. It is flaws in the stroke, not necessarily any lack of power, that will spoil a triathlete's hopes of swimming a mile in under 30 minutes.

Once a satisfactory stroke has been attained, four miles of swimming per week for about two months is the recommended minimum amount of preparation for a first triathlon. You could conceivably get by with less, but it is better to do more. It is worth the trouble if you can afford the two hours per week it will take to swim four miles, but it is just as important to enjoy the time spent in the pool. Some triathletes tend to become masochistic about their training, and piously spend seven days per week in the pool, swimming from 10–14 miles each week from a background that previously included no swimming at all. Sure, they may have become proficient swimmers in a relatively short period of time but, psychologically, the mere thought of a swimming pool has become anathema. Moderation is vital, and a slow but steady build-up.

Many often discover a pleasant surprise with swimming four or five times per week, be it in the morning before work, or during a lunch break. It can provide an uplifting and, after a time, a much-looked forward to part of the day. Unlike a run, which requires 30–60 minutes of running and a 15-minute cool-down period to be of value, the swimmer can spend a vigorous 20 or 30 minutes in the pool and climb out feeling refreshed, clean and invigorated. Within a few minutes, you can be back in the office or wherever.

Minute for minute, swimming is a highly 'cost-effective' undertaking. The former Canadian Premier Pierre Trudeau swims nearly a mile every day in the early morning, and despite his age, his wife claims he has the body of a twenty-five year old.

Training ideas for the proficient swimmer
There are several schools of thought on what training the moderately proficient swimmer should undertake. One idea is interval training: that is, relatively short

bursts of 100–400 yards or metres, followed by a short period of rest, from a few seconds to a few minutes. Others advocate long-distance training, and over-distance training (i.e. greater than your race distance) to build strength as well as endurance. Marathon runners do not train for 26.2 miles by running 100 yards sprints, they point out. Yet another mode of thought is fartlek training, in which the swimmer covers about one mile and varies the pace at which he or she swims. Once again, there is no unanimous agreement on the training triathletes should undergo. Rather than lay down any sort of law, however, I recommend to you to try the different training methods, and stick with what works best for you. But do give each method enough of a chance to be effective.

Speed work
First of all, it is vital that the swimmer swim a mile (1600 metres) non-stop and in relative comfort. To consider interval or fartlek training before a swimmer is proficient enough to swim a mile in 35–40 minutes is probably a waste of time. Never sacrifice style for speed.

Once having leaped that hurdle, however, the prudent swimmer may want to explore fartlek or interval training or other methods to bring his times for the swim down even further. It is almost unavoidable to improve in the water, especially if you are just beginning. Good technique and good training work wonders.

If you can swim a mile in 30–32 minutes, some experts say, you should not continue to plod along at a constant pace for a mile at each work-out. You will be quite adept at swimming that exact pace, but you will never become any faster. Some form of occasional speed training is crucial.

'Swimming long and slow like that might be all right if you're just starting out,' says Juliet Smith. 'But I really think you need to push yourself in sets of shorter distances to get anything out of it.'

Fartlek
Fartlek is a Swedish term meaning 'speed-play' coined by the athletics coach of the 1948 Swedish Olympic team. Although it was originally designed for the benefit of runners, there is no reason why swimmers cannot use fartlek as well. By interspersing relatively short bursts of fast training with periods of moderate swimming, the swimmer can expect his aerobic capacity to enlarge sometimes considerably.

The attractive quality of the fartlek method, as opposed to the interval, is that you can continue to swim your continuous 1,000 metres or mile, theoretically without interruption. You can push when you want to, and glide at normal effort when you do not wish to. Fartlek in the water can also deflect some of the mind-numbing dullness that underwater conditions can create.

Intervals

This is the password for many swimmers, particularly triathletes with swimming backgrounds. They have trained for years with intervals, and undoubtedly they have become faster swimmers thereby. Interval sets are ideal for the oxygen intake, for building strength, and for morale, but if you are not used to them, they can be devastating for the mind. The body, after the third or fourth 100-metre or 100-yard set, starts screaming for oxygen after the first 50 metres. The pain is appreciable and the stroke may begin to falter because of it. The improvement will no longer be dramatic at this point either. Whereas, before, whole minutes seemed to come off your times in a matter of weeks, it now takes months, even years, beyond the 30-minute-per mile pace to take even seconds off. This is no reason to give up on improvement, on the contrary, this is where the good swimmers start to separate themselves from the average swimmers. With training, almost anyone can swim a mile in 30–35 minutes. To reach 27 minutes for the mile takes a great deal more practice.

'Most triathletes make a mistake by going into the pool and just swimming a mile or more at a constant pace,' says Don Kortmann, a Master's swim coach in Seattle and a graduate of Dr David Costill's Human Performance Research Laboratory at Ball State University. 'By doing that, you are only working your body at about 60 per cent of your maximum oxygen capacity. You are working all the muscles, but you are not subjecting them to the physiological stress needed for strength gains.'

Intervals can be done in two ways: one is to do an interval, say, every 90 seconds or every two minutes. So if you finish 100-metres in 1:45 and are going on every two minutes on the clock, you have 15 seconds to rest. If you finish 1:30, you have 30 seconds. Peter Moysey, one of England's top short-distance triathletes, regularly does 100-yard interval sets on 80 seconds, that is swimming the distance in 75 to 78 seconds, and then five or two seconds later he dives back in for another 100 yards.

Other swimmers prefer longer-distance, longer-rest intervals. Dave Scott for example, chooses 200-metre and 400-metre interval sets, with between one to three minute rests in between. To increase his aerobic capacity, he tries to shorten the rest interval.

Whatever distance you use, the goal during the rest period is to allow a partial, though incomplete recovery. Thus, your pulse rate should fall down below 120 or closer to 100 (or 30 to 40 per cent of its resting rate) before beginning the next sprint.

'There are,' says Scott, a former swimming coach, 'three types of aerobic training which should be integrated into a weekly, monthly and yearly swimming programme in order, first of all, to improve the maximal oxygen consumption

(VO$_2$ max) by interval training; second, to elevate your anaerobic threshold, also through interval training; and third, to develop stroke rhythm and pace through continuous, over-distance training.'

If you cannot spend at least five hours per week at the pool, Scott says, then you should get the most out of your swim work-outs by incorporating all three types of training into your weekly programme. Interval sets of 3–10 minutes of continuous effort are his favourite distance to work with, although he finds interval sets of from 15 minutes to 40 minutes the most conducive to building up the anaerobic threshold. For triathletes who prefer 100-metre, 150-metre of 200-metre intervals, he says the rest in between should be limited for the first few repetitions, and then increased gradually in the work-out so that the performance level does not fall off.

The other major part of training, Scott says, is the over-distance training from 20 non-stop minutes to several hours non-stop. 'The advantage of this training is to develop a sense of pace and stroke rhythm, and to train your body to race at a pre-determined speed.' One or two such work-outs per week are usually enough of a supplement to the intervals.

Interspersed in Scott's work-outs are 5-15 minutes of warming up before each swimming session and an equal amount of time after the swim to wind down. A second phase of his swim work-outs includes a warm-up set of intervals to start accelerating his heart-rate gradually. This is followed by a main set, either the work on the anaerobic threshold, or the shorter intervals (3–10 minutes), or the over-distance training.

'Be innovative in your daily work-outs with a logical rationale,' he says. 'If you do so your swimming programme will be self-motivational and certainly challenging and a lot more enjoyable.'

Bill Kooser, a triathlete and swim coach from Chicago, also recommends variety. 'To vary my work-outs I usually break up the session into a warm-up, stroke work, a hard set of intervals, some work on other strokes, and some work on kicking and pulling (swimming with only the arms). I try to change the distance I swim in the hard sets every work-out, and often play speed games, such as swimming every other lap hard, or making each swim faster than the one before. The whole idea is to keep your enthusiasm and make the work-out as much as fun as possible.'

Swimming in open water is obviously different to swimming in a pool. The water is invariably colder, sometimes much colder, you cannot see the bottom, there are no walls to push off of, and often there are waves to contend with as well as wind. Many races are held in salt water too which of course is a quite different element to the neighbourhood pool.

If you have never swum in open water, and are planning a race which involves an open-water swim, it is essential to get in some open-water practice before the race, ideally swimming (with a friend in a boat) the course itself. You should never swim alone in open water.

Swimming in a straight line is one of the most difficult aspects of open-water swimming. In a pool, it is easy. All you have to do is follow the black line painted on the bottom. In a lake, or ocean, you obviously have no such lines, so you have to use some other form of alignment to keep on a straight course. At the 1983 National Championships in England, a one-mile swim turned into a 1.5 mile swim for many competitors because of a strong, though unseen, current in the middle of the Kielder Reservoir. Some swimmers managed to swim, in spite of the current, a relatively straight line, and were spared the extra distance.

Strong swimmers recommend a 'water-polo' type of stroke to stay aligned. By raising their heads out of the water every five or ten strokes, they can periodically check their course. It is a good idea to aim for landmarks, especially when swimming in wavy water. With practice, however, it is possible to be able to swim through currents without too much difficulty – you just have to stay straight and calm. Some triathletes like to follow other swimmers, and let them do the sighting, and aligning. This works well if you are following or are to the side of someone who knows where they are going. But if they do not, you are both in trouble!

Because it is legal in most races to draft or pace on someone else in the swim (though expressly forbidden on the bike course), many triathletes do it, and claim it makes the swim a lot easier. 'You can let someone else do all the sighting, and set the pace,' says one female triathlete who wins most of her races. 'If you can find someone going your pace, grab a hold of them.

Cold water can be a special nemesis for the triathlete. Swimming in water as cold as 12°C (52°F) can be accomplished, but prolonged periods in water that cold, or indeed any colder than 16°C (65°F) can cause major problems. The better prepared a swimmer is for cold water races, the fewer problems he or she will have.

Salt water tends to have an insulating effect, so that 13°C (56°F) water in the sea is roughly equivalent to about 16°C in a lake. When you first get into cold water, it can be a very unpleasant experience. You may even at first have trouble breathing. But do not panic. Relax. Let your body gradually acclimatise itself to the water, perhaps by using a side-stroke or breast stroke for a few minutes, and then switch over to the crawl.

It is vital to wear a rubber swim cap in cold water, preferably two. Cloth caps do not insulate your head nearly as well. Much of your body heat is lost through your head. If you plan to do a race in cold water, prepare for it by increasingly longer swims in cold water. You will be amazed how much easier it becomes if you gradually work up from 10 minutes, to 15 minutes to 25 minutes in cold water.

After the initial shock of the first few minutes, you may even begin to enjoy the numbing cold.

In the ocean the waves can really pummel you if you let them. On the other hand, they can help you if they are going in a cross-direction, and you can time your strokes to coincide with the wave's motion. I had the fastest two-mile swim of my life at Nice one year by riding on the waves, and because of the salt water, not kicking at all. It just takes a little practice a day or two before the race, making oneself acquainted with the waves on the course, how they break, when they break, and how you can utilise to your advantage the mammoth amount of energy stored in each wave.

There are on occasion other natural obstacles that you have to watch out for, such as jellyfish. Most fish or other sea-borne creatures will be more afraid of you than you are of them, but jellyfish, perhaps because they cannot escape in time, are the exception. If you land on one, it may sting you. The best way to prevent yourself being stung is to watch out for them. While many swimmers reported being stung half a dozen times or more at Nice one year, others, including the best swimmers, said that they saw a lot of jellyfish, but did not get stung by any. Even if you are unfortunate enough to be stung, it is often a relatively minor pain that, after a few minutes, wears off.

Finally, at the end of the swimming portion of a triathlon, it is a good idea to switch to a side-stroke or breast-stroke for the final 15 metres or 20 metres, to enable your blood to balance itself throughout your body, and to stretch your leg muscles a bit. If you stand up right away after swimming hard into the shore, the sudden rush of blood from your arms to your feet can leave you dizzy.

Chapter 7

Biking

Contradictory though it may at first appear, bicycling is perhaps the most exciting part of the triathlon. It has already introduced thousands of people to the joys of the sport, and has similarly introduced thousands to the agonies of the sport. For that matter, triathlons have introduced bicycle manufacturers to enormous profits.

Certainly, the transition at any triathlon from the swim to the bike produces some of the sport's outstanding moments. Hundreds of nearly naked bodies rising out of the sea, gradually regaining their upright positions on land, sprinting with increasing velocity to the glistening two-wheeled machines, adding clothing on the way, and ultimately pedalling off on the wheels. It is, in a sense, an illustration of man's evolution, as he moved from the sea to the land.

Words, unfortunately, usually fail to do justice to describe the cycling portion of many triathlons. It has to be seen to be believed. Normally, the cycling portion of the triathlon is the longest part. And it does not take a genius to realise that, if most of the time is spent on a leather seat, then the greatest potential for improvement is also to be found in the saddle. It is quite simply a matter of logistics. In a nine-hour event, even the best triathletes spend four-and-a-half hours, if not more on their bikes. That is half the race.

Even if you ride 1 mph faster, which for neophytes will not be a difficult hurdle to overcome, that will cut from 3 minutes to 20 minutes off your time, depending upon the length of the race. 5 mph faster over a 112-mile course will save two hours! Even with a shorter course of, say, 30 miles, the triathlete travelling at 20 mph will finish the bike section 30 minutes ahead of an opponent travelling at 15 mph. Try taking 30 minutes, or two hours, off your swim or running time! Indeed, cycling speeds can, and usually do, show remarkable improvement in short periods of time.

'I had never biked in my life,' relates 21 year old Gareth Caldwell of Stafford. 'I'd been running for a few years, but it was getting quite boring. The first marathon I ran had been all right, but by the time I'd run my fifth, I'd had enough. A friend let me borrow his 10-speed bike one day, and it was great. At the time I didn't know the difference between a chain ring and a key ring, but you figure out pretty fast. Biking doesn't bore me at all.'

As even many of the top American triathletes are finding, one need not have spent years on a bike to become a good rider. Dave Scott and Scott Tinley, who have five Ironmen titles between them, have only been cycling for a few years, and yet they can ride with the best cyclists. Although some people consider that it takes five to ten years to become a great cyclist, a few become excellent bikers within just a few years.

Two of the most crucial aspects of cycling are handling technique, and efficient pedalling. In their zeal to get fast quickly, many beginners tend to overlook these. Although most beginners handle bikes poorly when riding, an equal number pedal with astonishing inefficiency. Even top triathletes are not immune to such pitfalls.

'If I were to do it over again,' confesses no less a triathlete than Scott Tinley, the winner of the February 1982 Ironman, 'I would try to learn more of the basics of cycling at the beginning, before putting in heavy mileage. I started doing too much heavy-duty mileage before I should have. I got into shape faster than I learned how to become a competent cyclist.'

Novices under estimate the value of technique. Even small children can ride a bike, they think to themselves. But the difference between riding a bike and racing is immense.

Some bikers talk about the 'kind of line' a person rides, that is to say, how straight an imaginary line a rider follows. Is it relatively straight, with hardly a wobble, or is it a sloppy, weavy, rough, unpredictable line? Many miles in the saddle will help a bike rider straighten his or her line, but concentration, especially in the early weeks and months of biking is essential.

Riding a straight line is not something that can be mastered in a day. It can, however, be mastered with patience, practice and concentration. By riding with good cyclists, and observing not only their 'lines' but how they maintain such beautifully *straight* lines is an excellent way to learn. Although the legs of the cyclist are cranking merrily away, the upper body should barely be moving at all. This is one of the keys to riding a straight line: minimising excess motion, especially the upper body.

Because the centre of the body's gravity on a bike is somewhere above the waist, that is to say relatively high up off the ground, it is imperative to limit side-to-side movements in this part of the body. Even when a good cyclist climbs out of the saddle to use his body weight to crank his way over a hill, or into the wind, and seems to throw his weight back and forth from side to side, he or she is still maintaining a straight line with the wheels. You can always spot the novice; the front wheel wiggles. One way some cyclists improve their lines is by riding on white lines painted on vacant parking lots, or even along the side of the road. Simply by practising the straight line, even where no physical straight line exists, can be of value to the beginner.

A second way cyclists improve their lines is by carrying a back pack with a single shoulder strap, containing a few light items. At first it seems impossible to prevent the upper body, and especially the shoulders, from wiggling. But after a few dozen miles you discover that the back pack, once so infuriating and seemingly dangerous as it wobbles from back to front, no longer leaves the back. But it is not the back pack that has adhered itself to you; it is you who have kept your line straight.

There are many other areas of technique where cyclists can improve. Knowing when to climb out of the saddle, how to corner smoothly, how to shift gears for optimal results, and how to brake wisely, are areas of cycling that lend themselves to improved performance, and which distinguish good from mediocre cyclists.

'Bicycling is a fairly technical sport,' says Tinley. 'Probably a lot more technical than most people think. You can't just jump on and start plunging on the pedals. You can get real good on the bike in a year, but you have to learn technique and style first.'

Knowing when to sit and when to stand are skills that are acquired over the course of hundreds, if not thousands of miles. Top European cyclists know exactly when to rise out of the saddle and use their body weight to apply more power to the pedals for brief outbursts. Though used primarily on hills, climbing out of the saddle is a useful technique for overtaking someone on flat terrain, or even to help spark a tiring cyclist to regain a faster cadence. 'It's necessary sometimes,' says Tinley, 'to climb out of the saddle when riding against the wind. Sometimes to get a gear going, you'll have to stand up.'

Standing also has another big advantage: it stretches your muscles, and, particularly over a longer course, can give your rear-end a much needed respite. Occasionally, too, standing during the bike portion of a triathlon helps to alleviate some of the potential trauma you will experience at the next stage, the start of the run.

'I couldn't believe how rubbery my legs felt the first time I ever did a triathlon,' says Chip Rimmer of Reading. 'I'd never imagined it could be so hard. It felt sort of like I was a bit drunk, and was trying to run fast, but was moving in slow motion. Everyone passing me by made the situation even more desperate. But the next time I tried stretching on the bike a bit, and it helped considerably.'

Biking

One of the most exciting and even artistic moments in cycling is cornering. But to master cornering is not as easy as it might seem, and knowing when to slow down, when to change over, when to brake, and how to use your body weight are just a few of the adjustments a cornering cyclist must take instantaneously. As he travels at 20 mph or more around a sharp corner the biker has to act and think fast. Hesitation can lead to hospitalisation. Because no two turns are alike, it is impossible to say how a biker should handle any particular curve. Even top riders vary in their approach to a turn, depending on, among other things, their size, their weight, the type of tyres they have, the condition of the road surface, and their own particular level of courage.

This is one area where quality tyres pay for themselves. They seem literally to grip the road and allow the biker to lean further into the curve at noticeably higher speeds.

As is the case with a car, it is wise to allow the speed of the bike to decrease *before* (and change gear if necessary) entering the corner. If this is done properly, you do not even need to brake. Merely by easing off the pedals for a few seconds you can slow the speed sufficiently. On the other hand, if you are travelling too fast into the curve, and then have to brake in the middle of the corner you can run into problems. If the brakes are suddenly pulled hard, the bike may slow sufficiently, but its rider and his or her weight will still, according to the laws of dynamics, be travelling in the original direction.

Once into the curve, to the point where you can see it beginning to straighten out, jump on the pedals and regain your momentum. You have lost mere seconds, when it is correctly done, but at the same time have given your legs a brief and valuable rest. The cyclist who pedals hard into the curve, and has to brake hard, has lost far more momentum, and has wasted far more energy.

Once in the curve, it is important, again, to maintain as parabolic a curve as possible. If it is a sharp curve, loop out before you reach the bend to widen the angle you must turn. The wider your angle, the faster you can go. Try to make the turning as gradual as possible, and watch out for the other cyclists riding around you. A glance over your shoulder not only gives you a quick picture of your surroundings but gives the other cyclists a warning that you are up to something.

For maximum control steering, your hands should be placed on the drops just below the brakes so that, if you have to stop quickly, you can reach the brakes by simply and quickly extending your fingers. Some riders even ride corners with a finger or two on the brakes. This is not a bad idea, especially on an unfamiliar course. To add even more stability on a corner, you can turn your inside knee out into the side of the curve to place more weight in the direction you want to go.

On rough, bumpy surfaces you may even wish to take your weight off your saddle and place it on your pedals, thus lowering your centre of gravity.

Gear shifting, and selecting the right gear, is also a skill. When you are travelling at 18 mph, a full 80 per cent of the effort to maintain that speed is used to overcome wind resistance. And that is when there is no wind at all. Even a 5 mph wind against you can make 18 mph feel like a nightmarish task to ride through. A 20 mph headwind can make a mountain look easy; and a 35 mph headwind can leave a bewildered cyclist calculating the trade-in value of his bike.

Nonetheless, thanks to the different gears available and to the evolution of the derailleur, (a small device which moves the chain to different gears, i.e. De-Rails) cycling into the wind, or over a hill, can be made a lot easier. Choosing the right gear is crucial. Many novices try to push too big a gear.

A technique known as 'spinning' can help a novice cycler to travel faster with less effort over longer distances. Incredible as it may seem (almost too good to be true) spinning, that is maintaining a steady count of between 80 and 100 revolutions per minute (rpm), is a method superior to what is known as cranking, that is, 45–60 revolutions per minute in a high gear and therefore using strength.

There are two main reasons why spinning, or high revolutions of 80 to 100, are superior. The first is that the high cadence allows a fast return of blood flow and causes less compression of blood vessels in the muscles, whereas a low lugging cadence causes compression of the blood vessels and delays the flow of the blood for longer periods in between the pedal strokes. The second main reason is that, when you push the pedal at a slow rate (40 to 50 rpm), you can damage the joint surface of the kneecap. Furthermore, the slower cadence leads to an anaerobic condition more quickly than does the spinning.

Spinning may feel odd at first. You may feel as though you are not moving as fast: while the benefits are not apparent until you realise that, at the higher cadence, you can pedal much further without a break. Just keep your legs spinning around somewhere between 80 and 100 rpm, and by selecting a gear just below what would constitute a hard effort, you can pedal for hours with apparent effortlessness.

Controversy has erupted between the proponents of spinning and the proponents of cranking. The latter argue that 80 rpm or more wastes energy. They prefer to turn at 50 rpm crank revolutions per minute, and claim they travel faster and save more energy. Bike racers invariably disagree. Moreover, the few bike racers who have entered the world of the triathlon spin 100 rpm or more. The spinning technique makes it possible to save the legs for the ensuing run, as well as keeping the pulse slightly lower. Naturally, there are points in any course where the cyclist will want to push hard. A triathlete may not want to yield any ground, for instance on a steep hill, so he will stay in a relatively big gear, jump out of the saddle, and crank 60 or 70 rpm for a few minutes up the hill in the bigger gear. Apart from breaking the monotony, it works different muscles and gives the over-exerted ones a brief respite.

The argument will most likely never be resolved. Some cyclists swear by spinning. Some swear by cranking or 'power-caming'.

To get the best results from shifting gears, it is wise to anticipate the gear you are going to need. Neither words, nor books, nor lessons, nor examinations can teach a rider which gear to use. Time in the saddle is the only educator. The observant and discerning biker will gradually develop a sort of sixth sense, a tacit understanding of when to be in which gear. The factors that the brain will soon automatically be digesting and computerising include the grade you are on (flat, downhill, uphill) and the road surface (from bumpy to smooth), to wind direction, wind speed, distance of journey, pace, and energy level.

'Most people wait too long to shift gears going up a hill,' notes Bob Curtis, winner of the New York United States Triathlon Series Race in 1983. 'You have to learn to shift just before you need to. If you wait too long to shift on a hill, you end up losing a lot of momentum and have to pedal too hard to compensate for it. You have to learn to anticipate.'

One final factor to keep in mind when shifting gears is that you will temporarily have less control as you reach to shift. Some bicycles have shift levers built right into the lower grips of the handlebars. It is a useful feature, but after a short while the extra cable can stretch and you lose the smoothness in shifting. If you keep your one arm on the drops as you reach down to shift, your loss of control will be negligible. It does, after a while, become second nature.

Braking is another misunderstood and oft-overlooked aspect of the bike. Contrary to popular wisdom, most of the stopping power of the bike is on the front wheel brake, approximately ninety per cent. Although the rear brake is not nearly as effective, it is important for preventing the rider's weight from sliding forward too quickly. A good rule of thumb is a sixty per cent pull on the rear brake, and forty per cent on the front. When you are forced to brake hard, it is wise to stiffen your arms, otherwise the chances of a head-first fall without the bike are high.

Biking, as many triathletes discover, is a fascinating sport. Powering over a hill, flying deftly around corners, or overtaking another cyclist in an exciting duel all offer some of sport's most exciting moments. Although it is perhaps difficult for some people to fathom, the ecstasy that one experiences while riding a bike up a one-in-four grade (25 per cent) for four miles to reach the top of a mountain, and then cascading down the other side in a fraction of the time required to climb, is surely unmatched in sport.

The heart steadily thrumbs along, beads of perspiration sprout from the forehead and slide merrily off the nose, and the lungs expand and collapse in a happy unison. As the climb continues up, up above where the lesser mortals dare, it suddenly dawns on the cyclist how spectacular the scenery is, how close the clouds are, and how much more brilliant the colours seem from these mountain perches. The blood zipping around the body eight times per minute seems only to heighten the moment, for mountain peaks never seem so fantastic, the colours never so brilliant seen through a car window as when on a bike. It has to be experienced to be believed.

In its first year in 1982, the Nice Triathlon lured some of the world's top triathletes from across the Atlantic, largely because of the spectacular, breathtaking bike course at Nice. From the swim in the Mediterranean, the bike course wends its way up into the Alps behind the city, rising to staggering heights through little French villages, and then plummets back down to the city some 75 (120 kilometres) later. 'I came here for the bike course,' said Rick Kent, 'I'd heard so much about it, that I just decided I had to see it for myself. I've never ridden up hills like these. It's tremendous.'

How do you get better on the bike? 'The most important thing is time on the bike,' according to Gerd Uhren, a West German triathlete who is perennially one of the top German finishers at Nice, thanks primarily to his sterling bike rides. 'Once you've developed a good technique, you've got to put in a lot of time on the bike to get better. It takes kilometres, and lots of them.'

There is, it seems, no way around the fact that triathletes who manage 200 or 300 miles per week on their bikes are going to perform better nine times out of ten than their counterparts who spend half, or less, time than that. This is not to say that a minimum of 200 miles per week on the bike for fifty-two weeks per year is a pre-requisite to enjoy triathlons, or even to be competitive. On the contrary, many have not only finished but have won triathlons on 100 miles per week on the bike and less.

West Germany's Regina Schwarz won the women's division of the West German national championships in 1984, despite the fact that she had never, ever, ridden a racing bike before the race. 'I run a lot,' she explained. 'But I had never been on bike like that before. I still don't know how to use the toe clips. I had never biked at all before that.'

However, the days of victory for triathletes who do not train at all on the bike are fading. When the sport was first reaching Europe, and few Europeans even knew what a triathlon was, any reasonably fit runner or swimmer could turn up, and if not win an event, certainly challenge for first place. The contending triathletes of the mid-1980s are all now putting in at least 150 miles per week, but closer to 250 miles per week. Many are even putting in up to 300 miles or more per week.

For the triathlete who is looking for a good time, good fitness and a decent finishing time, anywhere from 50 to 100 miles per week will in normal cases suffice.

That is of course in ideal circumstances. You should not be discouraged, nor fear to enter a triathlon, if you have not been able to bike more than a few times per week. Some triathletes, such as Newcastle's Terry Mason, do not train at all on the bike, and yet they still manage to finish respectably somewhere in the middle of the pack. Chrissie Barrett usually rides just 20 miles per week – two 10-mile rides – in the month or two before a triathlon, and has no trouble finishing races.

Beyond the weekly mileage totals, beyond the calloused palms and sore bottoms, there is one other major aspect of improved cycling, and that is riding on the right size of bicycle. Before you worry about the size of your chain wheel, or the few grammes of weight you might spare by drilling out the inside of your derailleur, it is important to make sure that your bike properly fits your body. Incomprehensible though it may seem, race directors at many triathlons where bike inspections are mandatory are finding that triathletes are riding on frames two inches too large or too small. Countless other misadjustments, from seat positions to handlebar height, have been reported. Proper positioning of the seat and the handlebars is paramount. A saddle that is just an inch or two too low can reduce the efficiency of the leg muscles by nearly 25 per cent. When pedalling 100 miles or more, 25 per cent is a lot to throw away on a poorly adjusted seat. Further, the likelihood of injury is magnified. Some European bike racers are so obsessed with optimal seat adjustments that they carry Allen wrenches in their back pockets, and will, depending on the terrain coming up, adjust the seat up or down millimetres to ensure the maximum efficiency of the legs. Such fine attention to detail is a big part of biking.

A basic rule of thumb for finding the optimal seat and handlebar is comfort. Experimentation also is not a bad idea. Basically, what you should be looking for when adjusting the seat post is a slight bend in the knee on the down leg at its furthest point of extension. The toes on the pedal slightly bent. In other words, the extended leg should form something just short of an 180° angle, or appear as five minutes to six on an imaginary clock. This height positioning will extract maximum efficiency from the powerful leg muscles. But why, the reader may be wondering, slightly bent, and not fully extended? Answer: because the greatest amount of power from the muscles is released precisely at this point – just short of full extension. The energy output of the legs increases and decreases in a parabolic arch: bent at the 12 o'clock position at the top of the cycle it is contributing zero power. As it straightens out, its power output rises steadily and inexorably until it reaches its zenith just prior to full extension. From that point, the power output tapers off quickly and the opposing muscle group works to protect the joint. Similarly, boxers try to land their punches on their opponents well before the full extension of their arms. At that point, even if the boxer did connect, the punch would do little damage.

On most quality bikes, the seat can be adjusted horizontally (forwards and backwards) as well as vertically. Because body sizes vary as well, the adjustments will once again be able to maintain a slight bend in the arms (for greater shock absorption), and feel comfortable, then you are well set. If you are in doubt, ask a knowledgeable friend, or someone in a bicycle shop, to confirm it.

As far as the position of the handlebars goes, common sense should dictate their approximate position. Depending once again on the individual, the tops of the handlebars should be just about one inch lower than the seat. It may seem uncomfortable at first to ride with your rear end up higher than your hands, but if you let your arms hand down at your side, you will notice that your arms extend down considerably further than your waist. Also, you want to maximise the drive of your leg muscles, unquestionably the most powerful parts of your body. By placing your handlebars slightly lower than your seat, your centre of gravity will lie more directly over your legs, and your heart is in a more efficient position. Therefore if you do place the handlebars too high, you will probably notice a distinct lack of power.

A final reason for keeping your handlebars as low as possible is wind resistance. Even an inch or two higher can add an appreciable amount of wind resistance. It seems trivial, but really it is not. Top cyclists maintain that even half an inch higher than necessary will create sufficient drag to mean the difference between winning and losing.

You will notice the wind resistance factor as you begin to ride faster. The energy required to overcome wind resistance at 15 mph is relatively low. But increase your speed by 5 mph and the additional wind resistance makes it twice as difficult. Increase that speed up to 25 miles per hour, and, suddenly, it is eight times harder.

Thus it becomes crucial to avoid the wind, or 'cheat it' as much as possible. When faced with a strong headwind, or when riding really hard, it is best to ride with your hands down on the drops, and perhaps even with your elbows bent, and your head tucked down as low as possible. If you experiment yourself with this and other wind-cheating positions you will discover how sapping the wind can be, and at the same time, ingenious ways to minimise its effects.

The same applies when riding down a hill. If you want really to fly down a hill, where it is a safe, smooth surface – then lower your back parallel to the top tube and feel the difference. Similarly if you need to slow down slightly, you can try sitting back up straight, and you will see how effectively your chest works as a 'parachute' (as on a dragster) to slow you down.

The size of the bicycle frame is also quite important. Whereas some of the top triathletes, and those who wish to become contenders, on occasion spend large sums on custom-made bikes, such extravagance is not a pre-requisite for success. All that a custom-made bike can guarantee is bank-book shock.

'I've ridden £1,000 bikes that I wouldn't have paid £100 for,' one bike mechanic confided. 'I think it's a mistake to think the more you spend on a bike means the better it's going to be. You can get some excellent bikes, with the same equipment as a £1,000 bike, for less than half that.'

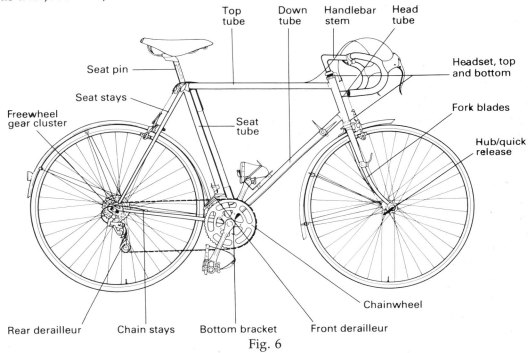

Fig. 6

A guideline for choosing the correct size frame is to divide your height in inches by three. Thus, if you are six feet tall, or 72 inches, a 24-inch frame, or perhaps slightly smaller (23 or 23½ inch) is optimal. It is better to lean towards a slightly smaller frame than vice-versa. The reason has to do, once again, with wind resistance. The lower the body, the less wind resistance, and the less wind resistance, the faster you can go. A smaller frame will naturally be slightly lighter as well.

Although until the late 1970s quality bikes could cost nearly as much as an economy car, technology (and perhaps to some extent the triathlon) has worked wonder on their prices. To purchase a light-weight (circa 21 pounds or less) bike, with quality alloy components, racing wheels, and light-weight tyres (to reduce moving weight as greatly as possible), would today only cost about £300 to £450.

By shopping around, and asking a lot of questions, you can more than likely find what you are looking for. It is important to have alloy rims, not only for their lightness, but for riding in wet conditions as well. Steel rims lose their breaking power when wet. It is also important to have as good a derailleur as you can afford. Without a doubt, it is the heart of the bike. If it malfunctions in a race, your race is over. Mark Allen's hopes of victory at Hawaii were suddenly ended in 1982 when his derailleur broke.

The frame is another vital part of the bike – try and obtain one as sturdy and light as possible. A good bike is a life-time investment if you take care of it.

Aleck Hunter had been riding on a bike that he has had for more than twenty years. It cost less than £50 when he bought it, and its value has quadrupled in the ensuing years. If you learn to love your bike, and care for it as if it had feelings, it will not let you down. You only need to guard against becoming too attached to it. 'If I watched after my lady like I do my bike I'd be all right,' said Mark Kleanthous.

A new breed of 'triathlon' bikes has crept on to the market. It is just a gimmick. Although the bikes are usually of excellent quality, they are race-touring bikes with a second water-bottle. And race-touring bikes have been around for years.

Basically, a race-touring bike is a cross-bred between a racing bike, which is used primarily for short-time trials of 10–50 miles, and a touring bike, which offers a far more comfortable ride than a racing bike, although it sacrifices, of course, some speed. Triathletes need a little of both. A racing bike has a front fork which drops almost straight down, whereas the touring bike has a front fork which loops way out in front. The race-touring bike comes somewhere in between the two.

Racing bikes often have extremely light, ultra light, (and ultra-expensive) tyres; touring bikes usually have sturdier, though heavier, tyres. Once again, the triathlete needs something in between. There are, however, plenty of relatively light-weight tyres of quality on the market. The Wobler Invulnerable, to name just one, is an excellent sew-up tyre. Technically it is a sew-up tyre and nearly as light, but it has steel thread wound in it to prevent punctures. Many triathletes glow in their praise of it.

When purchasing a bike, do not hesitate to shop around, and negotiate. Many bike dealers can reduce the price by at least five per cent, if not more, particularly if you offer cash. You have absolutely nothing to lose. Instead of worrying about a 'triathlon' bike, simply ask the dealer if he will throw in a second water-bottle cage, and strap the pump underneath the upper bar.

Understanding the bike

It is baffling, at times, how seemingly simple, and yet complex, a bike can be.

Some repairs that seem easy enough for a child to manage become nightmarish endeavours. Others that seem to require a PhD in Physics to solve can be put right in a matter of minutes or seconds. It is a good exercise to learn, and learn thoroughly, how the bike functions, and how to maintain and repair it on your own. For the 'uneducated' triathlete, who has no idea how to fix his or her bike, disaster may occur in the middle of a race. Sometimes even the simplest of repairs is all that is required, yet the triathlete has no idea where to begin, and has to retire, unfortunately and unnecessarily.

One now-experienced triathlete remembers: 'I had been training for months for this one triathlon. Months! And then a spoke broke, and I had no idea what to do. I was doing really well until then too. I had to drop out. What else could I do? It still hurts to think about that.'

The most logical way to avoid such an experience is to join a cycling club. The chances are good, particularly in Great Britain, that there is a bike club in your own community, which will be glad to have a new member. It is from their members' cumulative years of experience, amounting to decades if not centuries, of on-the-road miles, that you can acquire a wealth of knowledge about the art of cycling. Even if you do not know how to change a flat tyre, do not be bashful about joining a club. More than likely, someone will be glad to show you how. Smart bikers, you will soon discover, are not afraid to ask stupid questions. Pick the minds of the good cyclers; imitate their style.

Apart from the cameraderie and wealth of information that bike clubs provide, the races they hold throughout the year can also be of invaluable assistance for budding cyclists. Time trials of 10, 25, 50 and even 100 miles are run in dozens of cities and towns each week. There are even occasional 12-hour races, in which the cyclists try to bike as far as possible in twelve hours. The winners frequently get close to 290 miles. The twelve hour races are, incidentally, an excellent warm-up for a full-distance ultra triathlon. The day-long struggle to find energy, as well as learning how much and when you need to eat to keep going, are all part of the 12-hour or 200-mile time trials.

Time trials, or other forms of racing, also serve as an excellent barometer, telling you how much you are improving. If it took you, for example, 30 minutes to ride 10 miles on your first time out, and after a few weeks of training on the bike you can manage it in 28 minutes, you would understandably be delighted. And in this sense, the time trials will spur you on to train more. Success breeds interest.

Malcolm Kelvie, of Maidstone, was thirty years old when he joined a bike club. He candidly admits he joined it primarily to become a better triathlete. He had run for a few years, and considered running to be his forte until he began biking. 'It was tremendous,' he recalls. 'I'd never have imagined how much I enjoy biking. The club has helped me so much, and I've enjoyed just about every minute of it.

Biking has become without a doubt my number one sport right now. It's just got into my blood. I do more bike racing now than triathlons.'

Not surprisingly his zeal has already paid some handsome dividends. At Nice his first year he crashed and was one of the last triathletes to finish the race (despite a trip to hospital, he managed to finish). The following year, after joining the bike club, he finished seventh among the 40 British competitors there, and 66th among the 300 finishers, boosted by a strong ride (despite losing five minutes to a flat tyre) on the mountainous 75-mile bike course.

Another one of Britain's top triathletes, Alan Bell, also extolls the advantages of riding with a bike club. 'The best thing you can do is to ride with a club,' he says. 'You have to find riders who are better than you, and train with them. You may find that you can't keep up with them after 10 miles the first time out, but each time you'll be able to stay up with them a little longer. The next time out you'll make it maybe 30 miles before dropping off, then 40 and then 50. After a while, you'll be able to stay with them the whole time. That's a good feeling, then, because you know you're improving. But you have got to go out with a group. Alone it's just not the same. You don't push yourself as hard when you're alone. When you're fighting to hang on to someone's wheel, that's when you're gaining something.'

Aside from the camaraderie and the intangible push which riders in a group tend to give each other, it is usually safer to ride with a pack as well. Cars and trucks seem to respect a group of three or more bikers more than the solitary rider. It is amazing how often cars and trucks pull out in front of bikers, forcing them to grab madly for the brakes, but with a group of half a dozen or more cyclers, you tend to form a 'vehicle' all your own, and, according to the unwritten rules of the road, you seem to earn a lot more respect if you are in a group.

Interval training for cyclists

Runners swear by it. Sometimes they swear at it. Swimmers also swear by it in their work-outs, claiming it is the only way to improve. It follows that interval training can benefit the cyclist as well, indeed, many top long-distance runners, triathletes or not, spend time furiously pedalling bikes to improve their cardio-vascular fitness.

An interval, by definition, is an intense period of effort, be it in a pool, on a bike or on a track, followed by a period of rest which does not allow the body to recover completely. The push-ease-off, push-ease-off pattern is repeated, generally with from 1 to 3 minutes of pushing, and an equal or shorter period of recovery. Supplementary cycling has long been a haven for injured runners. Now with the triathlon, it has become an objective in its own right.

For newcomers to cycling, it is not wise to begin interval training on the bike too soon. Before beginning interval training a person should be able to complete comfortably long bike rides of at least 50 to 60 miles. Ideally intervals on bikes are performed on flat stretches, with few potholes and little traffic. Intervals over hills can also be beneficial, but for prolonged interval sessions, the flats are better for consistent measurement.

After at least 30 minutes of steady riding by way of a warm-up, pick a gear at which you can turn at least 10–20 rpm above your normal crank rate, yet is big enough to extract effort from your thighs. (A 52–14 might be optimal for some riders). The higher your rpms the better, optimally more than 110 yet, on the other hand, you do not want to spin so fast that you wobble or bounce.

You should stand up to start the session, in order to get your legs moving faster. Then, when in normal circumstances you would be ready to settle back into the seat, stay up and pedal hard for another 10 or 15 revolutions. Cranking as hard as you can without sacrificing technique and a straight line, push for a minute to begin with, and then ease off for one minute. Repeat the process as much as you can, but remember to build up to longer times gradually.

Times and distances covered in each interval should be increased (at a sensible rate, i.e. not more than a 10% increase in any one week). Ideally one does fast intervals by riding in chain (that is four or more riders taking one minute turns at the front each and the rest slip stream), which is extremely effective for speed improvement. For a triathlete who has to ride alone longer intervals are probably best done on Time Trial races or over pre-selected distances and repeated.

Tyres, which type should you use?

There are two types of tyre, tubs or high-pressure. Each tyre has its own particular advantages and disadvantages. In Europe, the tubs are used by most triathletes. In the United States, on the other hand, high-pressure tyres are more common.

Bike racers in Europe say that tubs, being lighter, offer superior handling and traction, are easier to change, fit over lighter rims, and create less rolling resistance.

What more could a triathlete want, you ask? Unfortunately there are drawbacks with tubs. Though lighter, they puncture more easily. Though easier to change when flat they require glue or sticky tape to hold them onto the rims. They are also expensive. The high-pressure tyre advocates, on the other hand, point to the fact that the high-pressure tyres are generally less expensive than tubs, are easier to patch, and with improving technology, are becoming nearly as light as the tubs. The greatest advantage, they add, is that they rarely puncture.

Because there is a tube inside the rubber tyre holding the air, objects that puncture have to cut through the outer rubber and then, if they can successfully remain pointed into the inside gap between the rubber and the tube, the object must then puncture the tube as well. Not impossible, of course, but not as likely as with the tubs. With the tubs, the sharp object needs only to break through the one outer surface.

Tyre manufacturers have responded to the needs of the triathlete, who naturally can ill-afford to lose five minutes changing a tyre. Wobler, for instance, has produced a tyre called 'Invulnerable' which, though far lighter than most high-pressure tyres, provides nearly as much durability. Many triathletes who use Invulnerables have yet to experience a flat tyre.

The choice of which type of tyre remains the rider's. With improving technology, the rider on the high-pressure tyres may not really be losing so much any more.

Chapter 8

Running

The running portion of most triathlons is where the fun begins. Although technically two-thirds of the race has been completed, in actuality it is only the beginning. This is a painful lesson for many newcomers to the sport.

'It was my first full triathlon, and I thought it would probably be my last,' explained one slightly bewildered competitor after a particularly hard race. 'I've only been doing this for a few months now, but wanted to see what a full triathlon was like, and much to my surprise, I was in first place at the midway point, 56 miles into the bike race. I've been running for about five years, it's my background, so I began thinking that I had first place all wrapped up.

'Was I ever wrong? A few miles later another biker caught me up, and, without saying a word, began to pedal past me. "Half-way there, eh?" I shouted over to him. He just looked back at me sort of strangely, and a few seconds later, he grinned and said, "Ha! This is where the fun begins".'

'I found out what he meant later. I was dead before the marathon even started. How was I possibly going to run 26 miles. It was awful. I've never felt so much pain in my life. I've never been happier either then when it was over. I said "never again", but you know, I can't wait for the next one.'

The run is usually the last event in the triathlon. There are, alas, exceptions to every rule. The Association of Professional Triathletes, an American organisation, stages a series of races in the Western United States, which are aimed mainly at professional highly trained triathletes. In these races, which are usually far less than even half-Ironman distances, the swim is followed by the run, and the race ends with the bike ride.

It is primarily for safety reasons that the run is generally the last event. Tired swimmers can drown. Fatigued bikers can seriously injure themselves, or someone else, if they lose control of their bikes, or bodies. But fatigued runners, no matter how delirious a condition they're in, do comparatively little damage to themselves or other people when they collapse.

Thus, the running portion of the triathlon is normally relegated to the end, systematically converted into the proving ground for serious runners, the burial ground for tired runners, and the play ground for good runners. Relegating the run to the finale has also become the source of a minor, though unsolvable, controversy: some runners claim, oddly enough, to be at their greatest disadvantage because everyone is spent by then, and thus good runners are unable to gain as much of an advantage as good swimmers or bikers. This is such nonsense, as anyone, especially a good swimmer, who has watched a good runner rocketing by them at the end of a triathlon will attest.

The run can do strange things. It has made previous lovers of running hate it. It has helped mediocre, but versatile, athletes become champions. It has humbled good swimmers, devastated good bikers, and even broken many good runners into hobbling plodders. It is often the deciding terrain, the turf, where races are more often than not won and lost. The championship round. If the swim is the quarter-finals, the bike ride is the semi-finals, and the run is the final.

'The triathlon is an interesting event,' comments Barry Turner of Essex, the dentist who tried his hand at a score of other sports but dropped them all once he discovered the triathlon. 'You can come out last in swimming and work your way up through the field, or vice-versa.'

To the non-athlete, the idea of running after biking and swimming seems preposterous, even insane. The legs are already tired. The body is largely drained of its energy reserves. The heart and lungs have already been working overtime. And now you ask your legs to carry your weight even further, pounding away 800 times per mile on an unyielding surface. Why push on? Why subject the body to further torment and misery when it has already been healthily challenged? This is the 'big why' of the sport, and it is, of course, not easily answered. Klaus Klaeren, the West German and European Champion in 1984, usually wins his races by catching opponents on the run, sometimes coming from miles behind. It is obviously his forte, the portion of the triathlon that he, one imagines, would look forward to with greatest relish; yet even he confesses to having doubts on the run. 'In longer races I ask myself at least a hundred times, "What am I actually doing here?" and "Why am I doing this?" There's just no easy answer. You just have to keep going, and think of other things, concentrate on something else. Sure it hurts, but you just have to keep going.'

There is something almost miraculous about the triathlon in the way the competitor will find hidden reserves, those pools of energy that even the body may not realise it possessed. If you pushed too hard on the bike, left little for the run, then you will naturally find the run a devastating experience. Your one consolation in such a case might be that, the next time you run a marathon, or longer distance road race, you will be so skilled at running on 'empty' that you will feel strong, relatively, to those struggling around you. However, if you pace yourself sagely on the swim and especially on the bike, and succeed in getting through the first few difficult moments of the run, you will find that miracles do still happen. For there is indeed something wonderful about discovering that, despite swimming, and biking, the muscles used to run have been 'preserved' on the bike course. In the water, of course, it was (or should have been) mostly an exercise for the arms. So, after nimbly changing into your running shoes, getting through those difficult first few wobbly minutes of the run as the gyroscope in your head reorientates itself, running can successfully, and joyfully, be accomplished. At first, it will seem impossible. After a few perhaps painful, slightly uncomfortable minutes, it will seem 'improbable'. A few minutes later, the chances of finishing the run will be further up-graded to 'maybe', and before you know it you will start estimating how many people you can catch before the finish line. One of the triathlon's most splendid, yet infinitely subtle, pleasures lies in this. You can be in front of a rival in the early going, be passed on the bike, and still manage to overtake him or her again on the run.

Getting Started

Anyone can run. You do not need a licence, nor an invitation. You do not even have to be of a minimum age. When historians of a later age look back at the twentieth century they will surely write of the world-wide running boom of the 1970s and 1980s as a not insignificant aberration. Millions of people, have discovered the joys and the healthfulness of this simple sport.

'I was running in a forest in the early hours of a Sunday morning not too long ago,' explains co-author Aleck Hunter, one of Britain's original triathletes. 'And I can still vividly recall the scene. The sun was just rising and glimmering through the trees. The dew was dripping down, and gathering the sun's rays with it. Rabbits, squirrels, and birds were all actively hopping about. There wasn't an unnatural sound to be heard. I was in another state, completely relaxed, flowing freely, and running more comfortably than ever before. How near paradise can one get?'

Running does offer invigorating pleasures to its regular patrons. It does, however, take at least 20–30 minutes three times a week to net appreciable benefits. What is important is to establish some consistent routine, running three or four times per week. You need not run every day. Even the top triathletes rarely run more than four or five times per week.

Where do you begin? The key is to start small and build gradually. This axiom applies to swimming and biking, when you are beginning, but particularly to running. Because of the immense pounding the body undergoes while running, even one mile, it is advisable to proceed sensibly.

Much depends on the original condition. Can you, without unbearable strain, run a mile non-stop? If not, remedial work is necessary. You may even wish, particularly if you are over 35 years old and more than 25 pounds overweight, or have a history of heart problems, to have a stress test performed before you begin. Those who are anxious to start right away, yet still wish for some sort of guide to the relative shape of their cardiovascular system, can administer the 'Harvard Step Test' (see Appendix 2) to themselves.

A first goal is to run 15 minutes non-stop. That is roughly one mile and a half, perhaps a bit more. There is no need to run it fast, nor is it vital to be able to run it non-stop the first time. Start by running a few hundred yards, and then walking until you feel ready to run again and then carry on running, interspersing walking whenever necessary. Try to run steadily and easily. Many beginners believe that they have to run fast, that if they are not running fast enough to become winded, they are not running fast enough. Why this occurs is a mystery, but it is common with beginning runners (and swimmers and bikers as well). So just run slowly, easily, and without strain.

You should be breathing easily enough to carry on a conversation while running, even if it means talking with yourself. Some of the world's fastest triathletes have described running as nothing more than 'fast shuffling'.

You will undoubtedly find that, in a short while, you will be running more and walking less. It might take a week before you can run the 15 minutes non-stop. It might take longer. The important thing is to keep at it. You will be surprised how soon your body responds and delivers its exhilarated owner to the goal.

Once the 15 minute non-stop run has been accomplished, keep adding five-minute increments. You will be startled how quickly you are able to run 30 minutes, or approximately three miles, non-stop. There will certainly be initial discomfort, even at first, in running for five minutes. But with regular practice, within a few weeks, you will begin to enjoy it. You need not believe me; just ask any one of the millions of happy runners today. The chances are that they all suffered from the initial 'What-am-I-doing-this-for?' doubts while slogging through the first painful weeks, but if they are still running, and most do continue with it, then the doubt has obviously been eradicated.

Speed, at this point, is *not* of the essence. Endurance is. You should be trying to lengthen the time you can run non-stop, not the speed in which you can run a given distance. Many runners fall into this trap. If you are covering three miles in 30 minutes, your next aim should be to run four miles in 40 minutes, not three miles in 25 minutes. Once you have established a sound 'base' as runners call it, that is to say a solid foundation, a point when your legs and heart have developed some strength, then you can, if you wish, start thinking about running faster. But to do this prematurely is to court disaster. More than a few impatient runners have suffered injuries that have needlessly soured their outlook on the sport. The 'base' takes months, even years to develop. It depends, once again, on the level of your fitness when you began. But as a guideline, even the fittest non-runners should not worry about speed before distance for *at least three months*, and preferably not before six months of regular running. A 'base' might be roughly defined as a point when a person can run, comfortably for 45–60 minutes consistently, non-stop, without any great pain or ill-effects.

'The more gradually you go about it, the better it is for your body,' says 25 year old Robin Ryan, who has been running for eleven years. 'It took me five years to build up to six miles. I just didn't push it. I still don't run much faster than eight-minute miles, but even to that speed I built up gradually. I've never been hurt, and I'm sure it's because the build-up has been gradual.'

Once you are able to run 45 minutes non-stop comfortably, then you are probably ready for a first short-distance triathlon. Regardless of your age, you should feel confident, providing that you can swim and bike the distances involved as well, that you can successfully complete the shorter-distances races, that is to say, anything up to a 1,000-metre swim, a 25-mile bike ride, and a six-mile run. It might not prove easy, but you should be able to finish.

The old-age myth, that is that older people should not continue to dabble in fields thought to be better suited for youth, has been chisled at in recent years, and seems finally to have been exploded in the summer of 1984, when the 37 year old Carlos Lopes defeated a field of the world's greatest marathoners, most of whom were considerably younger, to win the Olympic gold medal. Lopes' victory surely must have warmed the hearts of thousands of middle-aged people around the world. That age need not be a deterrent to successful running is shown not only by Bob Robinson who at 71 wins triathlons in his age group, but also by Bryn Jenkins. He is 63 years old, and runs marathons in 2 hours and 50 minutes. He runs a 10-mile race in an improbable 62 minutes, yet he did not begin running until he was 49.

The notion that women cannot handle stress of endurance running has also been destroyed, thanks in part to the triathlon. At the 1983 Ironman triathlon, Chrissie Barrett had the fourth fastest marathon time among the women (3:22), and 32nd fastest marathon time overall. 'I never find it tough to go to the run,' she says honestly. 'Maybe because I do a lot more running than cycling. Many triathletes, it seems, are good cyclists, and put a lot of effort into cycling. I feel sorry for them on the run. It's only natural that they feel frustrated struggling on the run, especially after biking so well.'

All you need for equipment is a pair of comfortable running shoes, comfortable shorts and, depending on the weather, a comfortable shirt.

The intensity you put into your runs is entirely up to the person in charge – yourself. There are no coaches with whistles (or whips), and there need be no stop watches. Running can also help your body in an extraordinary way, no matter how long or how much you have abused it with excessive eating, smoking or drinking. Minute for minute, there is no greater burner of calories than running. Swimming and biking come close behind, but only cross-country skiing, rowing, and chopping wood burn up nearly as many calories as running.

Running can also help you mentally. Although the source of 'natural highs' is still somewhat disputed, there are several intriguing theories. One of the more widely held beliefs today is that the massive amount of blood circulating through the body triggers the release of a chemical known as endorphins, which is perhaps responsible also for the pleasant mental stimulation you experience in the midst of runs. Besides it makes you feel good with yourself.

Running can, along with aerobic exercises such as swimming and biking, significantly lower your blood pressure and concentration of food fats in your system, for it increases the amount of blood pumped with each contraction of the heart, which thus lowers your pulse and blood pressure. Running greatly increases the efficiency of your heart and the ability of your muscles to remove the oxygen needed for energy from the blood. In his book *The Complete Book of Running* Jim Fixx asserted that heart disease has fifteen likely contributing factors. The most important of these are high blood pressure, cigarette smoking, diet, stress and heredity – all of which, with the exception of the latter, can be reduced or eliminated through regular aerobic exercise.

Running is not only one of the most sensible ways to lose weight; more importantly, it keeps it off, and much more so than any 'miracle diets'. When a person enters a diet, he cuts the intake, of course, of food into the body; but the body, sensing a forthcoming famine automatically sends messages to the brain to eat more while at the same time protecting even more tenaciously its stored-up fat. Dieting alone can be often, as many belatedly discover, a fruitless chore. The fat cells within the dieter's body may shrink a bit, temporarily, but the same number of fat cells remains. As soon as the famine is over, the body starts to replenish its spent reserves and, in no time, the weight lost will soon be back on, with perhaps the later weight gain exceeding what was originally lost. It is a vicious cycle.

With exercise such as running however, you can cure the *cause* of excessive weight, not merely the symptoms. The body, for all its marvellous complicity, is remarkably simple in this one sense: it is a remorseless counter of calories. You may be able to sneak down a cheeseburger when no one is watching, but your body will not miss it, and you will count every one of the calories. It is also an equally accurate counter of calories you burn. No one else may have seen you run those seven miles at 6 am, but rest assured, your body noticed. The good news is, as the accompanying chart reveals that the more you weigh the more calories you burn.

Regardless of your speed, if you weigh:

120 pounds	you burn	82 calories per mile
130 pounds	you burn	90 calories per mile
140 pounds	you burn	98 calories per mile
150 pounds	you burn	104 calories per mile
160 pounds	you burn	110 calories per mile
170 pounds	you burn	116 calories per mile
180 pounds	you burn	124 calories per mile
190 pounds	you burn	130 calories per mile
200 pounds	you burn	136 calories per mile
210 pounds	you burn	144 calories per mile

How much weight you lose through running (or swimming and biking) depends on how long you work. If, starting from a completely sedentary, overweight, non-athletic background, you gradually build up 20–30 minutes of running per day, (and 15–20 minutes of non-stop swimming, and 30 minutes of biking within a few weeks), that is more than one hour's worth of exercise a day, and without the stress of a single sport wearing away too severely at any single muscle group.

If you can manage one hour per day of non-stop aerobic exercise, in which your pulse is elevated to 50–75 per cent of its maximum, you will be burning 650–850 calories per hour. It may not seem much at first, but you could, without cutting back on your eating at all, lose six pounds per month at this rate of an hour per day. Should you supplement the exercises by reducing calorie intake as well, even by as little as 500 calories per day (one bowl of ice cream or two beers), you will doubtless find the weight loss even more dramatic. The vital ingredient here is patience. The body will shed itself of the extra baggage if you give it time, at least a month, but if you expect instant results you will find instant frustration. For good or for ill, the body changes slowly.

The triathlon may well be one of the ultimate weapons against obesity. Take a look around at the next (or first) triathlon. Rare indeed is the obese or even marginally overweight triathlete. The sport demands so many calories that it is impossible, even for top triathletes, to keep weight on.

For triathletes who have already been running for a while – and somewhere from 50 to 70 per cent of triathletes come from a running background – there is little that can be added here to the literature of running that has assembled since the 'running boom' began. Yet, the simple act of running itself remains something of an art form to connoisseurs. There is scarcely a sport which does not involve running in one form or another, and to watch natural runners just floating, seemingly running without touching the ground, is a pleasure unto itself.

'Some people are just natural runners,' says Julie Moss. 'They can just start out running, even in a triathlon, and start flowing naturally. Scott Tinley is a beautiful runner. Just watch the way he glides along. He just floats. Ah, it's just fabulous, a pleasure to watch.'

Most people are not, unfortunately, born with this special talent. This is not to say, however, that a decent running style cannot be developed. What is required is patience, suppleness and practice. It takes years, even decades, to develop a good runner. But that is one of the good points about running; its effect is cumulative. Even after a lay-off, a person can return to running and, after shedding some initial rust, can regain most, if not all, of his previous form.

A vital ingredient to running is relaxing. Many runners, especially in the latter stages of a triathlon, travel with clenched fists, stiff shoulders and gritting teeth. They may scare away werewolves, but they will not win many races. When muscles in the body tighten (even the lips), they cause tension elsewhere in the body, and require extra energy and oxygen. Thus blood needed for the working muscles has to be diverted from its main task to alleviate a secondary one. The entire body should ideally be as relaxed as possible, including the breathing.

Admittedly, this is not always easy, let alone possible, in the final miles of a long triathlon. After swimming and biking for half the day there is, to say the least, a detectable amount of pain, and our natural reaction is to tighten up. Pain can be combated, some people mistakenly believe, by literally clenching their fists and fighting their way through the agony.

The mind, which informs us of the pain, can also be a powerful force, however, to distract us from it. There are a myriad tricks and mind games that can be played when the pain becomes seemingly unbearable. Some triathletes figure out what time it is in different time zones around the world and speculate what people are doing, in say, Tokyo. Others conjugate verbs. Some hum classical music to themselves. Some review, in as many details as possible, the days of the past year or month or week. Research has found that endurance athletes, who are best able even partially to nullify the physical pain, perform significantly better than those who are unable to channel agony away.

There is no one right way or one wrong way to get through this barrier of exhaustion; what works for one may be worthless for another. But be ready for it.

The discomfort in running on the triathlon, particularly the longer events, exceeds running almost any distance. It has been estimated that completing the 2.4 mile swim, the 112-mile bike ride, and the 26.2 mile run at Hawaii is tantamount in terms of energy demands, to running more than 80 miles. Whatever your method is of running through this barrier, it is important that you stay calm and aim to finish alive!

'The secret of style is to run naturally,' wrote Fixx in his *The Complete Book of Running*, 'just keep your body straight and your head up, and lean slightly forward. Don't exaggerate arm motion. Run with your elbows bent, but not held tightly against your chest. Your hands should be relaxed, not made into fists. As you run, don't worry about the length of your stride; just do what feels natural. Keep your hips, knees, and ankles relaxed.'

It is important also to breathe naturally. Unlike swimming, in which breathing for obvious reasons can only take place at prescribed intervals, runners can take as much air and as often as they wish. The key is to do just that. By opening both air-intake orifices – your nose and your mouth – you can increase the flow of air into your lungs. Breathing on the bike is not nearly as difficult as on the run because the arms take much of the load of the upper body off the abdomen, enabling the lungs to expand and contract much more freely than while running.

'People used to come up to me and ask me how you breathe when you run,' recalls Kevin Gill, the fitness instructor. 'I'd be baffled. I just couldn't understand the question. I'd always assumed that it was the easiest thing there was. Just breathe. It's just so natural and so easy. After a while you don't even have to think about it any more. You just breathe.'

What you might occasionally need to think about when you run with your mouth open is bugs. Some runners harbour a death-like fear of swallowing bugs or other air-borne insects. Bugs usually tend to congregate mainly in moist areas, such as in marshes or along river banks, or after a rainstorm. There is no need to worry much about bugs, however, if the worst comes to the worst, and a bug becomes lodged in your throat and will not come out, just swallow it. It will not hurt you and unless you're a vegetarian, you should consider yourself lucky, after all, you have just had a free snack.

One of the exciting things about the triathlon is the effect that the supplementary swimming and biking can have on your performance. Many people who entered the sport as runners report that their running times, even after years of stagnation, are suddenly falling again. Others find that they can run far fewer miles than before they added swimming and biking to their routines, but discover that they can run just as fast, if not often faster, than when they were just running.

Kevin Gill used to run 70 miles per week – 10 miles each day. He now runs just four days per week, a fortnightly average of 70 miles (or half his previous total), and claims that he is faster now than before he began swimming and biking on alternate days.

Bernie Mulvanie, from Epping, experienced a similar phenomenon. 'The thing I noticed the most was how much triathlon training was helping my running,' he recalls. 'It was amazing. I don't know if the swimming helped much, but the biking has helped bring my running times down dramatically. I ran a 1:32 half marathon before, and just couldn't seem to get any faster. Now I do the half in 1:19. I just couldn't believe all the extra power, especially running up hills. It's just amazing.'

Chrissie Barrett finds the swimming sessions have helped her the most. 'I don't know about the cycling. I don't think that cycling has helped me much, but that might be because I only bike about twenty miles per week. A good swimming work-out, though, is just as good as a good run. If you work hard in the pool, you come out feeling just as drained as after a long run. And the nice thing about swimming hard is that it doesn't put any strain on your body the way running does.'

Getting Faster

Once you have developed a good base, and can comfortably run for 45 minutes to an hour on a regular basis without undue discomfort, you will want to start thinking about speed.

The three factors which determine your speed are heart-lung power, technique, and length of stride. Although all three are to a large extent influenced by heredity, training intelligently can greatly improve a person's ability to run faster.

An increase in basic speed will help you improve, no matter how slow you are or how slowly you intend to run in the race. In endurance races, how fast you go depends largely on the ability of your heart, arteries and veins to transport oxygen from the lungs to the muscles, and remove the waste products from your muscles back to your lungs where they are exhaled in the form of carbon dioxide (CO_2). By using what is known as the 'overload principle', that is periodically running slightly faster than comfortable in training, the body will gradually adapt and, after a while, what was once considered a pace faster than you were capable of running becomes your new comfortable pace.

Initially, of course, your faster-paced runs will not last as long as your normal-paced runs, for you should not expect to run, say, 15 seconds per mile faster and still be able to run as far. It is also not advisable to try to run fast each time you run; one or two hard runs per week at an accelerated pace will without a doubt net an improvement. To run hard is to challenge your cardiovascular system, to strengthen it. In the process, however, your knees, joints, ankles, hips, back and feet all endure a heavy, almost unbelievably brutal, pounding. Running long slow distances (of at least an hour) is invaluable for building endurance. For the triathlete, these types of 'over-distance' work-outs are vitally important. Your general endurance capacity will grow rapidly with increasing weekly mileage.

Once a certain level of fitness has been achieved, the stress has to be increased gradually by increasing the intensity or distance of the work-out. In the process, your heart will strengthen and actually enlarge so that it can more efficiently pump greater quantities of blood throughout the body. Running at even an eight-minute per mile pace the blood circulates through the body nine times per minute! Muscles become stronger and stamina will increase. Fat within the body is not merely conglomerated around the waist or on the thighs; it is spread out throughout the body, in between muscle fibres and within the blood stream. The fat in excessive quantities (five per cent body fat for men is considered optimal; 10 to 12 per cent for women) hinders your performance. As you gradually burn it off, the body is able to operate more efficiently.

In order to become faster, research has consistently found, an athlete needs occasionally to intersperse faster-than-normal training between regular endurance training. By periodically running an-aerobically, that is 'without air', for relatively brief periods from one minute to five minutes, the efficiency of the cardiovascular system is strained and thus enhanced. Over a period of time, considerable improvements in overall speed will be noted. There are several different ways to do these 'high-intensity' work-outs; where one type of weekly high-intensity work-out might be of enormous benefit and satisfaction for one person, it might not work for everyone. Therefore, the following three popular forms of high-intensity programmes – Intervals, Fartlek and Repetition training – are briefly described below.

A final bit of advice on the speed work. Do not 'hammer' yourself too soon. If you push yourself so hard the first time out that you cease to have any desire to try quality sessions thereafter, the value of the exercise will be nil. The value, on the other hand, of occasionally trying different speeds is immense. Once your body learns to run at a certain tempo, it can lock itself into that particular pace. To improve on it is difficult; you have to 'un-learn' one pace before you learn another. Peter Tegen, the women's track coach at the University of Wisconsin, devised a programme which he calls 'Dynamic Training' for Cindy Bremser, the first American finisher in the 3,000 metre race at the 1984 Olympics. Bremser has run different distances and at different speeds every day for the past ten years. The idea behind the dynamic training is to keep her mind and body from ever getting too set at any one pace. The programme worked so well with Bremser that

Tegan now applies it to all his distance runners, and in the past eight years Wisconsin has won seven Big Ten track titles.

Intervals

Credit for the development of Interval training is most often attributed to two pre-World War II German physiologists, Woldemar Gerschler and Hans Reindell, who first developed it in the late 1930s. Credit for popularising intervals, however, must go to Emil Zatopek, the Czechoslovakian 5,000-metre and 10,000-metre Gold medalist at the 1952 Olympics who, despite never having run more than twelve miles before in his life, won the Gold medal for the marathon as well that year, setting a new Olympic record of 2:23 in the process. Zatopek had been a strong advocate of interval training long before many runners even knew about the programme; the Czech is said to have run as many as 60 sets of 400 metres (15 miles!) in a single day in 1948. His success triggered a great interest in interval training.

What, exactly, are intervals, you may be wondering? Running interval training consists of repeated hard runs over a fixed distance, usually on a track, with a prescribed recovery period, known as the 'rest interval' or 'interval' for short, in between. A typical interval session would be to run 440 yards (a quarter of a mile, or 400 metres) in 75 to 90 seconds, or at a pace that would be at least, but usually well above, 75 per cent of your maximum pulse rate.

After a slow jog or rest for a minute or two, the fast set is repeated. the whole process of running hard, running easy (or walking) is repeated from 4–5 to 12–20 times.

What the interval sets do is to force the heart to work hard during the period of exertion, pushing the pulse up to near its maximum rate, and then resting just long enough to allow the pulse to go back down to near 100 beats per minute, that is permitting a partial, though incomplete recovery. By doing this, you are duplicating the conditions at the end of a long race, that is, teaching your body how to continue running quickly despite mounting fatigue.

Another benefit of the interval session is that during the rest period (the interval) the heart, itself a muscle, actually is believed to grow. Regardless of the distances runners use, almost all top runners – from the 400-metre specialist to the marathoner – include some form of interval work in his or her training. Some runners do 20 sets of 200-metre intervals; others do 12 sets of 400-metres. Still others mix it up, and include a few longer 800 or 1600-metre interval sets a few times per week. The distance is not as important as the amount of time your body is going anaerobic, that is, trying to find oxygen to power the muscles despite a diminishing supply of oxygen in the body. This is a state known as 'oxygen debt'. The fitter you become, the higher your anaerobic threshold will be. Through training, you can increase your maximum oxygen consumption by as much as 30 per cent.

There are some important principles, however, which you should keep in mind. The most important is to be patient. You cannot expect instant results after one or two interval sessions. It will take at least a few weeks to begin to enjoy the benefits of the interval sets. Also, it is injudicious to begin running eight sets of 400-metre intervals in, say, 75 seconds with no gradual build up. For a beginner, if you run four 400s the first time out in under 90 seconds, that's a good start. Four days or a week later try five, and add on more from there.

Another important principle is to alternate hard and easy work-outs. You cannot do intervals every day and expect to improve. Your body needs time to recover, and to repair the muscles damaged in interval work-outs. Once repaired, the muscles will of course be stronger than they were originally, but the easy work-outs in between are vital. The concept of listening to your body is crucial. Experts say that no more than five per cent of your total work-out mileage should be devoted to running intervals.

Finally, it should go almost without saying that an interval session should only follow a good warm-up. For example in addition to a good 10–15 minute stretching period at least two, better three miles should be run at normal speed before commencing interval sessions.

Fartlek

An attractive alternative to interval training with many of the same benefits is the 'fartlek' programme. Fartlek or 'speed-play' was designed by Gosta Holmer, the coach of the 1948 Swedish Olympic team. Unlike the interval sessions, which are of course set distances and set times done in a set place – usually a track – fartlek sessions can be done anywhere, at any pace, and at any distance the runner chooses.

Fartlek sessions are often tucked into the middle portion of a longer run, and are in fact no more than occasional sets of fast stretches of anything from roughly 200 metres (or roughly 30 seconds) to 800 metres (perhaps two minutes). It is difficult to say how long or how fast the sessions should last because that is entirely up to the runner. It is just an occasional burst of speed, reaching at just below anaerobic state, and trying to maintain running at this accelerated pace for a few minutes. The speed of running then returns to normal pace, not below.

To gain any benefit the runner should, in the course of a longer run, try to get in at least four, and preferably up to six or ten such bursts. There is no prescribed distance or time, and because it is such an independent work-out an appreciable amount of individual self-discipline is a pre-requisite for the session to be of any value. Runners who need to know exactly how fast they are doing a given distance, or who might not have the self-discipline to push themselves on their own, might be wasting their time trying fartlek sessions. But those who prefer trails or country lanes to tracks might discover a utopia.

Fartlek bursts need not be pre-calculated either. Some runners report their best fartlek sessions came spontaneously in the midst of a longer run, either through feeling a sudden burst of energy that needed an outlet, or they were becoming bored with running at the usual pace and so spiced up their work-out (as well as getting home quicker) by lacing the run with a few quick fartleks.

Repetition Training

A further form of speed work that may be useful if neither intervals nor fartlek appeal to you is repetition training. Dr Kenneth Cooper, the American physiologist who devised his programme to increase the oxygen capacity of astronauts, is largely credited with developing it. Repetition can be a difficult work-out, but it can also be an invaluable exercise for some.

After measuring out a mile and a half loop course, you run it at near top speed, rest for six minutes, and repeat it a total of four times. What is being tested and improved here is your ability to take up and use oxygen. Physiologists often use precisely this distance to determine the cardiovascular fitness of a person; when running distances longer than 1.5 miles, factors other than oxygen capacity (such as muscle strength and will-power) come into play.

All your running training need not be a calculated, premeditated conglomeration of facts, figures, and pre-ordained distances to run. None of it need be, in fact. What is important, however, if you want to become a strong runner, is some form of occasional speed work. Anyone of the methods just listed will suffice. And speed work need not be more than five per cent of your total running time. One interval, or fartlek or repetition work-out per week will suffice, and in the process help considerably in time.

There are other even pleasanter types of training which may be attractive to you. Hill running, or running on sand along the beach, are both excellent surrogates for speed training, and do marvels for the cardiovascular system.

Sand may be hard to find for some but you will find it a delightful and completely natural surface on which to run – once you get used to its unusual and at first frustrating texture. Hills, or their civilised world surrogates, stairs, on the other hand are not difficult to find. Even if there is no hill in your vicinity, there are most certainly stairs to be found. By running up hills, you will place a strain on your cardiovascular system, as well as on your back muscles, abdomen and quadraceps, the big muscles in your thighs. A hard minute or two up, followed by an easy jog back down the hill (or stairs), or a continued ascent up a really big hill after a brief pause, can be an exhilarating experience. At the top of the hill, there is often a fine view, and even if your legs and heart are pounding away, your senses are usually so awakened by the extra blood racing through your body that the view will seem even more spectacular than usual.

The special demands of running in the triathlon

You will discover, if you have not done so already, that running in a triathlon is different from running in a road race. By the time you are lacing your running shoes up in a triathlon, you have already been largely drained. Thus, there are important points to keep in mind as you trudge through those first painful miles.

The first principle is not to panic. Running in a triathlon will seldom, if ever, be as easy as running alone. Even if some runners come waltzing by you in the first few miles of the run, do not despair. For every strong runner, there are probably at least ten who are running as slowly, if not more slowly, than you are. It may not seem that way but it is true. Most athletes are already well beyond the so-called 'wall' – that is, the point where their bodies have used up all the available energy reserves – by the time the run starts. Some triathletes move faster on the run because, quite simply, they are good runners.

Kevin O'Neil always runs past me in triathlons. The first time he did it at the London Triathlon I was stunned at how quickly he flew past me; I had thought I was moving well, at a steady pace, picking off a few people in the early going. I thought, 'Oh no, am I running that slowly?' His speed was improbable; it made me feel as if I were standing still. Afterwards I figured out my time for the eight-minute mile run and found it to be 55 minutes, a better-than-normal time for me after biking 35 miles. O'Neill had run the race in an astounding 42 minutes, moving from 20th place after the bike ride up to fourth.

'I ran out of time,' he said after the race. 'It was just too short a run to catch anyone else. I needed another few miles.' Since then, whenever I see his heels flying past me, I relax. He's got me again, I think to myself, for there is not much more you can do. You just have to stay calm, and hope to catch a few who are struggling more than you later on. And keep the faith. There are always – always, no matter how long the distance, or what the conditions of the day or the course are, how many are racing – a few who blow themselves out worse than you have, and who if they do not drop out of the race, will be easy game sooner or later along the course.

A second principle to remember is to work your way gradually into the run. The first mile or mile-and-a-half will be the hardest in most cases. The initial discomfort most often wears away, at least to some degree, once your legs re-acquaint themselves with the earth. Some triathletes eagerly look forward to the run, the point where their versatility finally pays dividends.

You can begin preparing, psychologically as well as physically, long before the run starts. In the later miles of the bike course, for example, you may be well advised to do some sort of make-shift stretching of the hamstrings, twisting your shoulders around to stretch your back, and perhaps even (on a downhill stretch) slipping your foot out of the pedal and grabbing your ankle for a few quick hurdler's stretches.

You can also begin preparing for the transition to the run by untying your cycling shoes, loosening your toe clips, and your chin strap (if you have a helmet). (For more details see the Transition chapter which follows.)

Just try to shuffle through the first mile or two of the run without undue concern. It will not be easy. Nor can you expect it to be fast. You will be lucky to

LONDON TRIATHLON, 1984

1 Nerves, adrenalin and . . . the London triathlon about to start, 19th August 1984

2 Taking the plunge

3 Swim

4 Stage one ending

5 False modesty Part 1

6 False modesty Part 2

7/8 Don't be put off by articles exclaiming you must have the latest models

9 You are not allowed to ride in tandem

10   You have to develop mental toughness in the triathlon particularly as you finish biking, others have already started running.

11   Fran Ashmole finishes as first woman

12   Glen Cook finishes as first man

13   Charon Groves
  Short-course Champion, 1984
           Reading

14   The swimmers prepare – they had checked in at 5am on Saturday 6th October 1984
ready for the off at 7am.

15   Meanwhile the one thousand or so bikes had been inspected the day before and lie
waiting for their owners who must first swim in the Pacific for 2.4 miles.

16   Sarah Springman (UK)
Ironman 11th (1984)
Nice 8th (1983) 6th (1984)

17   Dave Scott (USA)
Ironman 1st (1980; Oct. 1982; 1983 and 1984)
Nice 2nd (1983) 2nd (1984)

run faster than 80 per cent of your top running speed, indeed, in the first mile, you should count yourself lucky if you run 75 per cent of your normal speed. But be patient. If you are in pain, so are your opponents.

'The first two miles of the run are critical,' says Kevin Gill. 'If you trot off too quickly then you can blow up. There's a distinct difference, I think, in the limb action in cycling and running. In the first few miles of the run you might find it helps to shorten your stride a little, and you should also try to get your breathing together early in the run. I definitely think you breathe differently on the bike than you do on the run. Breathing on the bike seems a lot easier. You don't have to expand the lungs as fully as while running.'

How well you fare on the proving ground, that is, the final event in the triathlon, will depend on the condition you are in related to the distances of the event. Another factor in your ultimate success or failure on the run course will be how hard you pushed yourself on the swim and on the bike course. There is a fine line between pushing too hard and just hard enough in endurance events, and, in the triathlon, mastering this technique becomes even more critical. Push too soon, and you blow up. Hang back, and hardly push yourself at all and you trot across the finish line still feeling refreshed, but perhaps not fully tested.

This fine line is, of course, different for everyone, but is probably best for beginners to hang back a bit more in a first or second race until the start of the run, and then use whatever energy is left. Much depends on the distances, of course, but it is more important to play it conservatively the longer they are.

Assuming, however, that you have trained for the race, have started at a sensible pace, have taken in enough food along the course, particularly on the bike portion (if it is longer than three hours), you should be able successfully, if not painlessly, to finish the race.

'I'll never forget my first triathlon,' says Kathy Harvey. 'I'd run two marathons in the last two years, and it was getting, you know, a bit boring, just running. But this London triathlon came up, and I'd thought it'd be fun. But I never expected the bike part to take so much out of my legs. They felt dead after. I still had eight miles to run, but they didn't want to move. Next time at least I'll know what to expect.'

As excruciating and all-encompassing as the desire may be to retire after the cycling portion of the triathlon, there are ways to alleviate, if not fully obliterate, the rubbery feeling you have when you start the run. The most sensible course to pursue is simply to practise running after biking. Even if you only run for a mile or two after a hard bike ride, the practice you are giving your legs (unwanted practice though it may be) will be invaluable. 'No matter how tired I am after a work-out on the bike,' explains Julie Leach, a top American triathlete, and winner of the 1982 Ironman, 'I put on my running shoes and go out for a short run. I was wiped out one time on the run in one of my first races, and I decided I wasn't ever going to let that happen again.'

The more triathlons you do, the better you will become at this awkward physical transition as well. Your running will naturally improve too. As Steve Search of Ilford explains, 'I always felt tired at the end of runs before I started doing the triathlon. But now I don't get tired at all at the end of training runs. It's made long running almost easy. A two-hour run now seems comfortable. It seems pretty easy in comparison with a five or six-hour triathlon.'

So the next time you are struggling through the last few miles of a triathlon, just relax and keep in mind that you are not the only one struggling, and that you are not the first person to feel powerless on a triathlon. Practice may not make you a perfect runner, but it certainly helps.

Chapter 9

Transitions

It is staggering how much time can be gained, or lost, in that easily overlooked aspect of the triathlon. To watch some of the masters of the quick change operate can be a staggering experience.

'At my first triathlon my transition times were terrible,' confesses Malcolm Kelvie. 'I figured it out afterwards that it took me 16 minutes total. It was awful. I just didn't know what I was doing.' Consider that some triathletes can go from the swim to the bike in 15 seconds or less, or from the bike to the run in 10 seconds or less. 'I just didn't realise,' Malcolm Kelvie goes on, 'that the clock was still going. I went into the locker-room, dried myself off real well, had a look in the mirror, combed my hair, made sure I looked all right, changed my socks, the works. I even tucked my shirt in before getting on the bike. I just didn't know.'

Less than a year later, Kelvie was rocketing through his transitions, overtaking as many as 50 faster swimmers in the bike park, and another 20 before the run at one race in Cologne, West Germany.

'I began watching how some of the others were doing their changes so quickly. My wife began taking notes. Obviously I couldn't observe everything while competing, so Anne began telling me what some of the top triathletes, especially the Americans, were doing at Nice, how they were dressing on their bikes and that sort of thing. Gradually I've been working some of the ideas in and it's saving time. I can change in about 30 to 45 seconds now. That's still not great, but at least it's much better than 16 minutes.'

Great amounts of time, then, can be spared, but it is important first to assess the personal goals of the reader. If you have little interest in setting personal best records for the course, or have no illusions (or delusions) of winning the race at your age category or beating a friend, that is, the sort of person just out for a good time, you may in fact prefer to take your time in the transitions, have a bite to eat, a drink or two of juice, and maybe even a chat with another like-minded competitor. If that is your choice, fine. There is no law insisting that you rush through transitions.

But if you *are* interested in saving as much time as possible – and the shorter the race, the more crucial transition times become – then you may want to consider some of the following ideas. Some triathletes in fact consider the transitions a 'fourth event', and tacitly compete among themselves for the fastest changes possible. For some, having the fastest transitions is a greater source of pride almost than where they finish in the race itself.

Short-course triathlons, that is with distances of a 1,000-metre swim or less, 20-mile or less bike ride, and a 10-kilometre or less run, are obviously an entirely different breed of race to the ultra-distance triathlon. So the sort of transition a person plans should directly reflect the length of the race in which he or she is competing. Obviously, 16 minute transitions for a race in which the winning time is under two hours, will not do, but for an ultra-distance triathlon, where the first person across the finishing line will take nearly 10 hours, a blazing 10-second transition might be injudiciously fast. For in the long events, it is vital to eat and drink, and the few seconds saved now by passing up a banana, could be fatal later when the body, like the car running on empty, runs out of gas.

A few basic principles, for any event, exist for all transitions. First to simplify as much as possible. The transition is not unlike a pit stop for a car race. The basic ideas are simplification and speed. Be nimble, and be quick, as they say. The less you have to worry about, the less time the transition will take. If you do not mind biking in a running singlet, you have already cut your clothing needs by 25 per cent. You can, and should, run in the same socks that you cycled in. Even the most sweaty people, like myself, find the slight discomfort of running in soggy socks mild in comparison with the trauma of being passed 100-metres before the finish line by someone who elected not to change their socks when I did. Chip Rimmer once lost a race by three seconds. He had changed his socks. The winner didn't. 'I don't think I'm going to change my socks anymore,' he said.

Biking in a running singlet on days in which the temperature is 60° or above makes a lot of sense, particularly for those who warm up quickly and sweat profusely. The singlet worn on the bike course is in many ways far superior to the biking jersey. The biking jersey looks sharper, of course, and will provide more protection to the skin on the arms and shoulders and back in the event of a crash. On the other hand, biking in a singlet is a lot cooler and, aerodynamically, it does not have much more drag than a biking jersey. A bonus for wearing the running singlet on the bike ride is that there is one less piece of equipment lying on the ground that could be lost or stolen.

The Short-Course Triathlon

Speed is of the essence in the short-course triathlon, but nowhere is speed so important as in the transition areas. Seconds there are magnified to outweigh their normal time value. Ten seconds lost in a sloppy transition are 10 seconds never recovered. It might as well be 10 hours if you lose the race by 10 seconds. In the short-course or sprint race, 10 seconds can and occasionally has separated first from third place.

One big advantage which short-course triathletes have is that there is no need to worry about food. In fact, it is not worth while to eat any food in a race shorter than three hours. Not only will the food not be successfully digested; it will waste precious energy by directing blood away from the muscles and to the stomach in order to break the food down. For a sprint race, you want to run your stomach on empty. Longer courses are another story. You need food then. Liquids are fine for the shorter courses, for they are absorbed quickly and efficiently. Naturally, no two bodies are identical, and if you absolutely, positively need food in races shorter than three hours, eat if you feel you need to but preferably in liquid form. But in general try to avoid eating in races shorter than three hours.

The single greatest way for a sprint triathlete to save time is by investing in a skin suit. According to some triathletes these save up to three minutes off of your time. The one-piece lycra Spandex suits fit tightly and are worn throughout the race. Purportedly, the drag created is minimal in the swim, precisely because they are so tight. Some even claim that they add flotation potential. In any case, they virtually eliminate transition times. A skin-suit clad warrior can go from the swim to the bike in less than 15 seconds. It has even been done faster than that. A quick shake while running towards the bike to get rid of some of the excess water (think of a dog emerging from the water and it's not much different), a quick slip on the cycling shoes and you're off. Socks are optional. For some they are mandatory, for others unnecessary.

Peter Moysey, perhaps Britain's master of the quick change on the sprint triathlons, has won several short-distance triathlons, thanks in part to his fast transitions. To watch Moysey nimbly dance through the transition area is to watch an artist at work. He once won a sprint triathlon with a total transition time of 12 seconds. He swam the 400-metre swim in six minutes, and needed only 12 seconds to get from the last stroke in the water to the first revolution on the bike. His speed left observers awestruck. Swimming in the tri-suit, all he needed were a pair of socks and running shoes on the first transition, and that was it. It took about six seconds to slip each sock and running shoe on to each foot. His laces were already tied, and his shoes were powdered with talc to assist an even faster insertion. He covered the six-mile bike circuit in only 11 minutes, jumped off the bike and lost not a single second as he sprinted off directly on the three-mile run, which he finished in 16 minutes.

'It was such a short course that I had to eliminate everything that would take up any time at all,' Moysey explains, despite winning the race by 2 minutes, 45 seconds. The positioning of the equipment is really important. You need to know exactly where everything is beforehand. And you want to lay your things out in the order you'll put them on. It's also very important to have things as simple as possible. That's why I like the tri-suits. There's a lot less on your mind. The less you have to worry about the better.'

Moysey also talks about the need to hurl himself into a transition area, speeding up even rather than slowing down. Dangerous though this may be for the middle-of-the-pack people when there are scores or hundreds of other triathletes all changing at once, Moysey is often alone, or among very few others during his transitions. He can afford to be a bit reckless, he reasons.

'You have to really storm into a station to get the aggression going, but you don't want to go absolutely berserk. You really want to fly through those things though. You can't be timid, especially if the areas are empty and you're up near the front or holding onto a lead. Be aggressive, but stay under control. If you can ride no hands for a short period of time, then don't put the gloves or helmet on until you've already started rolling. In bigger races riding no hands could be dangerous, but if you practise it, and can do it without crashing, then do it. But whatever you do, don't waste time standing in the bike park fighting with your gloves or chin straps. Just get going.'

Part of the logic of remaining aggressive in a transition area is to combat the 'coffee break' mentality that naturally seeps into the mind of beginning, and even some experienced triathletes. You've completed the swim, a not insignificant accomplishment. You want to relish the moment for a while, savour the little victory. And after the bike section, you are ready to lie down, not go off and run. Dallying at these two crucial points of the race is common. However, you know what to expect, so try to postpone any thoughts of accomplishment until you are on the bike course or on the run. View the triathlon as a single race, not three separate ones.

If you do not own a tri-suit, it does not mean you cannot do well in the race. Many races, even sprints, have been won by non-tri-suit-clad racers. It just needs some imagination, forethought, and planning.

There is no law, for example, stating that you cannot run or cycle in your bathing suit, if you can stand the irritation to your inner thighs, or the discomfort to your rear end.

Even if you simply throw a pair of running shorts on over your bathing suit, you will only have lost perhaps five seconds at the most. If you can cycle and run without socks, you will save between 3 and 10 seconds. To dress quickly in running shorts and running singlet (with your number pinned to the front), and hop on your bike can be done in less than 15 seconds.

Without a doubt, the tri-suit-clad athlete *can* do this faster, but he or she has to contend with slightly more drag in the water, and will also be faced with slightly more discomfort in the run. Heat can also be a problem for those who wear tri-suits.

For triathlons shorter than a 30-mile ride, and a seven mile run, you almost have to be able either to run in your cycling shorts or bike in your running shorts. If it is impossible to do that, then it is better to put your running shorts on over your swim suit after the swim and then put your cycling shorts on over your running shorts before heading off on the bike. This way, all you have to do is drop your cycling shorts after the bike ride, and if you have been wearing running shoes for the bike, you're off and running.

It is indeed advisable, for triathlons shorter than 20 miles, to bike in running shoes. Some triathletes use running shoes in races up to 35 miles and experience no appreciable loss of power. It is a matter of individual taste and preference. If you can do without cycling shoes, then do not feel obligated to wear them, for shoe changes are the most time consuming part of any transition.

Several running shoe companies in the United States are currently working on a triathlon shoe, which could be worn on the bike as well as for the run. But running shoes and bike shoes are diametrically opposed to each other: the bike shoe needs to be stiff and inflexible and the running shoe needs to be flexible and relatively soft to absorb some of the shock of the road. Therein lies the fundamental contradiction and the reason why no shoe company has yet met with much success.

Whether or not you change shoes in a race, you will have to tie your shoes at least once, if not twice, and here a revolutionary little clip can save precious seconds. It is similar to the clips found on some sleeping bag sacks; you depress the little button and pull the laces tight, and when you let go, the laces are held in place. They are not yet easy to find, however.

In middle-distance events, that is any triathlon that lasts from 3 to 6 hours, different sorts of transition will naturally be needed. No longer is the second quite so crucial. The hungry triathlete can, and actually must, eat in between stages of the race. Bananas are the ideal source of quick energy, as the 100 calorie fruit is pummelled into an easily digestible mass before it even reaches the stomach. The breakdown is nearly complete. Dried apricots, orange slices, and raisins are also suitable.

The problem is up to you to solve. You either get these energy sources at food stations or bring them with you. If the food stations are strung out on the bike course at one or several points, then you need not worry about carrying your own food. Simply munch on what they have to offer. If however, the race organisers are not aware about the triathlete's need for food in 3 hour-plus events, then the onus is on you.

If you wear a cycling jersey, all you have to do is tuck a banana or two, or whatever foods you feel help you the most to stave off the 'bonk' and the 'wall' respectively. If you bike in a running singlet or a triathlon suit, and the organisers provide no food, it is less easy. One approach is to pack food and even a few important wrenches and a spanner into what the Americans call a 'fanny pack' (a mini-pack that straps around the waist). These can easily hold a few bananas, candy bars and tools. A further advantage is that you can pin your number to the back of the fanny pack, so when you emerge from the swim and snap the fanny pack around your waist, you're also eliminating the need to pin a number on your skin suit either before or after the swim. Another way to avoid this is to pin your number to an elastic band large enough to fit comfortably around your waist. After the swim, all you have to do is pull it over your head and down to your waist.

Because time is still of the essence even in a triathlon lasting six hours, valuable seconds shouldn't be wasted in the pit stop. Getting in and out within 30 seconds is a goal to aim for. You can begin preparing for the transition area in the last miles of the cycle ride. You can loosen your shoe laces, even pull your feet out of the shoes if they're attached snugly in the toe clips just before stopping the bike. You also might want to loosen or even take off your crash helmet, if you wear one, over the last few miles of the bike ride.

If you wear your running shorts underneath your cycling shorts, it takes just a second or two to strip off your cycling shorts and pull on your running shoes. You're off, with perhaps no other lost time than grabbing a banana on the way out to the run.

On runs longer than 10 miles, it is not a good idea to wear the cycling shorts. Some people may find it no hindrance to run in cycling shorts; others may, particularly on a hot day. So the longer the race, the more you may want to consider wearing cycling shorts for the bike ride and running shorts for the run.

Gloves may help to absorb some of the shock and pounding from the road on a long bike course, but they do not make you go any faster. So, if you are a safe rider, and don't often run the risk of crashing you might prefer to leave the cycling gloves at home for a short or middle distance race. If you really feel safer and more comfortable with gloves, you might find precious seconds can be saved by attaching them to the handle bars and pulling them on once you are on the way. The same applies to the helmet.

Long and Ultra-Distance Transitions

Triathlon suits are definitely not fashionable wear among the long-distance and ultra set. The few seconds spared in the pit stops begin to be rendered meaningless over a 10-hour race, and particularly if the course is hot, the tri-suit will enclose a lot of heat. A sensible middle-ground for the ultra-distance triathlons is to swim in a bathing suit; jump into biking shorts and a running singlet or biking jersey after the swim; then jump into cycling shoes, and socks if necessary, and you are off in under a minute. You might want to leave your bathing suit on under your cycling shorts. This way, by adding a fraction more protection, the swimsuit can actually help keep your rectal temperature lower, at least at the beginning of the bike ride, but it is more confortable if you can untie it after the swim. If there is no food on the course you can stuff the pockets before the race, or snap on the fanny pack.

To smooth the transition from the bike to the run, you might want to do some stretching. If so, stand up in the saddle of the bike and move about during the last few miles. You can reach down and massage your thighs as well. You could also try standing up over the final five miles of the bike course and lean forward to stretch your calf muscles. Easier spinning over the last five miles of an ultra event is also recommended.

You should remember to leave your bike in the right gear before starting out. Leave it in a lower gear, for higher revolutions per minute to make the first few minutes on the bike easy spinning. The chances are your legs will feel weak after the swim because they were not getting much blood supply, so easy spinning over the first 5 or 10 minutes expedites recovery and enables the athlete to give it some 'stick' as bikers call riding hard, sooner than the athlete who starts off pushing big gears when he is not really warmed up.

A transition that with luck you never have to make in a race, but one nevertheless should be practised, is fixing a flat tyre. With sew-ups, it is not difficult, but advance planning will make it easier. A few days before the race, take the sew-ups off the rims and put on new glue. Old glue tends to stick with a lot more tenacity than fresh glue, so you will avoid fighting with a tyre to get it off. Moysey once had a flat in the London triathlon, but nevertheless finished in second place, just a few seconds behind the winner! Take used tyres for spares. Not only will they have a little glue on them already, they will attach well to the glue remaining on the rim, which should hold the tyre on well enough for you to finish the race.

Women, naturally, have some different concerns in the transitions, although most of the points mentioned apply as much to women as to men. While men have few qualms about changing at their bikes, most women, at least in Great Britain, are not so prepared and are forced either to change in the crowded locker-rooms or marquees, or wear their swim suits underneath for the whole race. At triathlons in West Germany and Denmark however, women have stripped completely in the bike park.

Wearing the swim suit underneath works well for some women. Caron Groves, who has a 37-inch chest, says 'It's ridiculous to change after the swim. The swim suit gives adequate support. Particularly in running. After the swim, you're too cold anyway to change. It's best just to put some cycling clothes on top, and move on as quickly as possible.'

Especially on shorter courses, women find it quite easy to just pull on some cycling shorts (with the number attached to the rear) and then, at the transition for the run, switch to running shorts and shoes. No shirt is needed, many say, over the swim suit, unless it is a particularly cold day.

On longer courses, you may prefer to change out of the swim suit and into a regular biking outfit. 'I think it's definitely worth it to change out of the bathing suit,' says Sarah Springman, who finished eleventh among the women at the 1984 Ironman. 'It's a matter of comfort, and for me it's worth the extra few seconds, but only on the longer courses.'

With a little bit of practice, pre-planning, and imagination, transitions can rapidly be converted from clumsy, lethargic ordeals into a deft operation. Watch the best athletes, note what they do, and you will make some helpful discoveries.

Chapter 10

Improvement

Mark Kleanthous is an intense, aggressive young man. A few years ago, it was difficult for many other triathletes to take him seriously. He lived alone, usually trained alone, and often made a point of telling people he met how talented he was. He certainly *looked* like a triathlete, and seemed to have the right style clothes, but his 'big talk' prior to a race often turned into humbled silence afterwards. Just another talker, most thought.

But Kleanthous knew better. He trained hard through the following winter, cycled 22 miles to work in London and home six days a week, ran regularly in the cold and rain, and improved his swimming from a disastrous 50 minutes per mile to a respectable 30 minutes per mile.

The following summer he finished seventh at the National Championships, and third at the highly competitive London triathlon. He never had to tell anyone 'I told you so' because everyone knew.

Kleanthous was just one of a hundred triathletes who discovered how much improvement can be made in the sport. Unlike road runners, who can struggle for years to take a few seconds off their 10-mile times, and unlike swimmers who can train for years to lower their personal bests by a few split seconds, the triathlete can dramatically improve his or her performance at a seemingly never-ending rate. Improvement is the spice of life, whether in large leaps or in barely perceptible steps forward. Stagnation is the cloaked enemy of the athlete, for it can lead to complacency, and complacency often leads to regression. 'Success is an important stimulant to every competitor,' says Sarah Springman. 'Initially to complete a course is enough. Thereafter your performance can be measured against the others and against the clock. I get so excited when I swim a certain race faster, or bike faster, or run stronger. Improving is what makes it so fabulous.' Even runners who have spent years in search of a sub-2:45 marathon, have

106

reported that the supplementary swimming and biking, even while cutting back on their running, has proven to be enough to bring them across the finish line in their desired marathon or 10-kilometre times.

'I had never broken 39 minutes for a 10k,' said one triathlete. 'And then suddenly, after swimming and biking, I ran one in 37 minutes. I was shocked. I just couldn't believe all the extra power I had.' In the United States Triathlon Series people of all sorts of ability compete and from all sorts of backgrounds. From the seasoned pro to the first time athlete who has never swum more than 400 continuous metres, there is a common denominator: they are all gauging their improvement.

Run over the standard distances of 1,000 metres swim, 30-kilometres bike, and 10-kilometres run, they provide a sort of 'barometer' for the whole gamut of triathletes. 'How much have I improved?' they want to know. Have they improved? What are their weaknesses? Swimming? Transitions? Biking? Running? Did they start too fast? Did they start too slowly? What are they made of? Can they handle fatigue? Pain?

The top triathletes are driving for fame and fortune, and sponsorships. Each year the competition grows tougher, and the records for the various courses fall perceptibly. It is stunning, actually, to watch course records fall by two or three, or even 15 minutes, in a single swoop. The triathlete's bounds for improvement seem, at this point anyhow, limitless. The fastest marathon time in the Hawaii triathlon is an incredible 2:53. When some were still doubting whether it could ever go below three hours, Dave Scott shattered it by a full seven minutes.

The intermediate triathletes are also checking their 'pulse rate'. These are triathletes who have been entering triathlons for a while, have combat experience, but by no means consider themselves, nor necessarily wish to be, top contenders. They are interested primarily in having a good time, but a large part of that 'great time' is improving. Have they improved? Are races becoming easier? Is the swim becoming easier? Transitions smoother? Biking on hills less difficult? Running after biking? Such people are interested in overall fitness more than in glory or competition.

The beginning triathlete is perhaps the most anxious to gauge his or her improvement. The first race is often the most difficult, no matter what the distances. You are more than a little nervous, more than a little curious. Can you hold up for the distance? Can you remember to pace yourself? Can you remember where your running shoes are? You have swum a mile in a pool, but can you do it in a lake, with hundreds of others also scrambling for space in the water? Can you complete the bike ride? Can you run the distance? Have you done enough training to prevent injuring yourself?

The USTS races are held fortnightly in up to a dozen cities across the country, beginning in Florida in April and finishing with a championship race in California in late September. Anywhere from 400 to 800 participate in each of the races, and the post-race celebrations rival any New Year's Eve party. Friendships are forged among total strangers, training partners are linked, and everyone joins in a huge cheer for the last person across the finishing line. It is a display of community spirit of the sort that many Americans have forgotten. A similar series of seven races has been established in West Germany and Great Britain, while Ireland and Holland also have plans for a series of standard distance races.

Improvement generally parallels time invested in training. Although this is oversimplified, to a degree it is true that the more you train, the better you become. At first however, even with minimal training, the triathlete can count on great strides forward, particularly in the new sports.

'I never thought I'd be able to swim a mile,' remembers Andrew Colvin. 'It didn't seem possible. But I wanted to do the National Championships, so I started practising in the pool a few times each week. It was amazing when I discovered that, with practice, I could eventually swim a mile. I was over the moon.'

For the beginner, or for the relative newcomer to the sport who has not previously been able to devote much time to it, vast improvement can be expected by investing just a few hours each week. But moderation is important. From scratch you can build up to half-hour work-outs four or five days a week, alternating swimming, biking and running. From that base you might want gradually to build up in a few weeks to, say, four or six hours per week. Eventually, you might wish to continue escalating your training to eight or ten hours each week. Or more. There are no rules, no laws, but if you do increase your training it is probably best to do so by no more than 10 per cent each week.

The training must remain enjoyable. Not that every minute has to be a stroll in the park, but if after each work-out you find yourself so devastated that you cannot untie your shoe-lace, then you have gone too far! An occasional 'gut-buster' is great, but if the sport ceases to be enjoyable it follows that it will not be long before you cease the sport. Even so, he who trains better, moves faster. Listen to your body.

Even top triathletes have taken hours – yes, hours! – off of their times at Hawaii. The first winner, Gordon Haller, won the Ironman in 1978 in 11 hours and 46 minutes, which in the 1984 race would only have been good enough for 18th place among the women and 209th overall. Tom Warren won the event the following year in 1979, shaving a full 31 minutes off the previous year's time. The year 1980 saw Dave Scott's debut; he accomplished the triumph in his first Ironman, in a staggering time of 9 hours and 24 minutes. In 1983, Scott lowered the mark again to 9:05. In 1984, a further 11 minutes fell.

Improving, perhaps even more than winning, is what really captivates Dave

Scott, an_____ him through his legendary training routines. 'The sport has really open_____ s up,' he says. 'You're dealing with three sports and you're trying to pu_____ together. There are so many variables, there's always room for improvem_____

The startling_____ vements are not by any means limited to Ironman distance races either. Whe_____ irst began, I had no idea what to work on, or how to prepare for a race. I had a v_____ notion that I had to learn how to swim the distance of the race, but I had no io_____ hat an interval was, or how that could make me faster. Also how to run after b_____ seemed an impossible task at first. The amazing thing was how much easier ru_____ g after biking becomes with each race. The cumulative effect of the training and racing can be extremely satisfying: you remind yourself with each race you do. Your transitions improve, your swimming often improves, as do the biking, and, especially the running.

Interval sets will doubtless help in all three events. The individual swimming, biking and running chapters describe them more fully, but the basic idea is to improve your oxygen uptake capacity, that is the maximum amount of oxygen that the human body can deliver to the working muscles. The muscles need oxygen to fuel the breakdown of glycogen to produce energy for the muscle. The waste product of this exchange, lactic acid, is removed by the blood returning to the heart. The right side of the heart pumps blood into the lungs where carbon dioxide is given off and oxygen is taken up to repeat the cycle. The more efficient your cardiovascular system is, the more oxygen you can take in, the better you can perform. Intervals are an outstanding means to improve the efficiency of the oxygen transport system.

Genetic factors do play a role in how great the Maximum Volume of Oxygen (VO_2) will eventually be. But interval, or fartlek training can improve the efficiency dramatically. Michael Gross, the West German who dominated the men's swimming competition at the 1984 Olympics, has an oxygen uptake capacity considerably greater than normal.

Intervals are defined as working at a higher rate than normal, usually between 80–95 per cent of your maximum heart rate. The usual method to calculate your maximum heart rate (a theoretical figure) is to subtract your age from 220. A 20 year old would thus have a theoretical maximum heart rate of 200, and a 38 year old would have a maximum rate of 182 beats per minute.

The intensity of the intervals should be relatively high, and the rest interval should allow a partial removal of the lactic acid and a partial replacement of the oxygen debt. The sets last anywhere from one to 10 minutes, and the recovery periods from a few seconds to a few minutes. During the intense part, you want to get your pulse rate up to around 85 to 90 per cent of your maximum. You can check your pulse best by placing your fingers on your neck and counting the number of beats for six seconds, and then multiply by 10 (just add a zero). Once your pulse falls by about 30–40 per cent, usually somewhere between 100 and 140 beats per minute, you can proceed with the next set.

It is believed that the heart actually grows in the interval rest period, the minute or so between the sets. This training elevates the heart rate and blood lactate levels to uncomfortable highs, which strengthens your aerobic capacity and in time elevates your anaerobic threshold. The thickness of the heart wall increases and major arteries become more efficient as well, while at the same time a greater amount of blood can be efficiently oxidised in the lungs.

But a word of caution is needed, however, for those interested in pursuing intervals; running intervals exacts a far greater toll on the body than swimming intervals. Most authorities do not recommend doing intervals in running more than once or twice per week. Dave Scott rarely does any sort of speed work running; when he does run harder it is most often fartlek work. Swimming intervals, on the other hand, can be undergone much more frequently. Some triathletes say that you can spend as much as 80 per cent of your swimming time doing intervals or forms of speed work without damage. There is obviously far less pounding of the joints swimming, and the body can dissipate heat better in the water, and the heart is in a prone position. Biking intervals can be done somewhat regularly as well, because the wind keeps the cyclist cooler than the runner, and also because the pounding on the bike isn't as great as on the run. Biking up hills is a most common, and enjoyable biking interval.

Intervals, in any case, are not always easy for beginners. It is important to be able to swim the crawl stroke reasonably efficiently first. Whereas demanding pool work-outs may be well-suited for experienced swimmers, for beginners the increase of speed in the end leads to a decrease because of loss of style and then you may find your interest in swimming rapidly deteriorating.

If you are enjoying mile-swims five times per week, even if you are not bringing your times down rapidly, do not throw in the towel merely because intervals fail to excite you. Give them time. Later, as you gain confidence and strength in the water, try them again, or, alternatively, fartlek sessions in the pool.

Fartlek basically accomplishes the same as interval sessions, i.e. it raises the heart rate to near the top of its maximum. The major difference, of course, is that fartlek can be done whenever and where ever you wish. In the midst of a 1600-metre swim, for instance, you might decide, at metre 400, to swim 150 or 200 metres at a speed 30 seconds faster than normal. That could be followed by 200 or more metres of regular paced swimming and perhaps a second or third or fourth spurt could follow that. The important thing is to keep at it, especially at the sports you don't seem to enjoy so much at first. It often transpires that the weakest, or least-liked event becomes in time the favourite.

Barry Turner, who began from a swimming background, did not initially like cycling. 'It was probably because I wasn't ever very good at it.' But within a year, it had become a most enjoyable part of his training. 'I really enjoy running and cycling. You're outside, and there are things to look at. Cycling has become especially pleasant. But it might be because I'm getting better at it.'

One of the bonuses of the triathlon is the relatively new concept of 'cross-over training' or the 'cross-over effect', when the effects of exercise in one sport increase the strength and capacities of another. The swimming, biking and running 'triangle' are superbly suited for one another. When you improve in one sport, you will inevitably improve in the others. The whole triathlon is greater than the sum of its three parts.

'The triathlon has opened up new potential,' says Dr Edwin Boys. 'It works all the major muscle groups of the body. It just doesn't hammer any one system as severely as running, or just cycling does. I think the potential for improvement is going to be vast.'

While improvement can come with startling speed, it is important to keep a level head about how much and how soon. 'The triathlon world is full of dedicated triathletes who have done too much too early and seem to have lost their way on the improvement, or even the fun,' observes Aleck Hunter, a founding member of the British Triathlon Association, director of half a dozen races, and a triathlete himself. His advice to beginners is to build up over several years, not weeks. Improvement is cumulative. The first year would wisely be spent, no matter what your age or fitness level, working up to the point of completing a short triathlon.

In a second year, the triathlete could begin refining by occasionally working a bit more on speed and aiming not only to improve performance splits, but to become more comfortable in racing and training as well.

Short races can and should still be done, but gradually working in those middle-distance and long races which are impossible to complete. A third year could then be a year of competitive racing, if you're so disposed, but by no means has to be. If your aim is to do an ultra, a third year would be the reasonable point at which to attempt one.

Matthew Keogh, who won Smirnoff's 'Great Dreams' competition, and changed from a completely sedentary life-style to the Ironman in ten months, finished the ultra triathlon (as it is also known) but at the same time, hung up his running shoes as well. He had lost two and a half stone in the first six months of his training, and successfully managed to complete the race on a crash training programme. Harry Wilson, who helped coach Keogh on his running, was impressed that Keogh finished the race, but is convinced it was a mistake to try to stuff so much training into one year. Never would he do that again.

The idea that the Ironman distance triathlons are the only races worth competing in is nonsense. A lot of triathletes believe that the shorter and middle-distance races are far more satisfying, and comparably, just as difficult. 'It's like running,' says Scott. 'There are plenty of smaller triathlons around now. You start with a five kilometre race, not an ultra-marathon.'

Assessment Level	Swim ½ mile	Cycle 20 miles	Run 6 miles
Beginner/Slow	30 minutes	90 minutes	60 minutes
Improving/Low	24 minutes	80 minutes	52 minutes
Low/Middle	21 minutes	74 minutes	48 minutes
Middle Fitness	18 minutes	66 minutes	45 minutes
Upper Middle	15 minutes	60 minutes	40 minutes
Upper Fitness	12 minutes	55 minutes	36 minutes
Super Fitness	9 minutes	48 minutes	30 minutes

If you have been doing the triathlon for a few years, and are seriously interested in searching for new ways to improve, you might want to consider aerobics, for several American triathletes who take part in aerobics programmes insist that it helps improve the VO_2 maximum as well as improving their flexibility.

'Aerobics are beneficial in that you are stretching muscles to their limits, and working all the muscles of the body,' says Kevin Gill, who is an aerobics instructor as well as triathlete. 'Aerobics for triathletes need not necessarily be formally in a class, because they get just as much aerobic benefit from a good work-out, but what is valuable for the triathletes is the stretching. I've noticed my muscles have become shorter over the years. I think it's especially important for younger athletes to stretch thoroughly. 5–15 minutes a day of stretching is terrific.'

Gill thinks it is also important for triathletes to work on their abdominal muscles and back muscles as well. All-round body strength is important. Scott Molina stretches for at least 15 minutes (in front of a television) every day. He spends at least one work-out session a week strengthening his back and stomach muscles as well.

Aerobic exercise was actually first studied by Dr Kenneth Cooper, who devised the aerobic conditioning for astronauts, that is, working within oxygen for improvement in the efficiency of their circulation systems, and lowering their resting pulse rates.

Although the primary focus was originally on astronauts, thousands of people interested less in taking a tour of outer space or even in improving their health, but rather in reducing their weight, began taking part in the aerobic programmes. Triathletes have in recent years taken to weekly or bi-weekly aerobic sessions for reasons closer to those of the astronauts, i.e. increasing their aerobic capacities.

Improvement

Whatever steps you take, or do not take, you will doubtless experience one of the more stimulating aspects of the triathlon: improvement. For no matter what condition you are in, the triathlon guarantees improvement.

Chapter 11

Equipment

Some triathletes feel that a certain piece of equipment makes them a faster swimmer, or a faster biker, or a stronger runner. Others say they cannot compete without the very best product there is.

Equipment is, of course, essential. But gear for the three sports can both be very expensive or amazingly inexpensive. It depends on how far you wish to go. If you are just starting out, and are unsure how much you want to pursue the sport, you need not spend much. Improvisation with what you have or can borrow will certainly suffice to get you ready for, and through, a first short-distance race.

The basic needs are a pair of running shoes, a bike, and a bathing suit or trunks. From there, you can build up to your liking, but you do not need to spend a small fortune to win races. I have seen people win on bikes with no toe clips and which weighed over 35 pounds. People wearing old shorts and running shoes with holes have beaten triathletes clad in expensive tri-suits and £200 racing shoes. Having the best equipment, many triathletes are belatedly discovering, is no guarantee for success.

Better goggles will not make you swim faster, neither will a sharp cycling jersey make you ride any faster. What they can do however, is make training and racing more comfortable. Good, reliable equipment might also stave off fatigue slightly, but, with the possible exception of the bike, it will not in itself make you any faster. It can, however, help to prevent injury and excessive pain. Indeed, inadequate or poor quality equipment can damage your performance, if you're lucky, and if not, your body. As long as your gear is sound, though, and fits well, feels comfortable, and does its job– no matter how inexpensive or expensive – you need not waste your money on elaborate items.

To assist you further here are some suggestions on equipment.

Swimming Equipment

Goggles are a must. Although some triathletes and swimmers insist they can see better without goggles, there is little reason to believe this. With the eyes closed for much of the stroke, there is no way that swimmers can see better than someone wearing with goggles. Also the goggles that are made today mold compatably to the head, so that the old argument of non-goggle wearers about excess 'drag' is meaningless. Some goggles are so streamlined that the argument could almost be made that swimming without goggles creates more drag.

The triathlon boom has not been an opportunity overlooked by goggle manu-facturers. Which particular brand is best is naturally a matter of individual opinion. Some swear by one pair; others swear at them. The goggles which are best for you might not keep the water out for someone else. Try on as many different pairs as possible, but don't be too discouraged if nothing seems to fit. Stephen Russell, who works as the manager of a swimming pool in Rotherhithe, says that, without exaggeration, he tried on twenty pairs of goggles left behind each week, yet none suited his particular forehead-nose-and-eyebrow conform-ation. On the verge of despair, he tried a pair of Talbata anti-fog goggles. 'They're terrific,' he said gleefully. 'I love them. I must have tried on 500 pair of goggles before these. Where have they been?'

Like thumb-prints, no two foreheads or nose bridges are alike. Yet somewhere, as even Stephen Russell discovered, are a pair of goggles that fit. Speciality sports shops will usually let you try the goggles on in the store. When trying on goggles out of the water, you need to get a suction going. After a few moments you will know whether or not they will leak, for you can feel the goggles firmly adhering to your face. In a store, try to squeeze the goggles in towards your eyes. If there is no suction, then most likely water will come in. If, on the other hand, and despite pressing in on the lenses with your thumbs, no air escapes across your face, then all is well.

Of course, it is possible to adjust the nose strap and the elastic band to fit your own particular head, and just because the goggles leak in one position does not mean they are useless. Experiment.

When you pull the elastic band tight, it is important to remember not to tighten it to the point where your head hurts. If a searing headache develops, and maybe you feel a stroke coming on then perhaps the goggles are tight! But seriously, the better quality the goggles, the looser you can leave the strap and still ensure an airtight seal for your eyes.

A word of warning, however. Sooner or later, no matter how hard you try to prevent it, water will eventually get into your goggles. The first reaction is to panic, for it feels as though the submarine has sprung a leak, and is filling up with water. But there is no need to panic, nor even to feel sheepish for that initial reaction. Water seeping into your goggles is an unpleasant feeling. But stay calm, and if they really are filling with water, close that eye until you have the chance to finish the length or the interval. If you are in a race, float over on your back, and sort the trouble out by either lifting up the lens and pushing it back into the eye socket or adjusting the strap. Often, you can just lift up the bottom of the leaky lens while treading water for a second or two. But don't worry. You are not the first person it has happened to. Just stay relaxed.

Some swimmers prefer large goggles or even diving face masks for open water swims; they contend that they provide superior visibility and, in cold water, add a degree of warmth to the cranial cavity. True though that may be, bulky swim masks which protrude from the face add drag and weight to the swimmer, as well as a sense of clumsiness to the swimmer who is searching to prune any unnecessary baggage. Deep-sea style diving masks offer, apart from slightly improved vision, a crucial element of warmth in exceptional cold-water swims. Also, because the nose is fitted inside most deep-sea diving masks, the triathlete can occasionally breathe out through the nose which provides a warm cavity in front of the eyes, nose and part of the face.

That added bit of protection, because between 30 to 40 per cent of body heat is lost through the head, can help considerably, especially the warm-water swimmer who loathes the cold-water swims of England. Some long-distance swimmers, who have used the diving masks in cold water, would never use anything else; others have been disappointed. Once again, it is a matter of individual experimentation.

No matter what type of goggle or mask you use, it is important to be able to see through the mask after the first 50 metres, otherwise it does more harm than good. Fogged-over goggles are as useful as fogged-in airports. Inexperienced triathletes are often seen clutching angrily at their goggles shortly after a race has begun, damning the build-up of fog which has converted the turn-around buoy into a blurry white moist cloud. The source of the fog is the perspiration released from the skin around the eyes.

There are cleaning fluids available to coat the lenses of goggles. There are also anti-fog goggles available, which work well at first, although gradually they lose their effectiveness after a few months. However, no solution works as well as the natural solution, spit or saliva. Saliva spit on the inside of the goggles, mixed with a bit of water which is then dumped out just before the start of the work-out or race, is a method without peer. Nothing else is as effective. An impressive feature of that natural spit as opposed to chemically made anti-fog ointment is that spit will not burn your eyes as the chemicals might. It is a good idea incidentally to rinse your goggles with fresh water after using them in salt or chlorinated water. Both contain agents that can eat away at the rubber.

Good vision in the swim is vital because it is so easy to go off course. Your eyes are mere inches above sea level, and most of the time they are below sea level. Currents, the pitching of the ocean, and even a poor stroke can make a one-mile swim into a mile and a half ordeal. Because you may be following the person in front does not mean that you are on the right course.

A large tree or house, or beach, can be spotted more easily when standing up on the land before a race than trying to find a landmark in the middle of the race. Have your targets picked in advance and aim for them by checking your alignment at every tenth stroke. Some swimmers can simply continue swimming the crawl and pop their head up in front (instead of to the side) as a water polo player does for a stroke or two, to check the alignment. Some swimmers can switch from the crawl to the breast stroke without missing a beat, and then back to the crawl once they have checked their direction. Even if you have to stop for a second or two, it is worthwhile to check your alignment periodically. The stronger a swimmer you become, the less urgent the matter will be, but it is vital to check your direction because even straying off by one degree in the wrong direction amplifies itself rapidly.

Some swimmers wear coloured goggles, and some authorities claim that wearing blue, green or grey goggles protects eyes from bright sunlight. They also say that pink and yellow coloured lenses accentuate dim indoor lighting. Other swimming authorities admit that the colour is only for show, and many triathletes who wear clear goggles seem to agree.

Wearing glasses as well as goggles can pose a problem. Many triathletes wear contact lenses under the goggles; others put their glasses on once they get on their bikes. Others have had prescription lenses built into the goggles and put on glasses after the swim. Many opticians will be able to bond your prescription lenses permanently to any pair of goggles.

Nearly as important as goggles, as far as importance in the water goes, is a swim suit. A general rule of thumb is, the snugger it is, the better. But if varicose veins seem to start popping out of your neck and your legs turn white, then the suit is probably too tight, and you should try one a little larger. The idea, say the swimmers, is to wear one that is as tight as possible without being uncomfortable. The reason is obvious: drag. It is astounding what a difference swimming in a snug racing-style swim suit makes as opposed to wearing Bermuda Shorts. It feels almost as if flippers have suddenly been added to your feet.

Both Speedo and Arena have been making quality swim wear for a long time. Speedo tends to advertise its products in triathlon publications quite extensively, and these are normally good, if expensive, products. But so are Arena's. The best method is to sample as many pairs as possible. Try them on, and kick your legs; if you are a woman, do imaginary arm strokes standing up. If the suit rubs or slips, it is not a good fit.

Racing suits made out of nylon are slightly less expensive, but slightly heavier too, nor are they quite as snug as Lycra-sbandex suits, which hug the body better as well as being lighter. No matter what type of equipment you have, it is sensible to rinse them thoroughly with fresh water after using them in chlorine or salt water. Let them air dry, rather than dry them with heat.

Swim hats in cold water can be a lifesaver. In really cold water, below 58°F, two rubber swimming caps are essential because between 30 and 40 per cent of the body's heat is dissipated through the head.

Two rubber caps, which are often provided at some of the better organised races, should be worn in water below 64°. Cloth, or lycra hats do little more than protect the swimming pools from your hair, not vice-versa. The cloth cap offers little protection.

Wet suits, though initially forbidden at many races, are now completely acceptable. When purchasing a wet suit, it is important to keep in mind that the suit must be skin tight for two reasons: to prevent water from seeping in and to minimise resistance. Wet suits will keep you warmer but will add a degree of extra resistance. However, for ectomorphs, the wet suit may be vitally important.

Training Equipment

This is a subject with which the novice will not want to concern himself at first, but once the stroke is reasonably efficient, there are all sorts of devices that can help him to improve his stroke mechanics or, by creating extra resistance, increase his strength. Pull buoys, kick boards, paddles and even flippers can help the swimmer improve his technique, but it is for someone who cannot yet execute the fundamental crawl stroke to begin working-out with paddles.

Pull Buoys   This marvellous device can show a swimmer how powerful the arms are in the stroke, and how unproductive the legs are. The pull buoys consist of two styrofoam cylinders which are connected by two small cloth belts. The buoys are placed between the thighs, to give them support in the water, so you can concentrate on your arms. The flotation device is, in essence, a surrogate for the kick. Most people report being able to swim just as fast, if not in fact faster and with less effort, with the kick thus immobilised.

The buoys also magnify any wiggles or other flaws in the stroke. With the buoys tucked in between the legs, the upper body wiggle or the lower leg wiggle can be clearly felt. Corrections can be made more easily when the swimmer can feel the flaw as well as being told that there is a wiggle. Some coaches do not like the buoy or the rubber do'nuts which accomplish the same thing as the buoys when wrapped around the ankles because they feel that they raise the legs too high in the water.

Kick Boards   Yes, those things you played on as a child, are considered an important piece of equipment for serious swimmers. They are used, of course, by swimmers to work on their kicks. Even though the kick contributes little to the forward movement of the stroke, it is nonetheless important to maintain balance and stability, and so it should not be ignored. A bad kick will not go away! It will just get worse. Kicking sessions are also good for increasing the heart rate. Even when you are barely moving forward in the water, your legs are probably thrashing away and your heart is really thumping. Most swimmers recommend that ten per cent of work-out time should be devoted to kicking.

A kickboard, in any event, is not mandatory, nor is any of the other equipment mentioned in this section. You can, for example, work on your kick by simply floating face down in the water with your hands extended out in front of you and kick across the pool. Likewise buoys are not needed. You can simply let your legs drag motionless behind.

Paddles   These are pieces of plastic that fit over the palm and turn your fingered hand into more of a web. They are useful for building strength in your shoulders, chest, back and arms, for they increase the resistance, overload the muscles and make them work harder.

Simple devices though they are, they really make you work! Because the water resistance against the paddles is complete, i.e. water cannot slip through them as it can slip through your fingers and around the hands, the paddles make every stroke an effort. They help to build strength especially to the triceps, the strong arm muscles behind the arm that power the first half of the pull.

If you use the paddles, however, you have to be careful to avoid the tendency many beginners have to roll the wrist over or to bend the wrist in face of the increased water pressure. Undoubtedly that makes the exercise easier, but it also makes it worthless. If you lack the strength or determination or both to pull yourself through the water with the paddles, it is better not to use them at all.

Biking Equipment

The bike is the single most important – and expensive – piece of equipment you will possess. The chapter on biking (Chapter 7) gives greater detail on what to look for and what not to look for when buying a bike. It is, however, important to obtain the best you can afford; if you do so, you will thank yourself every time you take it out for a ride. 'I saved for five years for this bike,' said Wilfried Reichel, 'but I know I'll never have to save for another one. This one will last forever.'

You can get good advice on bikes from your bike club or bicycling magazines, or from bike mechanics or informed friends. Personally I have often found the most friendly help from cycling mechanics in the smallest, dirtiest, and least appealing bike shops. Although they might not be up-to-date on the latest sales techniques, they seem to know just about everything there is to know about cycling.

Bike Clothing   What you wear on the bike naturally depends on the weather. In the summer, the lighter the better. In the winter, however, it always feels, because of the wind chill factor even at slow speeds, 20 or 30 degrees colder than the actual temperature. 'I ride right through the winter,' notes Alan Bell. 'Why stop? If you wear the right clothes, there's no need to stop. You just have to be a bit more careful, that's all.'

Your Legs   In the summer, you need a pair (or preferably two or three) of cycling shorts. By having several pairs, either seamless or with seams in different places, you reduce the chances of getting painful rashes. The cycling shorts are cut long to prevent chafing of the thigh on the seat. Cycling shorts are either wool, which is slightly warmer and absorbs the perspiration from your body, or synthetic, which drys faster and is machine-washable. The chamois crotch pad has been a most beneficial invention. Its extra padding makes the seat much less abrasive.

In the winter, your legs obviously need more protection. Although some bikers spend money on the expensive wool cycling trousers, long underwear, tights or even sweat pants can be worn. The knees, strangely seem to become the coldest part and need protection, because they are exposed and have less blood circulating through them. Many women competitors wear leg warmers pulled up over their knees for cold weather cycling.

Your Torso   Because bikers are kept relatively cool even biking on the hottest summer days (as opposed to runners, who must view heat, not cold, as their chief concern) they need not worry about biking in hot weather. A light tee-shirt, or no shirt at all, might be the best course to take. Synthetic short sleeve cycling shirts let most of the heat escape, as do cotton-polyester ones which take the moisture away.

In the winter, however, you need a wool long sleeve jersey, and preferably even a tee-shirt underneath that. If it becomes really cold, you should wear a wind-breaker or down body-warmer on top of that as well. The cycling jerseys are good to wear, not only because the bright and attractive colours help motorists spot you, but mainly because they cover your lower back when you lean forward to grab the handlebars as well as having wide pockets to carry tools or food. It is best to layer the clothes fairly loosely because if they are too snug, no layers of warmth can build up around your body.

Your Extremities   These are the hardest parts of your body to keep warm: your hands and your feet. In very cold weather, it is nearly impossible for your hands and feet to feel comfortably warm; you just have to learn to live with the fact. Ski gloves on the hands seem to work the best, but in weather that is not so cold, standard wool or acrylic gloves can provide enough protection.

Wool-lined cycling shoes help to keep the feet reasonably warm. Wool socks help as well. Specially designed boots that slip over the cyling shoe, leaving a slit open for the toe clips, have been on the market for a few years, but if it is wet, your feet will not stay warm for long, no matter what precautions you take.

In the summer, cycling gloves help to absorb much of the road shock, and in the event of a fall, will protect your hands. They can also help you grip the handlebars better when you have begun to sweat profusely.

Lightweight cycling shoes (from one to two pounds) are best in the summer. Ideally the shoes should be comfortable, have ventilation holes in them and dry quickly when it rains.

Toe clips are essential. They not only lead to greater use of your leg and rump muscles, but they help smooth out your cycling stroke. Instead of one heavy push, the toe clips help to promote a smooth circular energy output. With toe clips and cleats, which clamp your shoe into the pedal, you can nearly halve your expenditure of energy.

The cleats and toe clips are a little 'scary' at first, but as Kathy Harvey and Barbara Head of London have found out, using them becomes second-nature after a while. 'We used to fall off a lot because we'd forget we had the toe clips on,' Harvey explains. 'But you pick it up real fast. If you do fall, it is usually more damaging to your ego than to your body.'

Cycling shoes are also important. Unlike ordinary running shoes which bend, cycling shoes do not. The energy exerted from the downward thrust of the leg is not, with the cycling shoe, lost as some of it is with your running shoes.

Your Head   A good, hard-shell helmet is potentially the best investment you can make. Unfortunately triathletes in Europe are only grudgingly wearing helmets. In the United States bike helmets are not only the standard fare, they have become fashionable as well. Those who ride without helmets are almost considered freaks.

Whereas soft-shell helmets will help you slightly if you hit the ground, if you are hit by a car or, for that matter, strike the ground hard, they will not protect your head very much. Hard-shell helmets are really worth a hard-sell here! Your head is the most valuable part of your body, and enough cyclists have had their skulls knocked open to prove that protection is needed. There are some excellent helmets on the market today that are so light and so comfortable, that you barely notice you have them on: for instance, Skid-lid, Bell, MSR, and Protec.

In the winter, a wool ski-hat underneath the helmet will help to keep your head warm. You may even want to put some vaseline on your face as well, or wear a face mask.

Wind-Load Simulators   This remarkable new machine was designed in 1978 by a West German born engineer, Wilfried Baatz. Living in Seattle, where it rains heavily, Baatz was an avid recreational cyclist, who was seeking a way to continue his training indoors during the winter. It is an ingenious invention. As the name implies, it simulates road conditions well, and far better than rollers. The bike is set up, with the front wheel removed and the front fork blades attached to the machine, the back wheel rests on a blower fan. The motion of your wheel drives the blower fan. Two fans on each side of the wheel draw in air and disperse it radially. The harder you pedal, the more difficult it becomes. It is the law of squares transferred from forward wind resistance to wind resistance underneath your tyres.

One of the greater advantages of the wind-load simulators, apart from their relatively inexpensive price (from under £100 up to £250), is the fact that you can train on your own bike. Unlike indoor stationary bicycles, which are expensive, you can simulate road racing demands far more closely on the wind-load simulator. The one draw-back of the machines is that they make a lot of noise, particularly underneath, and your perspiration will be immense as well. But one hour on a wind-load simulator, many triathletes say, is equal to two or three hours on the bike. More information can be obtained by writing to Racer Mate Inc., 3016 N.E. Street, Seattle, Washington, 98105.

Running Equipment

Running is clearly the easiest of sports to dress for. Aside from the running shoes, which next to the bike, are the most important equipment, running clothing is relatively simple.

In the summer, the idea is to stay cool. Nylon shorts, with slits up the sides, are best for releasing heat and drying quickly. Whether used for training runs or the races themselves, it is worth having at least one pair of the light-weight nylon shorts. In the winter months, however, you will feel more comfortable wearing cotton shorts, which offer a little more warmth than the nylon ones. If the weather becomes really cold, you may want to wear tights or long underwear or tapered warm-up trousers. But you will be surprised how far into the winter months you can get by with only wearing wool shorts and a sweat shirt.

In warm weather, if you are male, you may find it more comfortable to run without a shirt. Although considered uncouth as recently as ten years ago, this has now become widely acceptable. It makes sense, too, to wear as little as possible on hot days. Heat is the mortal enemy of the runner. A light tee-shirt or running singlet is preferable to a heavier shirt.

In cooler weather, you can add layers of tee-shirts, then sweat shirts and, for severely cold weather, even jackets or tank tops over the sweat shirts. Your body generates a lot of heat when running, so it is better to feel a little cold at first rather than warm from the first minute you walk out of the door. In cold weather, you might find it helps to do some push-ups and sit-ups to warm up the heart as well. A friend of mine, Jeff Hoffmann, used always to do this before runs in cold weather. At first it used to irritate me having to wait and watch him toning himself, but when it became apparent that he was running more comfortably from the start, I started to do it too. It helps to reduce the shock of the cold.

In cold weather, cotton gloves, or even socks, keep the hands warm and, if you really begin to heat up excessively, tuck them into your waist band. Wool hats keep in heat that escapes through your head but, once again, if you sweat harder than you would in mid-July, you might want to carry the hat or tuck it into your waist band.

Running Shoes   This is the single most important item of your running equipment. Consider what they do. In a single mile, a 10 stone person will place a cumulative weight of 60 tons on each foot. A 10-mile run would put 600 tons of weight on each foot. And a shoe weighing a few hundred grammes has to support that pounding. Your feet on average strike the gound 800 times per mile. Clearly, you need a quality shoe to support that kind of load.

There are more than 400 models of shoes to choose from, produced by scores of manufacturers. Nike, Tiger, New Balance, Puma, Converse, and Adidas are just a few of the many running shoe manufacturers. To inform yourself about running shoes, talk to runners, and to the people who work in running shoe stores.

To start with, look for a sturdy training shoe. Racing flats for triathletes are not a good buy. They are too light to stand the long pounding that a triathlete will put on them. Look for a snug, but not excessively tight, fit. There should be about a one half inch between your big toe and the toe box. The inside of the shoe should be smooth, with no exposed seams or rough stitching that might irritate your foot. There should be adequate cushioning in the forefoot, the mid-sole, and at the heel, but that cushioning should not be too soft. If you can press it together with just a little finger pressure, it is too soft. On the other hand, it should not be too stiff or unyielding.

The shoe itself needs to be flexible particularly at the ball of the foot; if it is not, you will find pushing off each strike considerably harder. A stable and firm heel counter at the back of the shoe is also vital. If it is too soft, you can develop (or accentuate) a bad habit of rolling the heel inwards (pronating) or rolling the heel outwards (suppenating). Take your time when buying shoes; look, ask. Quality running stores will let you take a 'test run' in the shoes around the block. If the shoe does not feel right then, it probably never will. More injuries could have been prevented by having the right sort of running shoes than any other single cause of injuries, so take the time now to find a good pair and do not be afraid to experiment until you find the shoe and model that works best for you.

Do not however, fall into the trap of thinking that a good running shoe will make you faster than you are capable of running. There are no mini-jets inside those heel counters! Wings may be stitched on the shoe, but they will not make you fly. A bad running shoe however, whether of poor quality or poor fit, can keep you from running as well as you are capable. And it could injure you.

Some runners recommend that you buy a running shoe late in the afternoon, because feet will swell during the day, just as they do in a race. Also, whereas shoes a decade ago were often made of leather and required a long breaking-in period, today's nylon shoes can be broken-in in no time at all. So long as you shop around, ask questions and familiarise yourself with the important points of the running shoe, and are also prepared to spend between £20 and £40, you will not go wrong. But remember, it is you who have to do the work. The equipment is just along for the ride.

'The biggest difference between running now and before,' says Field Ryan, however, who has been running since 1944, 'is the shoes. They just seem to get better all the time. Even in the last four or five years, they have been getting better.'

Chapter 12

Injury and injuries

Men do not die. They kill themselves
– Seneca

Eighty per cent of all injuries are preventable. I remember reading that assertion when I began running yet I have still managed to be injured several times. Words of wisdom just do not seem to sink in the first time you hear them. So let us repeat them: eighty per cent of injuries are preventable.

Undoubtedly the major reason why runners, bikers and even swimmers are injured is lack of stretching beforehand, and failing to warm-up sufficiently before work-outs. Athletes are often more anxious to start running or cycling or swimming, rather than take those extra 5–15 minutes preparation beforehand to stretch.

'Stretching is so important,' notes 37 year old Kevin Gill. 'I think it's crucial for triathletes to stretch thoroughly. At least five minutes a day. I've noticed my muscles have become shorter over the years, so I need to stretch even more. I'm sure it helps prevent injuries.'

The next major cause of injuries is over use. This happens particularly in running and cycling, when the athlete trains too hard and too long. Rest, as many belatedly discover, is a vital aspect of endurance training. Your muscles need time to repair. Pushing through pain is valuable for the athlete; and teaching your mind to tolerate, even appreciate, pain is an important part of the triathlon. There is a fine line however, between pain that is beneficial and pain that is detrimental, even harmful.

A third source of injuries is carelessness. This is particularly true on the bike, where many triathletes have crashed because they were not paying proper attention to what they were doing, nor to what other traffic, animals or pedestrians were doing. Land-born creatures as we are it is unnatural at first for us to be travelling at six times our walking pace.

Prevention

Preventing injury is, surprisingly, easier than it may at first seem. The triathlon is, of course, a non-contact sport. Thus injury in the triathlon is, as Seneca describes it, the result of people intending to kill themselves. Once again, eighty per cent of injuries are preventable.

Running

Running, for all its simplicity, is where most can go wrong. The jarring that the body undergoes, even when only running a mile, is staggering. Legs and knees are the most vulnerable.

Runner's Knee
When pain develops in the knee, it is foolhardy for you to ignore the pain. Seek professional advice. However, runner's knee can often be remedied by temporarily cutting back on your mileage, performing strengthening exercises for the quadraceps.

Stress fracture
Stress fractures occur occasionally in the two bones of the lower leg (the tibia and the fibula), as well as in the longest toe bones (the metatarsals). It is a minor change in the bone's structure, usually caused by rapidly increased training mileage or intensity of work. Fortunately, if you curtail your running training for 3–6 weeks, and run only in races or on soft surfaces, the stress fractures will usually heal themselves.

Bone bruises
This is an inflammation of the heel caused by repeated pounding. Once again, it is not a devastating or debilitating injury in itself; however, by either switching to running shoes that protect your heels better, or by inserting heel cups, or running, at least occasionally on softer surfaces the problem will usually resolve itself.

Achilles tendonitis
A painful and irritating injury, Achilles tendonitis is the swelling of the Achilles tendon, the tendon connecting your feet to your hamstring muscles. Cutting back on your mileage invariably helps, as well as running on flat hard surfaces. Some people advise soaking the ankle in hot water as often as possible and applying ice to it after running. Asprin can relieve some of the pain. The best way to prevent this injury is by stretching thoroughly before and after running. If the pain does not diminish once you've cut back on your running mileage, seek professional advice.

Shin splints
Shin splints – inflamed muscles and tendons – often afflict beginners, or other runners who rapidly increase mileage. Shin splints can range in degree of pain from a slight dull discomfort to a throbbing pain that makes running, even walking, not possible. The problem often is caused by stiff shoes, or running on your toes, or adding too many miles too soon. The best cure once again is to stretch, and to cut back for a few weeks on your running mileage.

Blisters
Blisters, as long as they do not become infected, are by themselves a relatively minor problem. If you pop the blister with a sterilised needle and let the fluid out,

and cover it with vaseline and a band-aid, it should heel itself within a few days. Blisters are often caused by seams in running shoes, dirty socks, or running with wet feet. If you do pour water over your head in a race, either lean forward, or try to shake it off before it can run down your socks into your feet. You may look slightly strange, doing your little jig in the middle of a race, but your blister-less feet will appreciate it.

Cramps
In longer triathlons, especially on hot days, cramps are one of the major problems. They are probably caused by a deficiency of salt, calcium, potassium, magnesium, or vitamin B – all chemicals that are lost through sweating. Hot baths and massages offer some help, if only ephemeral. The real key is to maintain a sufficient level of potassium and the other chemicals in the body. Fruit juices, fruits and vegetables are good sources of potassium. Potassium is to the body's metabolism what a rudder is to a ship, it provides a stabilising element, and helps the body's cells maintain normal fluid balance and body functions.

Side Stitch
The first time you get a side stitch you fear it is a heart attack – it is so sudden and sharp a pain. It usually occurs when you have been running hard for some distance, and most often disappears when you either slow down or stop running for a few minutes. The fitter you become the less susceptible to it you will be.

Bloody Urine
Frightening though this sounds, it is not, once again, the beginning of your end. Although fortunately rare, bloody urine can plague runners occasionally after demanding work-outs. It is most likely caused by the destruction of small amounts of muscles, and is not supposed to be a major problem. However if it recurs, it is probably wise to see a physician.

Chafing
This is another gory, though relatively minor injury. It is caused by rubbing by new or improperly fitting equipment, and it can attack your heels, your groin, your waist, your nipples, or your underarm. If vaseline fails to eliminate the problem, then you should consider not wearing the offending equipment.

Cycling

Cycling is not quite the hazardous sport in terms of self-inflicted injuries that running can be. Not that cyclists are injury-free. Outside traffic hazards: poor technique on the bike (particularly in the pedal stroke), can lead to painful and irritating injuries. Accidents are of course, more likely on the bike than while running.

Stretching is just as important before biking as it is before running, but many cyclists neglect even five minutes of suppling before they pedal away. Having a properly adjusted, and the right size of bike is also important in the prevention of injuries. It is also important to make sure that your bike is in good working order, and that all nuts and bolts are tightened before setting out. Loosened bike seats and handlebars have led to serious accidents in races.

Knee pains

Most knee problems are caused either by over-use, or by poor cycling cadence. Try to maintain a cadence of between 80 and 100 revolutions per minute; otherwise if you push too big a gear you will put more stress on your knee joints. Over the course of several dozen miles, the accumulated fatigue – as well as potential for stress injuries – increases. The 'spinning' technique helps to spread out the workload and extend the length of time you can ride.

'If you've never seriously biked before, you should begin gradually,' warns Dave Scott. 'If you do a 60-mile ride right away, you'll be vulnerable to injury.'

The best cure for knee pains caused from cycling is, once again, rest, and cutting back on your mileage. If you are stretching, and spinning 80 to 100 revolutions per minute, have not built up your mileage too fast, and are still having problems with your knees, re-check your saddle height and the alignment of your plates on your cycling shoes. Even a mere millimetre too high or too low can lend to knee problems. Researchers at Loughborough University have found that the optimal distance of the frame size was the leg inseam of the cyclist multiplied by 1.09.

Sore backs

On longer rides, particularly on colder days, you can get a stiff back if you ride too long in one position. The logical solution naturally is to alternate your position on the bike, and to twist occasionally. Riding occasionally with no hands can also help alleviate pain.

Bottom pains

These are inevitable. The one consolation is that the more time you spend in the saddle, the more comfortable it will become, or, more accurately, the less painful it will become. In time, your rear end will toughen, and you will scarcely even notice the saddle's existence.

To prevent saddle boils or other forms of skin irritation, wear clean cycling shorts. Also rotate two or more different pairs of cycling shorts into your work-outs so that no one seam can cause too much rubbing.

Biking accidents

The best way to avoid an accident on the bike is to stay alert, ride on smooth surfaces, with as little traffic as possible, and avoid riding at night. Use hand signals too. Try to be predictable, and anticipate situations in advance. Because you obviously have no horn (unless you wear a whistle) do not be afraid to yell or scream or shout to make some sort of noise if you are approaching a potential trouble spot. Watch for potholes, railroad tracks (which can ruin your rims if you take them too fast), cobblestones, wet potholes, ice, side-mirrors, opening car doors, dogs, bugs and pedestrians. Few people are accustomed to seeing bicyclists travel as fast as triathletes move on the bike, and so underestimate the time they have to get out of the way. Try when ever possible, to make eye contact with pedestrians and drivers and, if the worst comes to the worst, slow down.

Sooner or later the chances are good that you will crash. As long as you have a helmet, cycling gloves, and protective cycling clothes on, the injuries will probably not be too devastating. Skin burns usually look worse than they are. Those who fail to wear a helmet display what little respect they have for their own heads. Cycling gloves also prevent painful abrasions to your hands, as do cycling jerseys to your shoulder and arms.

Clean any burns with cold running water to remove particles of grit: then dab on antiseptic cream or liquids or sprays. Deeper cuts may need stitches. When in doubt, see a doctor. You should keep the abrasions covered and as clean as possible in the first few days.

Swimming

Swimming injuries are rare. For this reason injured runners and cyclists often maintain their fitness in the water while allowing sore knees, ankles, or feet to recuperate. Allison Roe, who had held the world record for the marathon, became plagued by over-use injuries while running in 1983 and turned to supplementary swimming and bicycling to aid her recuperation. She entered a triathlon in New York on the spur of the moment, and finished a close second. 'Running fast and hard on the roads is a lot of trauma, and biking really helps the quads,' she explained.

The most debilitating injury that can afflict swimmers is 'swimmer's shoulder', a form of tendenitis in the shoulder caused by over-use. 'Most runners increase their swim training too rapidly,' notes Dave Scott, 'setting themselves up for injury. Well developed cardiovascular endurance causes runners to overstress their underdeveloped swimming muscles long before noticing any fatigue.'

In addition to weight training to strengthen the arms, Scott also advises using a variety of strokes at the outset – backstroke, breast and crawl – rather than concentrating too much on the crawl at first. As long as you build up gradually – from 300 yards in small increments of 10 per cent each week – you should not have any problems.

Another injury which occasionally afflicts swimmers is when they collide with another swimmer or hit their wrists or legs on the walls of the pools while doing tumble turns. Even the British national champion, Stephen Russell, admits to being side-lined for a few weeks once after banging his left leg while doing a tumble turn too close the edge of a pool.

Cramp is the most dangerous injury swimmers need to look out for. Leg cramps are the most common, stomach cramps are the most dangerous. If you get a slight leg cramp in a pool, perhaps from pushing off the wall, you can usually gradually work the cramp out by kicking lightly, and not exerting so much pressure on the push-offs. If the cramp becomes severe, you can stand on your toes (in the shallow end, obviously) and the leg cramps should disappear. In a race in open water, you can try switching temporarily to the breast stroke, back stroke, or side stroke, which stretch the leg muscles better than the crawl does. Cold water is a main source of cramps – if you are not used to it. If a triathlon includes a swim in cold water, it is essential that you gradually acclimatise yourself to the colder water. Cold showers are the least pleasant method. Swimming in outdoor pools is much more fun. Generally, if you can swim in the body of water where the race will be held, three or four times before the race (building up from 15 minutes in the water to half an hour or however long it will take you to swim the distance), you should be sufficiently acclimatised.

Stomach cramps

Mention these to long-distance swimmers, and they will roll their eyes, look towards the sky, and say they wished you had not mentioned that word. Fortunately, stomach cramps in open-water swims are rare. They are devastating, and can be fatal. The stomach knots right up, and the swimmer, even a good swimmer, has little chance to avoid sinking like a rock. Even when rescue boats are only a few yards away, it is sometimes not possible to save someone with a stomach cramp.

Obviously this is something you need to avoid. The best way is to refuse to eat anything three hours before swimming in open water. Secondly, it is not a good idea to swim in open bodies of water (especially cold water) if you have already put in a hard training day. The accumulated fatigue can increase the potential for stomach cramps. Also, whenever you swim in open water, make sure that someone with a row boat, canoe, kayak, or paddle board is nearby. If that is not possible, and you must swim in open water, at least swim parallel to the shore, and not too far away from it. If at any time you can stand up, you will be better off.

It is also important to have proper fitting equipment for swimming. The trunk or bathing suit should be as snug as possible to prevent drag, yet not so tight that it causes pain or chafing. The goggles, of course, must fit snugly so that water does not get into them. Chlorine can burn the eyes.

Finally, one ailment to which swimmers are especially susceptible is athlete's foot. Normally picked up at pools in locker rooms, this is an itchy, irritating problem, which can, however, be successfully treated with anti-fungal cream. Some pools in West Germany, France and Austria have foot disinfectant spray in the locker-room. But the best way to avoid athlete's foot is to prevent it in the first place by wearing 'flip-flops'.

Heat Injury
'Probably no single factor poses a greater threat to the distance runner's health and performance than does over-heating,' says David Costill, the Director of the renowned Human Performance Laboratory in Indiana. 'With the high rate of energy expenditure, heat production by the working muscles may be 20 times greater than at rest.'

During endurance activities, the body tries to direct the heat away from the core of the body by, first, bloodflow and then sweating, both of which facilitate heat loss. Heat generated by the muscles is first directed towards the surface of the body, where it can be released to the surrounding air. If the heat generated by the muscles is still greater than the circulatory system can cool, perspiration helps to cool the body further. 'Although surprisingly effective, this system of cooling is not without limitations, and often is no match for the high rate of heat production,' says Costill.

In extreme heat or high humidity the body's ability to transfer heat effectively from the inside to the outside environment will be drastically impaired. This is where lighter runners have a two-fold advantage: first, their bodies do not produce quite as much heat as those of heavier runners; second, with less fat interfering in heat dissipation, more heat can escape.

The danger of heat in endurance events was shown by Jim Peter's paralysing collapse at the 1954 Commonwealth Games marathon in Vancouver. The race was run at noon under cloudless skies, Peters, the world record holder for the marathon at the time, held an 18-minute lead when he entered the stadium for the final few hundred yards. But he never made it to the finish line, and it was the last time, in fact, that he ever ran. He had not drunk any water during the race, fearing, as some runners of the time did, that diarrhoea would set in. The heat exhaustion Peters suffered that day in 1954 was by no means just temporary: he has suffered from high blood pressure and hypertension ever since. 'I've never really been the same bloke since,' he says. 'I have still got the after-effects, but I've survived 30 years with them. I wonder, though, if I was a bit too enthusiastic.'

Fortunately, that 'fear' of drinking water during a race has long since abated. Not only will water not harm a runner, it is in fact vital to help keep the body cool and replace some of the fluids lost during competition.

The importance of taking in fluid regularly during a distance event cannot be overstated. You should begin drinking water, in small sips, *before* you feel thirsty. Once again, it is easier to prevent heat exhaustion than to treat it. Once thirst has set in, and if you haven't already been drinking, it may be too late, for your digestive tract may have already shut itself down. In any endurance activity longer than three kilometres, fluids should be taken. Even if you do not perspire, you lose an incalculable amount of fluid through exhaling.

On extremely hot days, light clothing can help deflect some of the sun's potency. However, extreme heat will exhaust many triathletes, regardless of the colour of the clothing. In extreme heat, therefore, slow down, abandon your normal split times, and try to bike and run at a sensible pace.

According to Costill's research, rectal temperatures (a measurement to core temperature) rise steadily from 37°C up to 38.5°C during the first 45 minutes of exercise. If water or glucose solutions have been consumed, the temperature then levels off at this point and, provided that 200 ml of cool liquid is consumed every 10 minutes, the temperatures remain at the safe 38.5° level for up to 100 minutes of exercise. When water is not taken in, the rectal temperatures continue to rise steadily up above 39°.

Danger Levels and Symptoms

Rectal Temperature (Celsius)	*Symptoms*
40°–40.6°	Throbbing pressure in the temple, cold sensation over trunk.
40.6°	Muscular weakness, disorientation and loss of postural equilibrium.
Above 41.2°	Diminished sweating, loss of consciousness.

Injuries, as we have said, are preventable, and the best way to prevent them is through stretching. It can hardly be stressed enough how important it is to stretch before and, optimally, after a work-out as well. Those with special zeal may even wish to sneak stretching sessions during the day. Peter Moysey, a pool supervisor in London, admits that he does a great deal of his stretching at work. 'My boss doesn't know about it,' he confides. 'But I can usually manage three or four good 10 minute sessions per day. I think it definitely helps.'

Even if you are not the sort of person who plans to put down your drink at a party and break into a vigorous stretching routine, it is worth your while – if you wish to avoid injuries – to devote 5–15 minutes before each work-out to stretching.

For running, too, stretching is most vital. Because running demands less flexibility, muscles not used in running – the so-called 'antagonists' – need special attention. These are your shins, your stomach muscles, and the quadraceps. Dr George Sheehan has advanced a programme which focuses on the six muscle groups. He maintains that not all six need be exercised each day, perhaps three on one day and three the next, but, if done consistently, the six-point programme will successfully reduce the likelihood of injury. This programme will, of course, benefit triathletes because three of the exercises focus on stretching (and maintaining flexibility) on muscle groups used running (hamstrings, lower back, and calf muscles), and three which are not used (shins, quads and stomach). If the latter three supplementary exercises are not undertaken to counter the effects of running, imbalances which can lead to injury may occur. The time taken to do the following six exercises is trivial compared to the time lost while hobbling around inactively.

1. To stretch calf muscles and Achilles tendons, stand approximately three feet from a wall (or tree). Keeping your feet flat on the ground, lean forward until your legs hurt slightly. Hold this position for 10 seconds, and then relax. Repeat five or more times.
2. To stretch your hamstrings, keep both legs straight and put one foot up on a waist-high bar or table. Bend your head down to your knee until you feel strain. Hold for 10 seconds, then relax. Repeat five times with each leg.
3. To stretch your lower back and the hamstrings, lie on your back, arms down by your sides and bring your legs (while keeping the knees straight) up over your head. Lower them as far as you can, touching the floor behind you with your toes if possible. Hold this position for 10 seconds, and then relax. Repeat five or six times.
4. To strengthen your shin muscles (antagonists) sit on the edge of a table and hang a five-pound weight on the lower part of the foot just above the toes. (Baskets or empty paint cans with bricks or stones in them are suitable surrogates.) Raise your toes slowly, keep them raised for a few seconds, and repeat the exercise until you tire.
5. To strengthen quadraceps (apart from biking and running up hills) sit on the table and, with the same weights on your toes, raise your feet up to a point

where they are parallel to your knees. Hold for a few seconds and then lower and repeat five or six times with each leg.

6. To strengthen your stomach muscles – the antagonists of the back muscles – do twenty or more sit-ups.

Another key to preventing injuries is to listen to your body. The maxim 'train, don't strain' applies to all three disciplines but particularly to running and biking. The longer you do the sport (or sports) the more in tune with your body you will become, and the less inclined you will be to push yourself needlessly. The other slogan 'no pain, no gain' may seem contradictory, but there is a fine line between the two ideas.

If you do not occasionally push yourself through levels of discomfort, you will reach a plateau and stay there; improvement will cease if you stop pushing yourself through pain altogether. Whereas it is not wise to push yourself through pain all the time, much depends on the type of pain you are experiencing. Pains in the joints and the arches, and especially in crucial zones like the knees and ankles should not be ignored. The pain symptoms in the joints indicate that something is wrong and, at the most, you should try running lightly. If the pain does not go away within a few miles, *stop* running or cycling. If after a few days rest, the pain still refuses to go away, go and see a doctor. Many injuries, so long as they are dealt with when they are minor, can be cured in a matter of days. What is required, however, is rest. I once had shin splints, and thought I would never run again, let alone walk. A week later, I tried running, and felt fine. The problem had disappeared.

'Listening to your body' is important, yet it is not an easy talent to nurture. There are hundreds of athletes who unfortunately have no sense of what their bodies tell them. Without doubt there are minor injuries, aches and pains that can successfully be worked out without any further attention, and indeed, many minor ailments disappear within the first few miles of a run or the first few minutes of a swim. But not always. When pain persists, the injured part of the body is sending messages, loud and clear, warnings that something is not right. To continue to push through insistent pain is foolhardy. Listen to your body, particularly as far as knees go.

Many minor ailments can be cured in their early stages by merely taking a day or two off, or by swimming instead of running for a few days. One of the greatest breakthroughs of the 1980s has been to discover the merits of rest. The body needs time to adjust; it is a far more patient instrument than the twentieth century mind. Naturally, you do not fall out of shape two days (nor even two months) after curtailing exercise, and similarly, you cannot possibly be expected to become really fit within a fortnight.

Even champion athletes in one sport are discovering the importance of augmenting their training gradually. John Howard, who has been the United States cycling champion six times, was looking for a new challenge when he first read about the Ironman in 1980. He decided to join the race the following year but although he was an accomplished cyclist, he had virtually no experience as a runner. This did not temper his zeal for the Ironman however. A mere three months after beginning running, he attempted his first marathon. 'It was too much too fast,' he recalls. 'My heart and lungs were ready for the challenge of running 26 miles, but my feet weren't. Of course, I got injured. I went out too fast, suffered shin splints, and had to walk the last four miles, and finished with a time of 3:10. I had to build my base as a long-distance runner by training for an entire year before I was truly ready to run marathons.'

Although most of the focus on stretching thus far has been directed at the running portion, stretching for cycling and swimming are just as important. The cross-over effects of stretching for running doubtless help many of the muscles used when biking: however it is important really to stretch the quadraceps before pedalling off. You can either grab your ankle while standing up and pull it up to your rear end and hold for five or six counts, or tuck it alongside your thigh in the form of a hurdler's stretch.

For swimming, stretch one arm at a time against a wall, twisting your body away from the wall as much as possible. Also, you can grab your hands behind your back, and keeping your arms straight, bend forward and raise your arms up over your head as far as you can manage.

One of the achievements of the triathlon is that the sport has remained relatively injury-free; indeed countless runners drift into the sport accidentally, as a result of injuries suffered on the road. The mere diversity of the triathlon prevents most overuse injuries.

'As terrific as just plain running is, by only running you're likely to run into trouble,' admits no less a magazine than *The Runner*. 'Injury trouble. Fatigue trouble. Motivation trouble. Stale-performance trouble. Well, yes, that's all part of the game, any game. But now it has become increasingly apparent that by spicing up your training mix – by running a little less and doing other forms of exercise a little more – you can become a better runner. It's called total fitness. You give your entire body a work-out. It involves elements of swimming, cycling, and weight training, at times even experimenting with the latest high-tech training equipment, good nutrition as always, and perhaps more than anything else, a changing attitude, a feeling that your body can do more than you give it credit for.'

Chapter 13

What and where to eat and drink

The triathlon, by a strange twist of fate has awoken in many a hitherto twentieth-century city dweller a fetish for fruits, grains, vegetables and fresh air. 'We reach directly back along the endless chain of history,' commented Jim Fixx. 'We experience what we would have felt had we lived ten thousand years ago, eating fruits, nuts and vegetables, and keeping our hearts and lungs and muscles fit by constant movement. We are asserting, as modern man seldom does, our kinship with ancient man, and even with the wild beasts that preceded him. This, I think, is our remarkable secret.'

No one has to tell triathletes to eat certain foods, that more natural foods are better for them. Instead triathletes are merely migrating to a healthier diet. It is a delightful discovery to find that your body can 'say' what it needs.

'It's been a gradual process, I guess,' concurs Malcolm Kelvie, of Maidstone. 'I just began eating healthier foods. I hadn't really noticed any great change in my diet, but I've realised over the months a tremendous change in what I eat. I'm eating much healthier foods now than I was a year ago, but I can't remember any concious effort to eat better. It just happened. My theory is that the body dictates what it needs. You just have to listen to it. The harder I train, the louder my body talks.'

Scores of other triathletes echo the same thought. To watch triathletes eating is often something of an experience in itself. Aside from consuming the usual massive quantities of noodles, bread, and water the amount of fruit and vegetables they consume is startling. Dave Scott eats on average 15 fruits each day. He has on occasion eaten as many as 17 bananas in a single sitting – just as an appetiser. As a vegetarian, he eats no sugars, no sweets, and only on occasion, perhaps five times each year, he will eat chicken. Despite the legendary training regime, from five to eight hours each day (which consume up to and beyond 5,000

138

calories each day), he finds his abstention from meat no hindrance. He maintains that a diet high in complex carbohydrates and low in fat is the optimal diet for endurance athletes.

In the middle ages, of course, there was no cancer, and heart disease was not the great killer it is today. The people worked hard in the fields, and in the process expended thousands of calories more each day than twentieth-century inhabitants. They were also eating from the land. Although largely ignorant of nutritional wisdom, they nevertheless had far healthier diets than we do today.

But in our pre-packaged, fast-food society, we are consuming far too little of the right foods, and we count on medical science to rescue us from our self-inflicted ills.

Yet there is no great mystery about good nutrition or a balanced diet. The only trick is to eat a variety of foods from our four food groups – milk and milk products, cereal and grains, fruits and vegetables, and meat and high protein foods. If a balanced diet is followed, there is no need for vitamin supplements, exotic energy foods or other nonsense. The one exception is among women, who may not get enough iron without iron supplements.

The Cereal and Grain Group

This is where the triathlete needs to eat most of his or her food. The cereal and grain group supplies carbohydrates, some protein, minerals and a number of vitamins. Bread, oats, barley, wheat, rice and corn are the basic sources of this group, and are used as ingredients in many foods, from bagels to cakes, from breakfast cereal to bread. The carbohydrates are provided via plants, which combine energy from the sun, carbon dioxide from the air, and hydrogen and oxygen from the soil. During digestion, all carbohydrates are broken down and converted to simple sugar, 'glucose', and stored within the muscles for use as the body's principal source of energy. Meats were once believed to be the best source of energy for athletes, but carbohydrates are better and now recognised as a far better source of energy. Dave Scott eats up to 80 per cent of his food from the grains and cereals group. He eats as much as 1lb or 2lbs of brown rice daily, and is perpetually in a state of carbohydrate loading. 'The diet had undoubtedly contributed to my performance in triathlons,' Scott says. 'I've been following a strict – but enjoyable – diet for the past seven years. I do enjoy eating.' Approximately 11 per cent of his calories are fats, 15 per cent protein, and 74 to 80 per cent carbohydrates.

Before the 1983 Ironman, Scott, Scott Tinley and Marc Thomson were part of a group of six triathletes who in the six weeks leading up to the race ate a carefully monitored diet of 80 per cent carbohydrates, with less than 10 per cent of the diet fat. They finished first, second and fourth respectively.

Fruit and Vegetable Group

Coming from the ground, this group is high in vitamins and minerals. Fruits, berries, leafy and other green vegetables, yellow vegetables (such as carrots, squash and sweet potatoes) as well as potatoes comprise this group. Nutritionists recommend two to four servings each day from this group. Although some leafy vegetables, such as celery, are not digestable by humans and thus offer no nutritional value, they nevertheless need to be included in the diet for the benefit of the digestive tract.

Milk and Milk Products Group

Nutritionists say that each adult should receive the equivalent of two servings from this group every day – either in the form of a drink or included in the preparation of other foods, or as an alternative milk product. Cheese, yogurt, and ice cream also satisfy the body's need for dairy products. The milk group is important for its rich calcium and protein content, which is vital for tissue repair. If taken in excess, however, milk and dairy products can add unnecessary fat, protein, and salt.

The Meat and High-Protein Food Group

Apart from beef, pork and lamb – poultry, fish, eggs, dried peas and nuts can satisfy the body's requirements from this group. Some triathletes, of course, eat no meat at all; instead they consume above-average amounts of nuts, peas and beans.

Nutritionists advise no more than three or four servings of red meat per week, and no more than four eggs each week. Although vital for tissue repair, you need not eat more than 15–25 per cent at the most, of your food from this group.

'Meatless diets can meet the needs of the largest and most vigorous athletes, if the diet is properly selected from the groups of fruits and vegetables,' writes Dr Nathan Smith in his book, *Food For Sport*. 'Adding milk, milk products, and eggs will increase the efficiency of protein use, and add variety and coloric density. There is only one essential nutrient which is available only in food of animal origin, vitamin B_{12}. A relatively small amount of milk, cheese or eggs will satisfy the normal need for vitamin B_{12}.

In place of the meat, Smith points out that at least one daily serving of fresh peas, lima beans, soy beans, split peas, red kidney beans, Navy beans, Black-eyed

peas or sprouted mung beans be eaten, as well as at least a half a cup of nuts –
almonds, cashew, roasted peanuts, pecans or walnuts.

That is it. Everything you ever needed to know about nutrition but were afraid
to ask! Naturally, it is all more complex than this introductory primer, but the
preceding four food groups are the essential foundation.

Clearly, the more you eat that comes directly from the ground or from the trees
(instead of from inside a plastic wrapper), the fitter you will be. But you need not
worry excessively about your diet. If you are like most people, and your training
starts inching up to five or six or seven or more hours each week, you will
probably notice that you gain an inclination towards healthier foods. Instead of
craving potato chips, you'll feel the need to reach for an apple; instead of reaching
for a beer, you will eventually prefer a glass of water.

Few triathletes who gradually convert from junk food to healthier foods

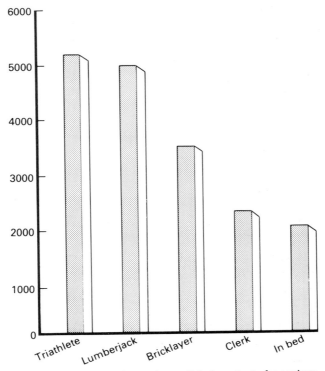

This Diagram shows Approximate Calorie outputs for various
activities. The Triathlete shown is in full Training and has swum
one hour, ridden two and run one. The total complete with his day
to day needs would be 5200 calories. A Calorie is the energy
needed to raise one litre of water one degree centigrade.

Fig. 7

141

remember which came first – the chicken (with green beans and baked potatoes), or the egg (salad sandwich on whole wheat bread). What they do know is that the foods their bodies now crave are quite different from what they craved before they began the triathlon.

As someone who has always enjoyed food, I not only enjoy eating enormous quantities of taste-bud tingling items, but I *have to*. This is just another one of the reasons that the sport is such an ideal activity for men and women into, and well beyond, the third decade of their lives.

After the age of 25, the caloric needs of men and women begin to fall. Whereas a 25 year old standing six feet tall and weighing 175 pounds needs 1800 calories a day to maintain his weight – to compensate for breathing, maintaining body temperature, and keeping body organs functioning – he or she will need 50 calories fewer each day by the age of 35, and 200 fewer calories each day by the age of 55. Although it may not seem like a significant amount, those 200 extra calories, if not either not consumed in the first place or exercised off, will result in a weight gain of 20 pounds each year. This is the primary reason why obesity is more common among middle-aged people. Their bodies need fewer calories, but they themselves fail to recognise the need either to reduce the amount they eat, or to increase their exercise. Indeed, most do the opposite.

A mere three to four hours total each week of swimming, biking and or running – in any combination or at virutally any intensity – can, if sustained for a long enough period, keep the 15 extra pounds away forever. For there is no secret to the arithmetic of weight loss, or weight gain: If you eat more calories than you burn off, you gain weight. If you burn off more than you eat, you lose weight.

Eating before a race

There are scores of different theories on the subject of pre-race nutrition. Many runners practise special pre-race diets in the weeks before a race, steadfastly believing a certain type of food will enhance their performance. Although prudent triathletes seem, by and large, to eschew most such diets, it may be worthwhile to look at some of the methods currently in vogue. The following are by no means a recommendation, for no two triathletes will respond in the same fashion to any particular diet or food. Once again, therefore, it is wise to experiment and find out what works best for you.

The Week Before A Race

The popular wisdom is to eat sensibly, as regularly as possible, and to carry on eating as you have been all along. If you taper your training down simultaneously, your body will already be storing up its energy supply, without any special diets. Two days before the world championships in Nice one year, Malcolm Kelvie, normally an exceedingly polite and calm Englishman, became uncustomarily nervous as noon approached and the car he was travelling in sped across France. Despite the cool weather and a cool breeze, Kelvie had begun to sweat by the time he somewhat frantically pleaded with the driver to find the nearest restaurant. 'Don't want to miss a meal now, not after all this training,' he reasoned after calmly devouring his 12 o'clock feeding. His attention to detail paid dividends; two days later he was one of the top finishers in his age group.

Naturally, during the course of your training, you may wish to experiment with other foods. However, the week preceding a race is not a sensible time to undertake something new.

Some athletes, particularly marathon runners, advocate what is popularly known as 'carbohydrate loading' diets in the six or seven days leading up to a race. Devised in 1967 by two Swedish scientists, Per Olof Astand and Eric Hultman, the idea of the diet is to pack in as many carbohydrates as possible in the days leading up to a race through massive consumption of carbohydrate on its own. The diet is still controversial. While some runners contend it works wonders in staving off what is known as 'the wall' – the point in an endurance event longer than two hours where the glycogen supply in the muscles is exhausted and the body must switch over to burning fats for energy (which because they require 10 per cent more energy burn more slowly and less efficiently than glycogen) – others contend its benefits are nil and its dangers many.

The diet programme is as follows: six or seven days before a race, the athlete exhausts his or her supply of glycogen with a long, hard training session. During the next three days he or she eats a diet low in carbohydrates and high in protein and fat. This first phase is known as the 'depletion phase', and light training continues.

During the next three days leading up to the race, the athlete switches over to a diet low in protein and fat, and high in carbohydrates – the exact opposite. This is the 'loading phase' and athletes normally consume augmented servings of pasta, bread, cakes, chocolate, and other foods rich in carbohydrates. The Swedish researchers demonstrated that the working muscles can, through this process of manipulation, actually trick the body into producing glycogen of its own during the depletion phase, so that when the loading phase does begin, the muscles will have a glycogen store far greater than normal.

Many marathon runners swear by the diet arguing that the carbo-loading can all but obliterate the deadening feeling one gets at around 20 miles into a marathon. Other marathoners, of course, such as Olympic Gold Medalists Joan Benoit and Frank Shorter, have met with tremendous success without using the system.

Although there are a few triathletes who subscribe to the carbo-loading school of thought (and most it seems, do not), they prefer instead merely to increase their carbohydrate consumption in the final three days before a race rather than undergoing the depletion phase. Apparently triathletes are reluctant to trick their bodies. They seem to have an instinct of what their bodies do in a triathlon, and appear by and large more reluctant to pursue any form of manipulation of their bodies. Unlike runners or cyclists, and other endurance athletes, triathletes seem to be immune from doping and other forms of drug-use that have fouled so many other sports. It is unlikely that doping will ever become a problem either. The athletes rightly have too much respect for their bodies to tamper with them for ephemeral gain.

Critics of the depletion phase of the carbohydrate loading system are also beginning to emerge from the medical community. Some physiologists, apart from doubting the wisdom of 'fooling' the body into something unnatural, have warned that the diet can damage tissue, lead to depression, and leave the athlete more vulnerable to influenza, colds, and other illnesses in the days leading up to a race. They also point out that the body eventually realises that it is being manipulated, and adjusts, which renders the whole depletion aspect of the diet nugatory. Nutritionists, however, have found little damage arising from the increase of carbohydrate intake – the loading phase – just before a race.

Dr David Costill the American physiologist, discovered a simpler, and for many endurance athletes, an attractive alternative in their quest to delay the arrival of, if not surmount entirely, the wall. By drinking two cups of black coffee (4–5 milligrams of caffein per kilogram of body weight) one hour before an endurance event, Costill found that athletes could extend their point of exhaustion by 19 per cent. The timing of the coffee intake appears to be critical, for when the coffee was consumed two hours – instead of one hour, before the event, the performance was increased by only seven per cent.

The caffeine apparently stimulates the nervous system to release more free fatty acids into the blood that, in the early stages of the race, the body burns *before* switching over to the glycogen store. Without the stimulant, the glycogen store is depleted *first*, and then, once that source is depleted, the body normally begins to search for fats to burn which, of course, are less efficient sources of energy because they require oxygen (unlike glycogen which burns without oxygen present).

Some triathletes, myself included, use the coffee trick zealously. There have been several occasions when like-minded colleagues have been seen, an hour before a race, desperately searching for black coffee. Others, on the other hand, find that it does not help their performances at all, in fact only increases their need to urinate just before the start of the race.

In general, but particularly in the week before a race, it is not a good idea to eat any fatty foods, such as sausages, pies, doughnuts, deep-fried fish or chips. Before I ran my first marathon, I thought that sausage and pancakes would be the ideal breakfast. The race was the longest four-and-a-half hours of my life. Other foods that should also be avoided are highly refined foods such as sugar, sweets, cakes and other fatty products. Convenience foods, even though they are often tasty, are also foods high in cost and low in value. So is alcohol.

Alcohol, particularly in hot weather, can be extraordinarily detrimental to your performance. Although popular wisdom leads many to drink large amounts of beer before a race, in the belief that it will add to the carbohydrate load, such benefits are usually outweighed by the drawbacks. This does not mean that you need to give up beer, wine or your favourite food or beverage. On the contrary. Because athletes burn off plenty of calories, occasional alcohol or ice cream splurges probably do little harm to their bodies, in any event, far less damage than they would do to a sedentary person. Indeed athletes seem, by and large, to be more immune to such harmful effects. However, because alcohol stays in the system for up to 48 hours or more, you will find it wise to abstain for that period before a race.

Grilled, boiled or steamed foods are more nutritionous than fried foods. Uncooked foods, especially vegetables, are excellent sources of nutrition in the week before the race. It is also good to eat larger than normal amounts of carrots or other raw vegetables *the day before* the race to clear out the intestinal tract. This is also a good time to eat as many smaller or normal-sized meals throughout the day as possible, rather than one huge, difficult-to-digest feast.

Race Day Nutrition

By this point there is little you can do to increase your performance considerably. However, it is not too late to damage your potential performance through misguided food consumption.

The pre-race meal should be eaten no less than three hours before the start. The inevitable nervous tension invariably makes digestion before a race difficult. It is a good idea, therefore, to eat lightly, perhaps a few rolls or slices of bread and toast. Cereal is also preferred by some triathletes, although many others prefer to stay clear of milk for the day or two before a race. Toast is also a good, if not extravagant pre-race diet. If you eat it without butter or margarine, you will probably be better off, but as long as you give yourself three hours before the start, the food should pass through your system.

What you should not want to eat is meat, or other heavy foods, which can remain partially digested in the stomach for 10–12 hours. Fatty foods are also digested slowly. Fruit juices on the other hand, are good to drink in the hours before a race, but not in the last 60 minutes!

In the final hour it is not wise to eat or drink anything that has sugar in it. Candy, pastries, ice cream, dried fruits, honey, soft drinks and even sport drinks, should then, according to Dr Costill, be avoided. The reason is that sugars, absorbed into the blood stream, stimulate the release of insulin, and once the athlete begins muscular activity, the glucose in the blood stream will be burned off at a faster rate. The exercising muscles, deprived of the important source of energy, blood sugar, begin to draw heavily from the glycogen stored in the muscles, leading to premature depletion. The condition, known as 'hypoglyce-mia', can impair performance dramatically. 'Our test subjects consistently fatigued earlier and found the running more difficult when they took a sugar drink 30 – 45 minutes before exercise,' observed Costill. He adds, however, that once the exercise has begun, consuming sugar drinks will not harm and may even enhance performance.

During the race itself, if it lasts longer than three hours, it is vital to replace your lost energy supply by eating and drinking. In races shorter than three hours in length, it is not necessary for most people to eat anything, although drinking 100 to 200 ml of water every 15 to 20 minutes is very important. Because the body is 50 to 60 per cent water, it is crucial that body fluids lost through perspiration and exhaling are regularly replaced. It is even a good idea to drink 13–15 ounces of water 15 minutes before a race, particularly in hot weather to 'pre-hydrate' yourself. Obviously, you cannot eat during the swim. And during the running portions of triathlons, your body and stomach are bouncing so hard that digestion will at best be impaired. That leaves the biking section as the obvious, and best, occasion to eat.

Eating while cycling is not unnatural. Bike racers need to eat, and have little trouble digesting foods such as bananas, raisins, and cookies. It is, perhaps, one of the sport's most devastating feelings to be cycling along, be it in training or in a race, and suddenly, inexplicably, to become the victim of 'bonk'. It attacks suddenly, and the feeling of fatigue is overwhelming. Few feelings are as nightmarish. You begin to dream optimistically about nuclear war, a quick flash to end your agony. Bonk is bonk, and if you are not prepared for it, that is, have not eaten, bonk can bonk you on the head harder than you can imagine. *What* food, then, should you eat? Most authorities suggest the banana, and other pulped fruits. Nutritious, full of energy, easily digestible, appetising flavour and colour, and easy to stick in a back pocket, tape to the frame, or reach for from a volunteer during the course of a race, the banana is indeed an ideal source of food for the bikers and the triathlete.

Other recommended foods are raisins and slices of apples and oranges, but here begins a controversy. Some so-called authorities repudiate the apple and orange slices, contending that it takes too long and too much energy to break them down and digest them to be of any energy value. But the choice is yours.

Doughnuts are also sometimes offered at races. Some claim that the grease in which the doughnuts are cooked will remain undigested in the stomach until the race is over. Others happily take the two forms of energy offered: quick energy, from the sugar coating, and slow burning energy from the bread content. Next to the banana, the doughnut is an outstanding source of energy, particularly in the longer triathlons. Other foods that could, and should, be consumed in moderation during longer triathlons, as well as raisins and cookies, include slices of watermelon, or cantaloupe, small meatless sandwiches, baby food, Mars bars, energy bars, or even hard candy which lets a slow steady trickle of glucose into your system.

When should you eat? Again, it is a matter of personal wish. Aside from the swim, you should begin to eat *before* you feel hungry, or at the very latest when you suspect you may be weakening. This is quite an art, knowing when to eat, for if you eat (too much) too soon, you can end up making an unscheduled pit stop at the side of the road. If you wait too long you can end up running (or crawling) on empty. One triathlete at the British National Championships one year was eating popsicles, chocolate bars, cakes, hard candies, and drinking grape juice by the litre. He finished the bike course, started to change and proceeded to throw up. The popsicles had not helped.

A sound idea which many top runners follow and which is worthy of emulation by triathletes, is to alternate drinking water and a sweet drink, such as Electrolyte replacement drinks. Too much sweet stuff early in the race can give you an early lift and leave your system depressed later in the race. Similarly, not taking any replacement drink can leave the triathlete spent long before the finish. Drinking water for as long as possible at the outset of the race and in the early stages, at least until well into the cycle ride, and then alternating the sweet stuff with the water is helpful. It is also preferable to take sips frequently from your water bottle rather than drain it in one or two gulps, for what you are doing is replacing water lost through perspiration.

Some triathletes particularly those from cycling backgrounds, claim that a constant slight thirst is preferable to water sloshing around in your stomach. Aside from being lighter, you will actually perspire less if you drink less, they claim. And because you are losing more than just water when you sweat, i.e.

minerals, you are unnecessarily taxing your system by over-drinking. Studies have shown that water drunk in the last four miles of a marathon remains unacted upon until after the race. Thus if, you avoid drinking water in the last few miles, or manage with a small mouthful (which can possibly be spat out) you will do yourself no harm. Promise yourself all of your favourite beverages later that night if you finish the race without having to reach for the last (unnecessary) drink.

Chapter 14

Dave Scott

It was the day before the World Championships and nearly all of the 600 tri-athletes from around the world who had descended upon Nice had long since put a cap on their pre-race training. There was not much that could be gained in the days leading up to a race. But out there in the Mediterranean someone was swimming a section of the course. And swimming it hard.

Many other triathletes had swum sections of the course easily in previous days. Actually, most had more than likely jumped into the water more to cool off than to work-out. The week leading up to the race is for most a vacation from their training, a four or five day respite, a time to lie on the beach, soak up the sun, and think about all the miles they had swum, cycled and run all summer long. Nevertheless someone was out there, swimming the course with impressive speed.

After about a half an hour, the red hat began heading toward the shore. Silhouetted in the turquoise water against a brilliant setting September sun, there was something distinguishing about the stroke, something quite special. Steaming closer to the shore at seemingly ever-increasing velocity, the distinctive wide flair of the left arm extinguished any further doubt as to the identity of the swimmer.

'Hi, my name's Dave,' said Dave Scott, arriving moments later on the beach. The introduction was superfluous. Despite its short history, the triathlon has already managed to produce a legend. Dave Scott was not only still alive by the time he became immortalised; he hadn't even reached his thirtieth birthday. It is not merely that Scott has won four Ironman races in five attempts but that he has won the race by as much as a full hour (in 1980) and that he has set a new world record with each triumph. No wonder then that people flock around him as if he were a saviour.

Why a legend? There are several possible reasons. Perhaps because like so many other triathletes he was versatile, but undistinguished in a host of other sports before he began the triathlon. Perhaps because he has won the Ironman four times. 'Winning an Ironman – merely finishing one – is an act of raw courage and athletic virtuosity,' wrote Dan Levin in a 1983 article for *Sports Illustrated*. 'Winning two, as only Scott has, is a feat for the ages.'

Perhaps it is that Dave Scott has had such a humble start, and a dynamic and explosive present and future (indeed like the triathlon itself) which makes him not only the maestro of the triathlon, but a microcosm of the sport as well. Perhaps because he trains alone, and trains hard, pushing himself through work-outs which leave some people tired just glancing at his training log. Perhaps, the fact that like many triathletes, Dave Scott has weaknesses and had never seriously biked nor run before beginning the triathlon, breathes hope into the lungs of every beginner. If Scott can bike that fast, and run so well after just a few years training, so can I, many people reason or, at least, hope. Perhaps he is a fable figure for many because he has become a champion from scratch, a modern-day Horatio Alger.

Yet when Dave Scott talks he sounds like anything *but* a deus figure. He is, surprisingly, slightly shy, but talks a lot of practical sense. You get the impression that he personifies the American spirit, that hard work and enough drive are enough to accomplish anything. His determination is infectious. 'He knows what he wants,' a friend once said, and indeed he goes after what he wants with irrepressible zeal.

He is, as they say in America, 'down-to-earth', meaning that despite his mounting fame and fortune, he's not lost track of himself. He lives in a small condominium in Davis, California, just down the road from where his parents live and where he grew up. In his spare time he plays the piano. And perhaps most telling, he's not ashamed of his flaws. 'My stroke is horrendous,' he readily confesses to anyone who enquires. 'But I'm competitive. I don't care about leading out of the water, as long as I'm close to the front.'

He became the world's greatest triathlete after more than two and a half decades of limited success in other sports. Certainly this serves as a model for countless thousands of other triathletes, some of whom have failed to distinguish themselves in other sports, but who have suddenly found the triathlon in their court. 'If he can do it, so can I.'

Scott had played football and basketball in high school with moderate success. He had swum as well – the 500-metre and 1500-metre, the longest races available – but even in the pool he never really had much success. He was tough in practice sessions, but he would only be getting warmed up by the time the race was over. He played water polo – once again with moderate success – in college as well, a sport which, more than any other, seems to be the most likely pre-determiner of success in the triathlon.

After graduating from the University of California at Davis, he stumbled into ocean swimming, and finally began to enjoy success over the longer distances. The 2.4 mile Rough Water swim at Waikiki became a favourite race. His wide choppy recovery seemed well-suited for the ocean. At the same time he launched on his own initiative a Masters' Swim Program in Davis, and oversaw its growth from a half dozen members to more than 400 by the time he stepped aside to train full-time in 1981. It was at the Waikiki Rough Water race in 1978 that someone first mentioned the Ironman to him, which had borrowed the very same 2.4 Rough Water Swim and combined it with the 112-mile Around Oahu Bike race and the 26.2-mile Honolulu Marathon.

'I thought it sounded pretty bizarre,' Scott confesses with self-deprecating humour. 'I couldn't conceive of anything like that. I never even dreamed of running a marathon, or riding a bike that far let alone back to back. But in 1979 a friend sort of conned me into it. He said "You train a lot, you run and swim every day, and you're in great shape." Being ignorant and naive about what went into the triathlon, I let him lure me into it.'

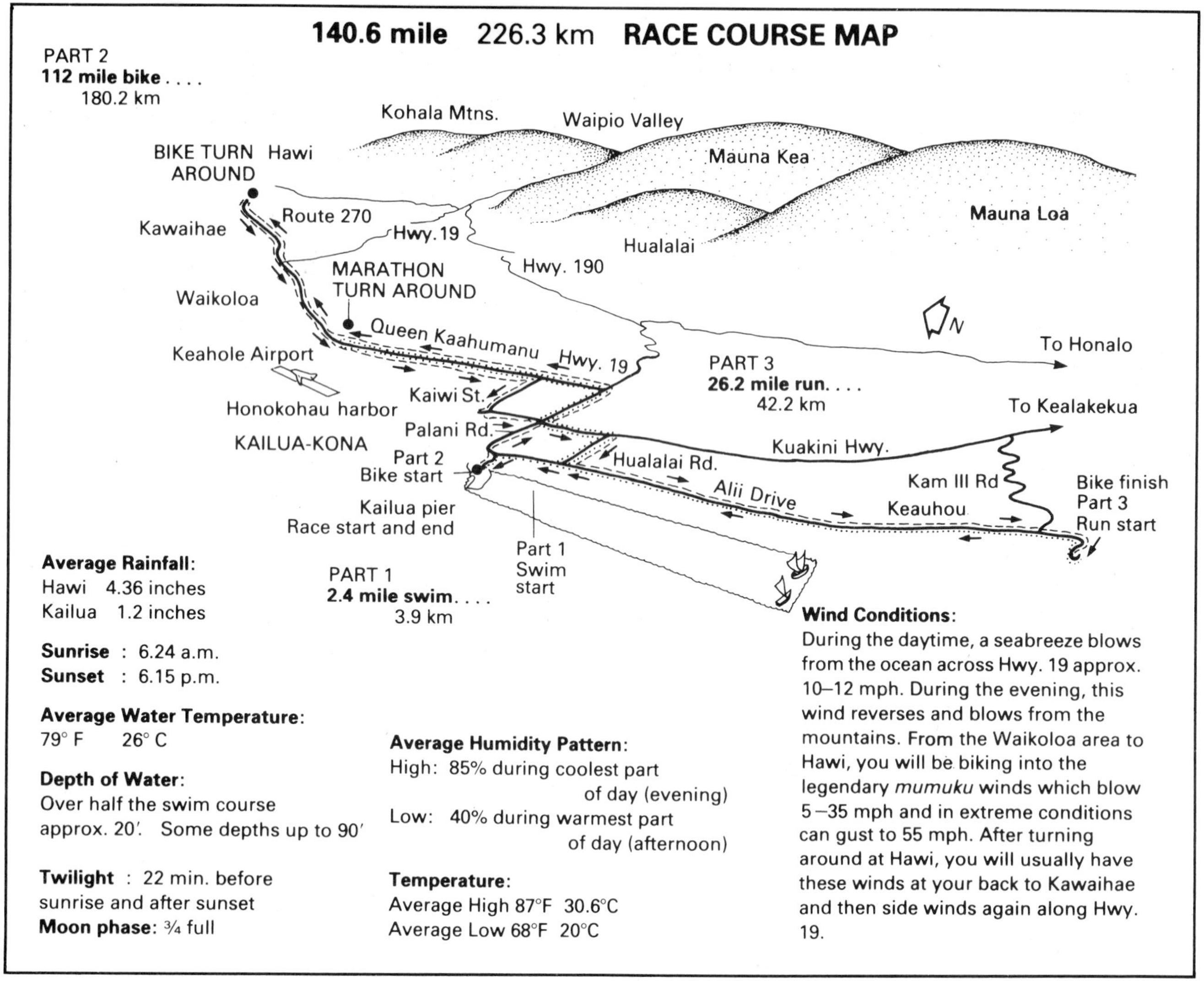

140.6 mile   226.3 km   RACE COURSE MAP

PART 2
112 mile bike . . . . .
180.2 km

BIKE TURN
AROUND   Hawi

Kawaihae

Route 270

Hwy. 19

MARATHON
TURN AROUND

Waikoloa

Queen Kaahumanu   Hwy. 19

Keahole Airport

Honokohau harbor

Kaiwi St.

Palani Rd.

KAILUA-KONA

Part 2
Bike start

Kailua pier
Race start and end

PART 1
2.4 mile swim . . . .
3.9 km

Part 1
Swim
start

Hualalai Rd.

Alii Drive

Hualalai

Mauna Kea

Mauna Loa

Kohala Mtns.

Waipio Valley

Hwy. 190

To Honalo

N

To Kealakekua

PART 3
26.2 mile run . . . . .
42.2 km

Kuakini Hwy.

Keauhou

Kam III Rd

Bike finish
Part 3
Run start

Average Rainfall:
Hawi   4.36 inches
Kailua   1.2 inches

Sunrise : 6.24 a.m.
Sunset : 6.15 p.m.

Average Water Temperature:
79° F   26° C

Depth of Water:
Over half the swim course
approx. 20'. Some depths up to 90'

Twilight : 22 min. before
sunrise and after sunset
Moon phase: ¾ full

Average Humidity Pattern:
High: 85% during coolest part
of day (evening)

Low: 40% during warmest part
of day (afternoon)

Temperature:
Average High 87°F   30.6°C
Average Low 68°F   20°C

Wind Conditions:
During the daytime, a seabreeze blows
from the ocean across Hwy. 19 approx.
10—12 mph. During the evening, this
wind reverses and blows from the
mountains. From the Waikoloa area to
Hawi, you will be biking into the
legendary *mumuku* winds which blow
5—35 mph and in extreme conditions
can gust to 55 mph. After turning
around at Hawi, you will usually have
these winds at your back to Kawaihae
and then side winds again along Hwy.
19.

Fig.8

152

The first thing Scott did was buy a bike. He had not cycled seriously at all, even though Davis, California is one of the world's Meccas for biking. The city is criss-crossed with bicycle paths and saturated with cyclists. It was a heavenly and futuristic foresight not lost on the city's myriad cyclists.

Within a few months, Scott had upped his weekly cycling mileage to 250 miles. He also doubled his running from 30 miles a week to 60. His swimming – at that time 20,000 yards per week – also experienced a healthy escalation, up to 30,000 yards (just over 17 miles) each week.

'I didn't have a cycling background, or a running background,' he says. 'I think everyone's a little naive when they start. But I felt I'd be able to apply to cycling and running the principles I'd learned with my swimming background and education. They're all aerobic activities. There are carry-overs from one sport to the other and specific things for each event that you need to be aware of. With running, for instance, I found you have to allow more recovery time on a daily basis and on a long-term basis because you're not as efficient when running. You're moving a much larger muscle mass and you're in a vertical position, as opposed to swimming, where you can dissipate heat easily, and where you're horizontal and thus able to recover much more rapidly. The same applies for cycling, because the wind cools you, and you don't have to move as great a muscle mass.'

Herein lies another contributing factor to Scott's tremendous appeal. He is the thinking man's triathlete, a personable prophet, fully aware of his body, its capabilities, its needs and its limits. He conveys such an impressive understanding of the body, a contagious appreciation that leaves you anxious to study physiology.

Despite his self-imposed seclusion in training, he unhesitatingly shares information and training tips with beginners and rivals alike. He has written articles on fitness, diet and swimming for various magazines. His expertise in swimming has been of particular value for many novices: he has written out training schedules for dozens of other triathletes, and even plans someday to write a book on the sport. Originally he wrote out the training schedules gratis for anyone who asked, but after word of his magnanimous nature spread, and he became deluged with phone calls, he opted to solve the problem by charging from $150 to $275 for those interested. He still writes out long-term training programmes for at least a dozen triathletes each year.

He has also popularised helpful information that has greatly aided discerning triathletes. He is, for example, cited, often, as the source for disseminating the information that it is better to switch from the free-style to the breast or backstroke in the last few dozen yards of the swim. Although less efficient strokes than the free-style, they can help the blood, concentrated during the swim in the arms and shoulders, recirculate throughout the body. Also, he adds, 'it loosens up the hip flexors, and calf muscles, causing the feet to dorsiflex, the position the feet are in when riding a bike.' Ask him a question about any aspect of the triathlon and he will invariably be able to provide a sensible, if technical reply, well-thought out and logical. What, for example, are the best ways to taper your draining down for a race?

'Tapering obviously depends upon the person's training programme and the individual's recuperation from day to day work-outs,' he begins, just warming up to the question, something he seems to enjoy in spite of the repetition of such enquiries. 'Running is the most demanding of the three activities and therefore the intensity and or distance should be gradually reduced during the last eight or nine days prior to the race with possibly one or two days of total rest during the last week. Cycling mileage should be reduced and also any interval or hill training should be stopped at least three days prior to the race. Swimming distances can be maintained, however, the percentage of free-style in the daily work-out should be reduced 20 or 30 per cent during the last three days with an emphasis on moderate intensity backstroke or breast stroke. Tapering is very specific to the individual and experimentation by the coach or the triathlete should develop an optimum plan.'

Ask him about diet, and he'll delve into some specifics, his daily intake of 5,000 meatless calories, his consumption of 10–15 pieces of fruit a day, and an incredible amount of rice, beans, and tofu. Complex carbohydrates, he enjoys explaining, are optimal for endurance athletes.

Recovery after a race, another topic once largely overlooked, is also a favourite of Scott's. 'It's important to eat a balanced diet after a race, with 10–20 per cent more carbohydrates to "re-load" your glycogen stores. Have a massage once a day, and swim easy, including walking on the bottom of the pool so that your legs can relax and also stretch out slowly without having the weight of the body. Swimming should begin immediately with only 30–40 per cent free-style the day after. Cycling should be started two days after the race and running can be started three days after. Don't allow yourself to just sit.'

Not surprisingly, many other triathletes now also talk about the importance of a defined recovery phase. Scott is without a doubt a trend-setter, but it is not so much because of his pontificating, rather it is the horde of triathletes who eagerly listen to and imitate whatever he says. Even his closest rivals, Scott Tinley and Mark Allen, sent him a telegram on 'Dave Scott Day' in his hometown in 1983 after he won his third Ironman, congratulating him and openly admitting that he was the standard to which they compared themselves, the model they strove to equal. They have invited him several times to move down to San Diego to train with them, where the warmer winters assist year-round training. He politely declined,

'You know why I live up here?' he once asked rhetorically, with a smile. 'Because the weather stinks. Those other guys are soft. They're not hungry, and they know what to expect from each other.'

He trains alone 80 per cent of the time, swimming with a club, and occasionally cycling with a friend, Mike Norton. He usually runs alone. 'That's one of the problems I'm having right now,' he candidly admits. 'I don't like being by myself. I may be a bit too selfish with my time. I want to work-out when I want to work-out. I like the cameraderie of being with someone else. I just like someone else there, even if we're not of the same ability. It just makes it more interesting. It's just really hard to do it by myself. I average about 5–7 hours training a day. You need a balance. You can't be inundated with one thing. The hardest part is the training every day. I enjoy training once I get going. The hardest part is getting out the door. But I think everyone must have that problem. The races are fun. There's a lot of incentive. It's the day-to-day rigours of training that's getting hard.'

It has become apparent in the triathlon that you simply cannot cycle and run as fast as you could in a separate time trial or a road race. Because of the accummulated fatigue, most triathletes need at least 10 per cent more time to run after cycling and swimming. Yet Scott, perhaps more than any other triathlete, has become intoxicated with the idea of smashing through this invisible barrier. He is forever trying to duplicate the latter stages of fatigue in his training, constantly aiming to cope successfully with the fatigue and to run through it. He has often been quoted as saying his most satisfying moments in the sport have been 'watching other guys drop off'. He is obsessed with improvement, and claims that he has not yet reached his peak.

'If conditions are right – the water isn't too choppy, the winds are light, and it's not too hot,' he said before the 1983 Ironman, 'I think an 8:40 is going to win this race.' The conditions that year were not right – it was hot and windy, and the ocean was choppy. Scott still won the race, in another world record time of 9:05. The following year, 1984, he shattered the hitherto thought to be impregnable three-hour marathon with a 2:53.

'I enjoy the mental perseverance and concentration and slowly wearing down my competitors,' he notes. 'I enjoy training just to stay healthy. The triathlon is such a challenging sport. I don't think people's potential is limited by what age they are or what age they start at. I think you can always improve your skills. It's really a wide-open sport. Physically, I don't see any limitation in myself, but I know I'm not going to be doing this for many more years at this level. I want to do other things. I don't think I've reached my peak yet, though. Swimming I've been doing for years and years. I'll never really get that much faster. I'll be happy if I can just maintain the level I'm at now swimming. I'll be happy and I'll be satisfied with that. I think, though, that I can improve quite a bit on my running. I know I can run faster.'

A good portion of his work-outs are devoted to matching the advanced stages of fatigue by doing lots of intervals, especially in the pool work-outs. He also employs fartlek on the bike and occasionally while running. His swimming intervals are especially demanding, usually from 2 to 8 to 10 minutes with just a 5–40 second (maximum) rest interval.

'Doing interval and or fartlek training can simulate race fatigue by working at a pace that is equal to or faster than your race pace. Additionally, incorporating shorter triathlons into your training and gradually reducing the transition period between events will simulate the race conditions. Interval training will expediate and maximise your time and efficiency in the pool. I think it is a most efficient way to train, short-rest intervals. A combination of short-rest interval training and repetition work to elevate the anaerobic threshold and oxygen consumption is paramount. Fartlek miles in the pool are okay for an ultra distance triathlon once or twice a week. However, fartlek swimming is terribly boring and it is difficult to monitor relative speed, whereas a pace clock gives you immediate feedback. When a lot of people start swimming just long distances they get stale and bored. You have to keep it interesting to stay with it.'

In diet he is a vegetarian, although he does eat fish, and chicken perhaps five times a year. 'But I don't have any withdrawals if I don't eat it.' He is convinced that meat and diets high in fats are the sources of many western societies' health problems. He eats upwards of 80 per cent of his calories from complex carbo-hydrates – wholewheat bread, brown rice, potatoes, grains, beans and pasta. He eats no sugar, and limits his fat intake to about 11 per cent of his diet. He eats a lot of fruit but no regular meals, rather a steady consumption all day long. Three slices of wholewheat bread and three bananas start the day, and the daily feast continues almost uninterrupted throughout the day. He's been known to have eaten as many as nine main courses before races. During the race itself, he usually eats figs and water.

'This diet has undoubtedly contributed to my performance in the triathlon over the years,' he says without hesitation. 'I watch my diet closely. I do take some vitamins, but I'm not sure whether they help or not. I don't think any nutritionist can really define whether you need extra amounts of vitamin C or E. Everyone's different. Everyone's body has different demands. I just think that anyone who is concerned about vitamin deficiencies should take some vitamins as a sort of insurance factor. It's just for insurance.'

At one point earlier in his career, Scott felt the media coverage of triathlons was appalling. 'I used to get disturbed by most of what was written about the triathlon, especially the Ironman. It might have been because of the way television covered it, where they showed it as a survival test, not a race. I was apprehensive at one point about talking to the media because they kept pulling out Julie Moss crawling across the finishing line.'

Even today, despite a warmer attitude toward the media, he still seems uncomfortable with the publicity. He gives interviews to essentially everyone who asks, yet still cannot understand why they want to talk with him. It is almost as if he keeps looking over his shoulder, expecting to discover the person the media really wants to talk to. There are, however, subjects Scott clearly enjoys talking about.

One day after winning his fourth Ironman, someone asked him what he thought of the growth of the triathlon. A wide smile quickly spread across his face.

'It's just unbelievable! In 1978, when I did my first triathlon, I couldn't possible envision the growth of the sport today. Even after doing the 1980 Ironman in which 108 people were entered, I had no idea that the sport would develop at such a torrid pace. It's just incredible.'

Dave Scott's training schedule: (a peak week leading up to the Ironman)

Sunday:
swimming	5,300 yards
cycling	65 miles
running	10 miles

Monday:
cycling	78 miles
swimming	4,800 yards
running	12.5 miles
weights	40 minutes

Tuesday:
running	9 miles
swimming	5,700 yards
cycling	65 miles

Wednesday:
running	14 miles
swimming	4,100 yards
cycling	90 miles

Thursday:
swimming	5,300 yards
cycling	65 miles
weights	50 minutes

Friday:
cycling	101 miles
running	12 miles
swimming	3,300 yards

Saturday:
swimming	5,900 yards
running	11 miles
weights	40 minutes

Seven day total:
swimming:	34,400 yards
cycling:	464 miles
running:	68.5 miles
weights:	130 minutes

Height: 6' 1" (1.87m)
Weight: 163 pounds (74 kg)

Chapter 15

Race Strategy and Tactics

It had been a tough race on a challenging course. A mile swim in the chilly North Sea, an 80-mile bike ride, and then a hilly 17-mile run. Martin Dyer, third out of the water, had quickly stormed into the lead and opened up an 18-minute lead over his nearest rival after the bike ride. Eighteen full minutes. He had covered the 80 miles in a scorching time of three hours, 29 minutes.

It was the National Championships at Durham in 1984, and the large crowd was assuming the race was all but over.

In second place after the bike ride was Klaus Klaeren, of West Germany. He had had 'a rough swim'. A bony 140 pounds, Klaeren had been pummelled in the North Sea and needed more than 30 minutes on the bike before he began to feel his normal self. He continued to fall further behind Dyer during the bike ride, even though he had moved steadily and inexorably up through the pack from 18th place to second.

But being eighteen minutes behind the leader did not seem to faze the German National Champion. He had been warned that Dyer was a fast bike rider. Dyer managed to hold on to a 7:42 pace per mile, far from spectacular, especially considering Dyer was formerly a runner, but on a hot day after a 23 mph bike ride for three and a half hours, it was reasonable. But Klaeren, who had averaged 21 mph on the bike once he had sorted himself out and pushed the cold of the North Sea from his body, managed to run an amazing 6:24 per mile pace for 17 hilly miles.

He rapidly began closing the huge gap, turning what had been a rout into a race. With just four miles to go, Klaeren spotted the fading Dyer, less than one mile ahead in the distance. He was able to gallop past him, and ended up winning the race by five minutes. It was an impressive display of intelligent race strategy.

'I had heard that he was a fast bike rider,' Klaeren said later. 'So I wasn't too worried when I heard that he had an 18-minute lead. I though I might be able to catch up with him. I've run a 2:26 marathon, and I felt pretty good about my chances. I just tried to relax, and see what would happen. I had had a rough swim. The water was quite cold, and it took a while on the bike before I got rolling. He did have a big lead, but there were still 17 miles to go.'

Hawaii 1984 was to produce a similar situation when Mark Allen, 12 minutes up on Dave Scott, faded badly to fifth place while Scott strode by to win in 8 hours 54 minutes.

There are countless examples such as these in the triathlon. Rarely is the first person out of the water the winner of the race. And likewise, seldom can the first person on the run course count on holding on to the lead. So much can be gained through intelligent race strategy. So much can likewise be lost through lack of foreplanning. It is perhaps precisely this aspect, this intangible appeal, this constant guessing game of 'but can he run?' or 'what kind of biker is she?' or 'can he last for five more hours at that pace?' that makes the triathlon such an alluring sport.

Strategy is crucially important. If for no other reason, it will give you something to think about during the last gruelling miles of the run, just one more mental game you can allow your mind to play in order to stave off or break through the 'wall'.

'Have I followed my strategy?' 'Have I stuck with my pace, and pre-planned time limits as I predicted?' 'Or have I started too fast and blown myself up?' 'Or am in shape relative to the others?' 'How are my legs doing?' 'How are the feet?' 'Do I need to stretch?' 'How much do I have left?' 'Do I need water now, or should I wait?' 'When should I eat?' 'How much should I eat?' 'Can I speed up here a bit?' 'Or should I slow down and save something for the run?'

These and an infinite number of other questions that you ask yourself can help maximise your performance. That is the idea of this chapter, Getting The Most Out of What You Have.

Some people feel that words like 'race' and 'strategy' are not part of their vocabulary. Perhaps 'race strategy' does invoke a competitive pale in which triathletes have no or little interest. But even if you have no intention of becoming 'competitive' and disdain the 'win-win-win' syndrome that some runners and triathletes have allowed themselves to fall into, the subject is important.

It is not necessarily important for those looking to shave a few seconds off their times, but it is significant for anyone who has done a triathlon and felt they could have done better or who are interested in maximising their performances and minimising what can go wrong.

The goal then is to pace your performance so that you use all your available energy to get to the finish line as quickly as possible. A steady burn of your energy will get you there faster in the long run than rapid bursts that leave you destroyed. It is no fun being passed by the entire field during the run, as you hobble woefully along. Nor is it very satisfying to cruise across the finish line when everyone else has gone home, including your spouse.

Nor does development of sound strategy begin an hour after the race has started. It should begin in the weeks before the race. You should assess your weaknesses and strengths, decide what your time splits should roughly be, taking into account any potential problems the weather conditions might pose: cold water, strong winds, or stifling heat. You also might want to plan out a tapering-down plan, when you start decreasing your amount of training, and when you stop altogether. You don't want to stop training completely a week before a race, yet you want to be at your physical peak on the race day, not after it.

Tapering down is truly an art. If it sounds inflated to call it an art, it nevertheless requires skill, talent, and patience. A rapport between the athlete and his body is also essential.

Much depends, as usual, on the distance involved, and on how much you train. If the race is a long or ultra-distance race, you might want to begin decreasing your work-outs gradually from seven days before the race until two or three days before the race, at which point you may completely stop.

Others may wish to taper first the running, which exacts the most from the body, then the cycling, riding no later than four days before the race, and then swimming right up until the day of the race. Dave Scott swims 1600–2000 metres the day before a race, and never seems to have problems.

What is not wise, in any event, is to stop training abruptly a week or so before a race. To do that could really be a shock to your system. Used to devouring mega calories each day, if it is suddenly left in a state of atrophy for a week, you can expect to lose some of your hard-won condition. A day or two days of total rest before the race should suffice.

'The taper period is defined as a sharpening of your training, due to a *reduced* exercise regime,' says Scott. 'Generally, there is a reduction in the duration or distance you train, the number of sets or repeats you do, and the overall intensity should be diminished. You should gradually reduce your training, but not completely stop until a day or two before the race.'

Barry Turner, who rarely finds time to train more than eight hours per week because he works as a dentist, was trying to better prepare for races by cramming up to 12 hours of training in the week before races. Not surprisingly, he came down with colds, and three times was unable to compete in the actual race. It was more than a little frustrating.

'I think my problem was that I was stepping up my training too much too soon before the race,' he observes. 'Tapering is an art, though, it really is. I tried doing the opposite for the next race, tapering down and doing essentially nothing in the four days before the race and it went very well. I almost felt guilty for not training for those days. I got itchy feet. But I learned the hard way that you just have to taper.'

You should have a fairly clear idea of how fast you can swim, bike and run the distance involved. Naturally, you will not be able to ride or run faster than you could bike or run the distances in a separate race, but by knowing how fast you can run a mile, and adding ten per cent, you should have an approximate idea of what your mileage speed should be in the run of any triathlon.

The first mile or perhaps two miles will be far slower than that, at least until you accumulate experience. But what is important is to know roughly what your splits should be for the various mileage points.

Be reasonable, too, when establishing your mile time goals. If you pick too fast a pace, and try too hard to maintain that speed, you could blow up miles from the finish line, and be lucky to walk to the finish line while others trot by. And if you find yourself slowing considerably below your selected time goals, you can become discouraged. The last few miles of the triathlon course is an unrelenting place, not the best time to add disappointment to a semi-disillusioned mind.

Be sensible when determining speed goals. Be fair. Try to inject some logic into it. The mental calculation during the race itself provides the mind with a pleasant diversion.

It is important as well to assess honestly your physical condition, your physical limitations, your strengths, and your weaknesses. By recognising your chances of success on the course involved, you should be able to formulate a reasonable 'road map' of where you should be at certain points. Some people can string the three sports together and perform marvellously. Others are devastated by the one-after-the-other facet of the triathlon. Generally speaking, however, if you are a good swimmer and a mediocre runner and cyclist, and you are entered in a triathlon that includes a relatively short swim (say 800 metres), a long bike ride (50 miles) and a long run (15 miles), then you must realise in advance that you will be almost literally a fish out of water for most of the day; the lion's share of the race will be run outside of your element. On the other hand, if you are a strong swimmer, and the swim course is challengingly long, and the bike and run courses are proportionately short, you may want to rethink your race strategy, and try to open up as large a lead as possible during the swim.

Similarly, if you are a good cyclist and a decent runner, and the swim course is relatively short (as is often the case in Great Britain), and the cycling course is a hilly mountainous ride, you can expect to do well, and should remain calm, even if you are the last person out of the water.

161

Knowing the competition

Whereas running races are often run against the other competition more than against the clock, the triathlete, conversely, is more naturally suited to racing against the clock, unless, that is, he or she knows the competition well. But because, most of the time, triathletes show up at an event not knowing many of the other competitors, let alone their strengths and their weaknesses, it is best to plan and swim, bike and run the best race you can: an even exertion throughout the race, unconcerned with the opposition, with, if possible, a slight crescendo beyond the midway point of the run.

When Martin Dyer tried to destroy the competition on the bike course at Durham, he hit speeds of more than 35 mph on certain stretches hoping to hold on to a big lead. He had the big lead. He could not hold on to it because he had paced himself badly. Klaus Klaeren, on the other hand, paced himself astutely. He biked steadily, getting stronger as the race wore on, and began to fly on the run, reaching his crescendo, his fastest miles, just before finishing the 17-mile run. It was a brilliant strategy.

When some people hear the words 'race strategy' they think of psych-out tricks, feigning weaknesses or fatigue, or feigning strength, all of which are part of the psychological world of track runners, who utilise every possible weapon to cause an opponent to worry, or to plant a seed of complacency. Races on the track can evolve into strategic as well as tactical warfare.

Except among the top triathletes, the psyching-out that occurs in a triathlon is rare. Even among the best it is used sparingly, if at all. The triathlon is much more a battle with the elements, the distances and one-self, than a struggle with the opposition.

Naturally this is an oversimplification, for 'psych-out jobs' do take place. At the 1983 Ironman, for instance, Dave Scott used a psych-out job on his younger, though outstandingly fit rival, Scott Tinley. Scott, a fantastic swimmer, had led Tinley by seven minutes after the 2.4 mile swim. But Tinley had flown on the bike course, moving up inexorably from 10th place to second, and closing the seven-minute lead Scott had had at the start of the bike race. Rather than speed up in the waning miles of the 112-mile bike race, Scott elected to *slow down*, let Tinley pass him, and hope to unnerve the younger challenger by blasting him at the start of the marathon.

Scott wanted to make Tinley think he had blown it by pushing so hard on the bike course. He let Tinley go by him on the bike, and then he did in fact storm past him early in the run. The idea of planting doubt in Tinley's mind worked exceedingly well. Scott quickly erased the 60 second deficit early in the run, and by the 10-mile point, he had built up a three minute lead. But he would begin to pay for his hard pace later, and Tinley would slowly begin to close the gap. Tinley eventually reached within 33 seconds of Scott before running out of time.

Tinley confesses that he waited too long to begin his kick. Scott also acknowledged that, had the race been 100 yards further, he might not have been able to hold on. That 33 seconds separated the two after 141 miles is astounding, less than one third of a second per mile. The psych-out in this case may well have worked. At other times, it might backfire. Among the top contenders, it is naturally one more weapon at their disposal, something to help nose out talented challengers. But for the vast majority of triathletes, this form of psych-out requires more energy than it is worth.

You are racing, of course, against the clock more than against anyone in particular. It is a fact that it is wise to *slow down* at the end of the swim, preferably switching to a side-stroke or breast-stroke for the final 30–50 metres, for that enables the blood that has been concentrated in the arms and upper part of the body to circulate more evenly throughout the body. By slowing down, you will only lose a few seconds, and in the process you make standing up after the swim much easier.

If anyone wants to sprint past you at the end of a swim, let them go. If they want to sprint past you towards their bike, let them. The few seconds spared here become meaningless as the race wears on. 'In an ultra distance triathlon, you should never go anaerobic,' observed Frank Shorter, the Olympic Gold Medal winner of the 1972 Olympics in Munich, while watching the Ironman. 'The way to win is to stay aerobic the whole way. Instead of going for the lead, you let the lead come to you as your competition drops off.'

At the 1984 London triathlon Kevin Gill was the penultimate swimmer out of the water. Since he is an aerobics instructor, he runs well but had only just begun to learn how to swim. The mile had taken him 56 minutes. But by the time the race had ended, he had passed 182 people on the 35 mile cycle course and 7 mile run, and had managed to finish a respectable 118th. He was happy, and said he would have to work on his swimming.

Passing people is a lot more fun than being passed. It is better, in this case, to take from someone than to receive. Refuse to believe anyone who tells you differently. Being passed in a race, whoever you are, is not as enjoyable as passing someone else. Some people, it is true, are not fazed *as much* when being passed as others but during a race, any race, the mind enjoys it when the body moves ahead of someone else, and does not enjoy someone else moving out ahead.

Juliet Smith, in that same London triathlon, was the first woman out of the Royal Victoria docks, and the fifth person out of the water overall. But she had been passed by more than a hundred people by the start of the run and, apart

163

from feeling physically ill, the mental disillusionment of being passed by so many (in stark contrast to Gill's experience) led to her retiring before the run began.

It takes a lot of experience and patience to realise that it does not mean too much to be passed early in an endurance activity such as the triathlon. Passing someone at the end of the race is where it counts. It is infinitely more enjoyable and satisfying also to pass someone on the run than it is on the transition between the swim and the bike. Smart triathletes will finish the swim in good shape, not too far back from their desired goals (if possible). Yet position at this point is irrelevant. The important thing, when leaving the water, is to be psychologically well-off.

To stumble out of the water, fatigued and shattered, as if you are the lone survivor from a shipwreck twenty miles off the coast, and when there are still hours of biking and running ahead, is not healthy. But leaving the water behind still psychologically fresh is a tremendous advantage. Experienced triathletes often cite this lesson: do not kill yourself in the swim, or in the early stages of the race. Find your comfortable pace, and 'float, coast, and shuffle'. Let your body shift into warp-speed later on. In terms of pain, the midway point of a triathlon is around the middle of the run, or the last event.

Getting Organised

Assuming you have selected, and registered for an upcoming race, say, four weeks away, you should in the next few weeks think about the game plan you want to follow. Is your aim to finish the race? Is it to finish ahead of half the other competitors or would you merely like to finish healthy? Would you like to challenge for your age-group championship? Is your aim to improve or is your aim to win the race? Or do you just want to see if you can do it? Once you have decided what sort of race it will be, then begin to focus on what your time splits might be. You want to draw sweat, not blood!

With your training eventually winding down, you should have, by this point, a good idea of what you will be doing on the race day. Most triathlons start early in the morning, so, if you are a late sleeper, you will either have to begin acclimatising yourself to earlier rising in the days or weeks before the race or miss the swim. When possible, it's a good idea to go over all your equipment the day before the race as thoroughly as possible. The bike is the most important item. Breakdowns on the bike can lead to psychological breakdowns shortly thereafter.

You might also find it useful to attach your running number to the front of your running singlet, your cycling number to the top rear of your cycling shorts (if you wear them), and, if distributed, numbers for your bike. If it is going to be an excessively hot day, you may choose to run without a running vest, if that is allowed. If you do this, then pin your running number to the front of your shorts. At the same time trim any excess paper away from the number, but if the sponsors' names are on it, be careful.

Many triathletes now change at their bikes. It saves a few seconds, and seems to excite the crowd and the media cameras. It is astounding how many pictures of rear ends have made it into journals and newspapers next to stories about the triathlons; it is almost as if they have never seen bottoms before! They view it as a sort of heresy, yet they lap it up. Women spectators particularly. 'Wait don't take a picture yet,' one 55 year old grandmother was heard to say at one triathlon just as one triathlete began to take his shirt off. 'It'll get better.' Most race organisers provide a changing facility, either a locker-room or a marquee. But locker-rooms can become tremendously crowded during a race.

Finding the right strategy is an individual matter. It has to suit the individual competitor's own needs. It would be pointless to prescribe here a definitive race strategy. Experience, trial, error, and simply knowing what your body is capable of, are the best guides to follow.

If you already have a competitive background in running, swimming or biking, you are already at an advantage: you understand the need to pace yourself, and have an idea what it feels like to be running on 'empty'. Bikers, particularly, know the 'bonk', and runners, the much-heralded 'wall'.

Strategies need not be complex, calculated formulae. The simplest plans are usually the best. But, in general, you want to devise a strategy in which you do not peak too early in the race, nor too late, but somewhere during the latter half of the run, the toughest part of the race. If you find you have a lot of energy left and the run is beyond the midway point, then you can start pushing even harder.

In a triathlon with a 1-mile swim, 50-mile bike ride, and 10-mile run, you should peak somewhere between miles five and nine on the run, and hope your momentum will carry you through to the finish line. Peter Moysey says he rarely has anything left in the last half mile of a race. He has long since reached his peak, and pleas from the crowd for him to run faster go unanswered.

A strong finish is unquestionably an awe-inspiring sight. It brings forth images of vast human strength. In the triathlon, however, a fast finishing kick is rarely seen, or needed. Except for the short-course races, fast kicks are rare. The triathlon is a race of endurance, and stamina. The race is more often than not settled a mile or more before the finish. To win a race by less than 20 seconds is rare. The most aerobically fit and mentally tough athletes who can push their bodies through prolonged periods of endurance and agony are the ones who are going to be the most successful.

Pleasure in pain is one of modern society's least understood and most under-rated sensations. Pain has acquired a negative connotation, and is regarded as bad or harmful. There is, however, much to be said in favour of the body's and the mind's love of pain. There is, for example, an appreciable degree of pain in sex. Rock musicians and singers also try to capture the emotion in pain when they squint their eyes, grit their teeth, and pretend they are in agony. Of course, it is usually merely an act; they are only portraying their imagined idea of what pain is, but the audience does not mind. They are fascinated by the image of pain, real or imagined.

'The most successful race strategy is based on the ability to finish relatively strong and to cope with the stresses encountered in the final stages of the race,' writes Brooks Johnson, a track coach at Stanford University, California. 'Assuming you accept the belief that excellence in the latter stages of the race is the best approach, it is imperative to recognise that it is in those latter stages that the pressures on the mind and body are the greatest. This is where the resolve begins to dissolve. This is where doubt tends to dominate. This is where the body begs for relief. Yet despite all these negatives, the proper strategy will help carry you through to the finish.'

Simulating the conditions of the latter portions of the race can be recreated in a work-out by doing high-intensity work-outs back-to-back. If you ride 30–40 fast hilly miles, followed by, say, a hard 10-mile run, and then perhaps by 1600 metres in the pool as fast as you can swim, your body will be learning how to function without much energy, and while in pain. If you can successfully train your mind to tolerate that degree of agony, and keep your pace faster than your normal race pace, you cannot help but notice improvement in your next race.

By occasionally duplicating as well as possible the conditions of the race you're planning for, you can anticipate good results in most cases when the race arrives. Of course, you do not want to leave your best race in practice, and you do not want to do as taxing a work-out as that within two weeks of a race; but by challenging your cardiovascular system, and your energy reserves, by faster-paced (though shorter) distances, you can successfully condition the mind. That is the key to success at the end of the triathlon. It is not necessarily the strongest bodies, nor the fittest, nor the fastest runners or best bikers who win. It is often the athlete with the strongest mind, the greatest determination to push on when the body would vote to push off. Mental toughness is as important to success in the triathlon, if not more important, than physical toughness.

Finding the right pace, be it in the water, on the bike, or during the run, is crucial. On shorter courses, in which the winners finish in under two hours, you can obviously push harder than in an ultra triathlon, where it takes the winners nine hours. But still the key in any race is to stay well within your aerobic capacity. For once the body slips over the theoretical threshold of 'anaerobic', that is to say the body metabolises 'without oxygen' and is using up its oxygen supply in the blood to remove the built-up lactic acid rather than using oxygen breathed in, it is a body in trouble. Burning energy anaerobically is many times more inefficient than burning aerobically.

Imagine a finely-tuned engine: it purrs comfortably along, burning a minimal amount of petrol, mixing oxygen and fuel with a tiny spark to coast along. But if you put your foot down hard on the accelerator, suddenly the consumption mileage drops off. The motor is no longer working as efficiently. It has to work harder and faster to burn the energy supply, much like the muscles of the body. Without a doubt you move faster, but the efficiency falls dramatically and you certainly will not last as long. You have to find the happy medium, the fine line between too fast and too slow. It is not always easy to find; trial and error, and a sixth sense are the only ways to know where your pace is most efficient.

Don't Look Back

Although it is tempting to turn around and have a look to see where your competition is, do not do it. You not only waste a split second, you waste energy, interrupt your stride slightly, and worst of all, you sent a tacit signal to the person trying to catch you that you are struggling. A fatigued athlete behind needs only the slightest hint that the 'game' he or she has been stalking for miles is fading and ready for the kill. Immense reserves of energy can be tapped, once you have given the game away. It is only natural to want to know where you stand, of course, particularly during the run when many a good swim and bike ride are rendered worthless by a feeble run. But whatever you do, do not turn around.

On curves it is possible to catch a quick, unnoticeable glimpse out of the corner of your eye. Or, while turning your head to a side to spit, you can catch a quick look behind you. But never turn around completely. You might as well pull out a white flag.

The time you waste, incidentally, by looking back behind you has been calculated to be one half second for each glance. The time loss stems from the slightly shortened stride you take when looking back. So if you have lost the race or a desired place by five seconds, and turned around a dozen times, you will know what to blame.

Catching an occasional glimpse behind you on the bike is not quite as damaging. It probably will not help, however. But if it is done discreetly, while looking underneath your armpit, or blowing your nose, or glancing backwards while spitting, the foe behind should not be fed any advantage. The chances of a biker's eyes transfixed on your head are not as great as on the run. Bikers have so many other things to worry about. Fatigued runners have often one-tracked minds:

their sole target is the back of the head of the person shuffling in front of them.

The key on the bike is to sneak the look when least expected. It is when you sense someone gaining on you from behind and sit up and twist your shoulders around, and offer anguished gazes, that the opposition will spring to life with newfound vigour. Like a vulture, the triathlete feeds off fading opponents.

This is perhaps why the occasional glimpse around in the swim is the least damaging. Who cares, after all, who is in front of you or catching you in the swim, the aim is just to get out of the water as fast as possible. Rather than look for dying foes in the swim, it is advisable to find someone who swims your speed, or perhaps slightly faster, and keep up with them.

Julie Moss, who swims a mile in 20 minutes, is forever on the hunt for slightly faster swimmers. Without someone pulling her along, physically, with a trail of bubbles, and psychologically motivating her to push, she feels she does not swim nearly as fast as she is capable of doing.

'You want to try to stay with a fast group in a race,' she explains. 'They really push themselves, and it makes you work hard to catch them at the start and stay up with them. Because once you lose contact with them, you're out of it, and you'll lose a couple of minutes per mile. But if you can keep up with them, swim in their trails, and not have to worry about sighting, you can swim some pretty good times.'

The psychological aspects of the triathlon, and any endurance activity, offer some of its most fascinating moments. Because so little is still understood about why it feels so good, why endurance athletes experience 'second winds' and other emotional highs, why swimming with faster swimmers makes you swim faster when swimming at that pace alone seems to beyond your outer limit, these problems, once stated, can only serve as a springboard for your interest and your understanding of strategy.

In any event, there are psychological games that you can play that may help. For instance, when you are exhausted on the run, if you run on a pavement or verge (if one is available), it will make you feel you are moving faster. Psychologically, especially at this crucial point in the race, running on a narrower strip rather than on a wide road, can provide a big, and much needed lift. You may discover other tactics that makes the distances more attainable – that is part of the fun of the triathlon: *You are the boss!*

Epilogue

What makes the triatholon such an enthralling, absorbing sport? There is an intangible aspect to the whole spirit of the triathlon, a sort of closely-knit kinship that often develops among triathletes which is hard to describe in words, but is palpable to all who are involved.

There are young triathletes, there are old triathletes. There are healthy triathletes, there are poor triathletes. There are triathletes who come together to have a good time, there are others who come to win, and there are yet others who come to challenge their own outer limits. The common denominators are the bathing suits, the bikes, and the running shoes. Anyone can come, and this, indeed, may be a big part of the delightful atmosphere that is associated with the sport. It is about as democratic a sport as one can find in Europe.

There are triathletes with all sorts of different backgrounds, different reasons for participating, and different goals. There is fortunately, no one particular mould or stereotype, or birthright connected with the sport. Anyone who dares can do it.

Appendices

Appendix 1

WEEKLY SCHEDULE

DATE	W/E	AIM:		
	Weather	Programme	Diet	Sleep(hrs)
Monday				
Tuesday				
Wednesday				
Thursday				
Friday				
Saturday				
Sunday				

WEEKLY TOTAL

WEEK NO:
COMMENT

SWIM } miles sprints		
BIKE } miles flat/hills sprints		
RUN miles		
WEIGHTS sessions		
YOGA time		
MENTAL REHEARSAL time		
SLEEP time		
CALORIFIC INTAKE		
WEIGHT		
BODY FAT		
PULSE (RESTING)		
ILLNESS		
INJURY		
ASSESSMENT OF AIMS		

MONTHLY SCHEDULE

	DIET	SLEEP	INJURY & ILLNESS
January			
February			
March			
April			
May			
June			
July			
August			
September			
October			
November			
December			

Appendix 1

MONTHLY SCHEDULE

	Swim	Bike	Run	Weights	Yoga	Mental Rehearsal	Competitions
January							
February							
March							
April							
May							
June							
July							
August							
September							
October							
November							
December							

PERSONAL BESTS

SWIM

50 m

100 m

400 m

800 m

1 mile

2 miles

2.4 miles

BIKE

5 miles

10 miles

25 miles

50 miles

100 miles

112 miles

RUN

6 miles

10 km

10 miles

20 km

½ marathon

20 miles

Marathon

TRAINING SCHEDULE USED FOR TRIATHLON September 1982

NAME Aleck Hunter

	SWIMMING			CYCLING			RUNNING		
DAY	DIS	TIM	REMARKS	DIS	TIM	REMARKS	DIS	TIM	REMARKS
1	¾			18			6		
2	1½		O.K.						
3							12		
4	1½		Steady	18					
5				18			5		
6	1½			34			8		
7				18			5		
8	1.2						5		
9	1½			18			8		
10				18			10		
11	1½						8		
12							14		Steady
13	1½		Steady	34		Fast	8		Steady
14				18			8		
15	1½	1.15					8		Steady
16		50m		18	53	Fast	12		Fast
17			Rest			Rest			Rest
18							3½		Jog
19							26.2	3.20	Canvey Marathon
20				38		Steady			
21	1½	1.15	O.K.				5		Steady
22	1.2	45m	Sluggish	15		Slow			
23	1	42m	O.K.		45m	Rollers	11	1½	Poor
24	1.2	56m	Steady				9	1.04	
25			Rest			Rest			Rest
26	1.2	52.2		68			18		
27	¾			8					
28	1½		Training				6+7		Bruised Fib/Tib and Ankle
29	1.2			18			6		
30				12			5+10		Severe bruising Fib/Tib. Stopped Running – injury

Monthly Totals   Swimming 23 miles   Cycling 371 miles   Running 223 miles
Weekly Average   Swimming 5¾ miles   Cycling 93 miles   Running 55 miles

N.B. Lack of understanding and personal listening to body. Poor notes. Injury inevitable.

Age 45   Height 5' 10½"   Weight 168 lb

The authors do *not* recommend you to copy this example. It is published here to give you an idea of how a triathlete began to keep a personal record.

TRAINING SCHEDULE FOR TRIATHLON (two years on)

NAME   Aleck Hunter   MONTH August 1984

DAY	SWIMMING DIS	TIM	REMARKS	CYCLING DIS	TIM	REMARKS	RUNNING DIS	TIM	REMARKS
1	1½ ml		A. ½m warm up 4 × 250	22 m.	1–10	A. Need more training	3½		A.
2	¾	38m	AM – Ilford / PM – Barking/cold			No time available			No time
3	1¼		Outdoor still cold slightly hypothermic	19		Lunchtime. Hilly course. Above A.	4¼		No improvement
4	1 ml		outdoor improvement felt	½ hr	Turbo T	Weak riding need more time	6		A. Tried Int. Unsuccessful
5	1.6	52 m	Barking open water cold acclimatising	52 m		Slow. P.	16		Steady run. Cannot catch up
6						REST DAY			
7	1¼		Open water. Beginning to enjoy cold	31		Morning ride	4½		Round Park
8	½ 1¼		Morning / Evening 4×10×50m	24		P. This is now a problem 1 mth too short	3¾		Ditto cycling too few miles early year
9	1¼		Open water G	18		P. Carry over fatigue must rest and tomorrow to avoid injury			
10	1½ 1		Indoor swim only today. Did not feel so bad by the evening. Outdoor						
11	1½		Outdoor. G.				4½		A little better twinge right PT muscle
12	¾		Outdoor pool crowded. Bad training	54m		Fair. Rest helped	14		Pain from pronating must take care
13	1		Swim only. No training. This injury problem must be watched, decrease weekly mileage, keep one long run						
14	1½		Indoor. Intervals 3×10×50m			REST			REST
15	1¼		Outdoor Intervals	32		Morning ride slightly better			REST
16	1		Tested Royal Vic. Doc for Sunday		30 m	Rollers	6		Steady
17	1½		Barking. G.	18		G.	12		Steady – leg better
18	1		Indoor						
19			Race Directed London Triathlon – Started 5.15 am						
20			No training. Fatigue from day before	4½				Steady	
21	¾ 1		Indoor Steady A / Outdoor steady G	26		Morning A	8¼	1 hr	G. No problem from legs
22	2	70 m	Outdoor cold OK	18		Hilly ride A	4		A
23	1	30.5m	G. outdoor cold				4		A. Feeling better
24	1¼		Steady outdoor		30m	Turbo training weak			REST
25	1¼		Int 4×10×50m			REST			REST
26	1		P. Crowded pool	55m		Steady. Some F.	14		Steady run Knee pain
27	REST			62m		Felt yesterday but OK			REST
28	1½		Outdoor steady			REST	6		A. Tried Ints but Tibial pain
29	1½		Outdoor 6×10×50m Ints	18m	53m	Felt Good			Pain in Tibia. No running today, sure it will be OK
30	1½		Outdoor 6×10×50m Ints				8	57m	G. Running steady
31		1 hour	Outdoor. G. but cold	26		Hilly – felt comfortable			

Months Totals
Weekly Average
Terminology:

Swimming 36¼   Cycling 505   Running 123¼
Swimming 9–06   Cycling 126   Running 30–81
G = Good   M = Muscle   I = Cold/Flu/Fever
A = Average   P = Pull   F = Fartlek/Interval Training
P = Below Average   T = Tear/Strain   E.T. = Steady Endurance
                                         PT = Posteria Tibial

A. Month. Trying to get in condition for Nice. Needed more time for this.
Date Aimed for 8th Sept. 'Nice'
Age 47   Height 5' 10½"   Weight 168lb

TRAINING SCHEDULE FOR TRIATHLON

NAME Sarah Springman

DATE	WEEK ENDING 10/2/85	AIM: Increase longest run to 15 miles Speedwork – pool Increase distance – bike		
	Weather	Programme	Diet	Sleep
Monday 4th	Overcast warm	Swim: 3000m inc 16 × 100m on 1:40 400m catch up, 400m legs, 400m arms. Run: 8 miles, 6 × 5 mins hard with 3 mins jog recovery. Weights: Increase reps to 10.3x	Muesli & skim milk, 4 Fruit, 2 granary rolls & cheese & salad. Quiche, potato, carrots & spinach.	7
Tuesday 5th	Raining	Swim: 2800m inc 400m warm up, 4 × 400m on 7m30s, 2 × 200m on 3m30s. Bike: 30 miles steady on exercise bike. Yoga; ½ hour	Muesli & skim milk, Yoghurt and fruit, Granary bread, taramasalata & tomatoes. Pasta & bolognese, salad.	7½
Wednesday 6th	Clear breezy	Swim: 320m with T.shirt 400m warm up, 8 × 200m on 3m30s, 400m legs with fins, 400m arms with paddles. 400m warm down. Run: 3 mile warm up, 8 × 400m on 2m15s, 2 mile warm down. Weights: 3 × 10 reps	Muesli & skim milk, Granary bread, fish, salad. Rice (brown), liver, onions, broccoli.	7
Thursday 7th	Sunny warm	Swim: club sprint session followed by 4 × 200m, 4 × 100m, 4 × 66m, 4 × 33m. Total: 320m. Bike: 10 mile warm up, 20 × 1 min with 1 min recovery, 10 miles warm down. Yoga: 1 hour	Muesli & skim milk, 5 fruit. Granary bread, pate, salad. Baked potato, fish, cabbage, carrots.	7½
Friday 8th	Freezing cold!	Swim: 3200m nonstop, steady 55 min. Run: 8 miles, steady, 7 min pace. Weights: 3 × 10 reps.	Muesli & skim milk. Lentil soup & yoghurt. Fruit, cheese. Pasta and veg. sauce.	7½
Saturday 9th	Windy! cold	run; 15 miles, steady. Hills 7 min pace. Stretching: ½ hour. Bike: 30 miles, hard with club.	Muesli & skim milk, orange, apple. Granary bread, pate, salad, banana. Baked potato, spinach, chicken.	8½
Sunday 10th	Fine chilly	Bike: 75 miles, steady, hills. Yoga: ½ hour. Mental Rehearsal: 1 hour	Muesli & skim milk. Toast, honey. 3 bananas. Roast beef etc, sprouts, potatoes, gravy, apple pie.	8½

Age 28   Height 6' 0½"   Weight 161 lb

American College of Sports Medicine Guidelines for the Prevention of Heat Injury

1 Distance races (longer than 16 km or 10 miles) should not be conducted when the wet bulb temperature/globe temperature exceeds 28°C (82.4°F).
2 During periods of the year when the daylight dry bulb temperature often exceeds 27°C (80°F), distance races should be conducted before 9 a.m. or after 4 p.m.
3 It is the responsibility of the race sponsors to provide fluids which contain small amounts of sugar (less than 2.5g glucose per 100 m water) and electrolytes (less than 10 mEq ounces) of fluid before competition.
4 Runners should be encouraged to ingest fluids frequently during competition and to consume 400 to 500 m. (13 to 17 ounces) of fluid before competition.
5 Rules prohibiting the administration of fluids during the first 10 km of a marathon race should be amended to permit fluid ingestion at frequent intervals along the race course. In light of the high sweat rates and body temperatures during distance running in the heat race sponsors should provide 'water stations' at 3–4 km intervals for all races of 16 km or longer.
6 Runners should be instructed on how to recognise the early-warning symptoms that precede heat injury. Recognition of symptoms, cessation of running and proper treatment can prevent heat injury. Early warning symptoms include the following: piloerection on chest and upper arms, chilling, throbbing pressure in head, un-steadiness, nausea, and dry skin.
7 Race sponsors should make prior arrangements with medical personnel for the care of cases of heat injury. Responsible and informed personnel should supervise each 'feeding station'. Organisational personnel should reserve the right to stop runners who exhibit clear signs of heat stroke or heat exhaustion.

Harvard Step Test

A method of testing cardiovascular fitness is the Harvard Step Test. You need a bench about 20 inches (50 cm) high; a small chair may suffice. If you are doing this at home, it may be advisable to do it in the garden. The test involves stepping up and down (ensuring that you fully extend the knee each time) thirty times a minute for a period of four minutes. It is helpful to use a metronome, or to ask someone to time you with a watch. The test is quite strenuous, so it is best to stop if you experience chest pains or acute difficulty in breathing. People who are much too fat, or who have a history of heart trouble should not try it at all.

After four minutes – or earlier if you have had to stop – you should sit quietly and take your pulse after one minute, two minutes, and three minutes, each time measuring it over 30 seconds.

It is then possible to work out your recovery index (RI) as follows:

$$RI = \frac{\text{duration of exercise in seconds} \times 100}{\text{sum of pulse counts} \times 2}$$

If your RI is 60 or less, your rating is poor

61–70	fair
71–80	good
81–90	very good
91 or more	excellent

If neither of these tests have put you off altogether, the next stage is to pay a visit to a specialist running shop.

Physical Benefits of the Triathlon

In the mid 1970s, the President's Council of Physical Fitness and Sports asked seven exercise experts to rank various forms of popular exercise in terms of their benefits

Physical Fitness	*Running*	*Bicycling*	*Swimming*	*Handball and Squash*	*Tennis*	*Walking*	*Golf*	*Boules*
Cardiorespiratory endurance	21	19	21	19	16	13	8	5
Muscular endurance	20	18	20	18	16	14	8	5
Muscular strength	17	16	14	15	14	11	9	5
Flexibility	9	18	15	16	14	7	8	7
Balance	17	18	12	17	16	8	8	6
General Well Being								
Weight control	21	20	15	19	16	13	6	5
Muscle definition	14	15	14	11	13	11	6	5
Digestion	13	12	13	13	12	11	7	7
Sleep	16	15	16	12	11	14	6	6
Total	148	142	140	140	128	102	66	51

towards cardiorespiratory endurance, muscular endurance, muscular strength, flexibility, balance, general well-being, weight control, muscle definition, digestion, and sleep. As you can clearly see for yourself, the triathlon was a clear cut winner even before swimming, running and cycling were even strung together into a sport.

Each one of the authorities were able to award anything from 0 points (no benefit) up to three points (maximum benefit), so that a score of 21 was the maximum an activity could score on any one count

Source: *The Complete Book of Running*, James F. Fixx p. 39

Appendix 3

Results

WINNING TIMES OF THE IRONMAN

1st Place – Men

	Name	*Swim*	*Bike*	*Run*	*Total Time*
1978	Gordon Haller	–	–	–	11:46:58
1979	Tom Warren	1:06:15	6:19	3:51	11:15:56
1980	Dave Scott	0:51:00	5:03	3:30:33	9:24:33
1981	John Howard	1:11:12	5:03:29	3:23:48	9:38:29
Feb. 1982	Scott Tinley	1:10:45	5:05:11	3:03:45	9:19:41
Oct. 1982	Dave Scott	0:50:52	5:10:16	3:07:15	9:08:23
1983	Dave Scott	0:50:52	5:10:48	3:04:16	9:05:57
1984	Dave Scott	0:50:21.4	5:10:59.1	2:53:00.2	8:54:20.7
1985					

1st Place – Women

	Name	*Swim*	*Bike*	*Run*	*Total Time*
1978	–	–	–	–	–
1979	Lyn Lemaire	1:16:20	6:30	5:10	12:55:38
1980	Robin Beck	1:20	6:05	3:56:24	11:21:24
1981	Linda Sweeney	1:02:07	6:53:28	4:04:57	12:00:32
Feb. 1982	Kathleen McCartney	1:32:00	5:51:12	3:46:28	11:09:40
Oct. 1982	Julie Leach	1:04:57	5:50:36	3:58:35	10:54:08
1983	Sylviane Puntous	1:00:28	6:20:40	3:22:28	10:43:36
1984	Sylviane Puntous	1:00:45.2	5:50:36.7	3:33:51.4	10:25:13.3
1985					

1985 Qualifying Times

A finish time in the 1984 Ironman Triathlon World Championship in the following age-group categories automatically qualified a participant for the 1985 Ironman.

Men			*Women*	
18–24	11:20		18–24	11:30
25–29	11:05		25–29	11:45
30–34	11:20		30–34	12:15
35–39	11:35		35–39	12:15
40–44	12:15		40–44	13:15
45–49	12:30		45–49	15:00
50–54	13:15		50–54	17:00
55–59	15:30		55–59	17:00
60+	16:15		60+	17:00

BUD LIGHT IRONMAN TRIATHLON WORLD CHAMPIONSHIP 1984

Top 20 Men

Place	Name	Nationality	Age	Total	Swim	Bike	Run
1	Scott, Dave F	USA	30	08:54:20.7	00:50:21.4	5:10:59.1	2:53:00.2
2	Tinley, Scott P	USA	27	09:18:45.0	00:55:54.7	5:18:52.6	3:03:57.7
3	Boswell, Grant C	USA	24	09:23:55.5	00:53:07.2	5:15:04.2	3:15:44.1
4	Barel, Rob R	Netherlands	26	09:27:11.6	00:53:03.8	5:10:22.4	3:23:45.4
5	Allen, Mark G	USA	26	09:35:02:8	00:50:22.1	4:59:21.4	3:45:19.3
6	Howard, John K	USA	37	09:38:39.3	01:07:52.9	4:56:49.1	3:33:57.3
7	Evans, David S	USA	23	09:43:55:8	00:59:00.6	5:21:32.0	3:23:23.2
8	Hinshaw, Chris E	USA	21	09:48:49.3	00:49:07.1	5:20:26.3	3:39:15.9
9	Sine, Steve M	USA	32	09:56:21.2	01:03:03.1	5:39:07.1	3:14:11.0
10	Skultety, Scott J	USA	34	09:59:02.5	00:58:45.8	5:33:37.7	3:26:39.0
11	Clifton, Eric V	USA	26	10:04:08.9	01:05:33.1	5:32:21.5	3:26:14.3
12	Mul, Nico N	Netherlands	38	10:04:31.3	01:09:53.8	5:35:15.5	3:19:22.0
13	Morath, Karl-Heinz	West Germany	30	10:05:32.7	01:05:27.7	5:31:43.1	3:28:21.9
14	Blaschke, Hannes	West Germany	24	10:12:21.1	01:03:36.5	5:19:25.8	3:49:18.8
15	Thomas, Duncan A	USA	35	10:13:14.5	00:56:05.0	5:29:30.0	3:47:39.5
16	Kraft, Mike T	USA	28	10:14:42.4	00:56:02.2	5:38:03.2	3:40:37.0
17	Nakayama, Toshiyuki	Japan	21	10:16:02.4	01:05:40.8	5:54:34.8	3:15:46.8
18	Seymour, Don J	USA	26	10:16:02.8	01:01:19.1	5:49:32.6	3:34:11.1
19	Kinlaw, Knox W	USA	23	10:16:35.7	01:03:09.6	5:43:53.3	3:29:32.8
20	Nihot, Ronald R	Netherlands	27	10:17:52.4	01:04:42.7	5:23:26.7	3:49:43.0

BUD LIGHT IRONMAN TRIATHLON WORLD CHAMPIONSHIPS 1984

Top 20 Women

Place	Name	Nationality	Age	Time	Swim	Bike	Run
1	Sylviane Puntous	Canada	23	10.25.13	60.45	5.50.45	3.33.51*
2	Patricia Puntous	Canada	23	10.27.28	60.51	5.50.31	3.36.05
3	Julie Ohlson	USA	24	10.38.10	60.33	5.38.00*	3.59.54
4	Joanne Ernst	USA	25	10.40.33	64.40	5.49.24	3.46.28
5	Moira Hornby	S. Africa	30	11.03.20	65.32	6.12.49	3.44.58
6	Jennifer Hinshaw	USA	23	11.05.02	50.32*	5.58.36	4.15.54
7	Juliana Harrison-Brening	USA	24	11.06.08	60.32	5.54.57	4.10.39
8	Karen Mckeachie	USA	31	11.07.37	69.11	6.10.11	3.48.13
9	Jacqueline Shaw	Canada	28	11.12.10	63.09	5.41.19	4.27.41
10	Anne Dandoy	USA	25	11.21.31	70.13	6.08.51	4.02.25
11	Sarah Springman†	England	27	11.22.24	67.00	6.09.30	4.05.54
12	Ardis Bow	USA	28	11.23.18	60.25	6.12.20	4.10.32
13	Claire Mcrae	USA	33	11.31.52	64.01	6.23.22	4.04.28
14	Leslie Landreth	USA	23	11.32.59	52.31	5.59.17	4.41.10
15	Samantha Steinbeck	USA	27	11.33.39	73.47	6.28.50	3.51.01
16	Tracy Kelly	Canada	25	11.37.33	79.50	6.22.14	3.55.28
17	Judy Glynn	USA	36	11.44.51	67.54	6.19.09	4.17.47
18	Anne Macdonnell	USA	22	11.46.49	64.44	6.17.03	4.25.02
19	Heidi Christiansen	USA	25	11.49.39	58.47	6.23.00	4.27.51
20	Shelby Hayden-Clifton	USA	24	11.52.05	82.49	6.02.02	4.27.13

† 1st European

Temperatures		Distances		SMS Ave Speed	SMS Position
Air	98°F	Swim	2.4 miles	28 min/mile	25th (app)
Tarmac	137°F	Bike	112 miles	18.2 min/mile	14th
Sea	75°F	Run	26.2 miles	9.3 min/mile	11th

Total number of starters 1153
Total number of women 155
Number in 25-29 age group 49

Sunrise: 6.24 am
Sunset: 6.15 pm
Moon: ¾ full

Transition times were approximately 3 minutes each between disciplines.
* Indicates fastest time for each discipline.

NICE TRIATHLON CHAMPIONSHIPS 1984

Top 50

			SWIM	BIKE	RUN	TOTAL
1	Mark Allen	USA	00h 42mn 45' 00"	03h 16mn 27' 00"	02h 06mn 10' 2"	06h 05mn 22' 23"
2	Dave Scott	USA	00h 41mn 24' 02"	03h 16mn 37' 98"	02h 09mn 56' 1"	06h 07mn 58' 13"
3	Scott Tinley	USA	00h 46mn 16' 00"	03h 21mn 56' 00"	02h 08mn 28' 5"	06h 16mn 40' 54"
4	Ken Glah	USA	00h 47mn 40' 00"	03h 28mn 44' 08"	02h 19mn 58' 9"	06h 36mn 22' 98"
5	Georges Hoover	USA	00h 43mn 38' 05"	03h 34mn 17' 97"	02h 25mn 58' 9"	06h 43mn 54' 92"
6	Gary Peterson	USA	00h 46mn 14' 00"	03h 24mn 56' 00"	02h 33mn 59' 7"	06h 45mn 09' 75"
7	Karl-Heinz Loot	FRG	00h 56mn 56' 00"	03h 34mn 22' 01"	02h 15mn 29' 3"	06h 46mn 47' 34"
8	David McCarney	AFS	00h 43mn 43' 05"	03h 40mn 45' 98"	02h 26mn 14' 3"	06h 50mn 43' 34"
9	Michael Schuler	FRG	00h 59mn 49' 00"	03h 23mn 47' 02"	02h 27mn 07' 3"	06h 50mn 43' 34"
10	Jorg Hofman	FRG	00h 47mn 58' 00"	03h 39mn 28' 05"	02h 24mn 41' 3"	06h 52mn 07' 44"
11	Gerhard Wachter	FRG	00h 46mn 12' 00"	03h 39mn 16' 02"	02h 27mn 16' 7"	06h 52mn 44' 72"
12	Stan Grebor	N.L.	00h 48mn 41' 02"	03h 33mn 58' 00"	02h 34mn 23' 6"	06h 57mn 02' 66"
13	Klaus Klaeren	FRG	00h 56mn 33' 00"	03h 36mn 05' 00"	02h 25mn 05' 9"	06h 57mn 44' 96"
14	Johannes Blaschke	FRG	00h 59mn 48' 00"	03h 22mn 55' 03"	02h 35mn 13' 3"	06h 57mn 56' 41"
15	Gerhard Roop	FRG	00h 56mn 35' 00"	03h 27mn 25' 01"	02h 35mn 06' 8"	07h 00mn 06' 82"
16	Colleen Cannon	USA	00h 45mn 54' 00"	03h 46mn 45' 00"	02h 32mn 36' 7"	07h 05mn 15' 73"
	1st women					
17	Julie Moss	USA	00h 51mn 00' 00"	03h 38mn 51' 07"	02h 37mn 10' 1"	07h 07mn 01' 18"
18	Mike Harris	GBR	00h 52mn 40' 00"	03h 52mn 24' 00"	02h 23mn 10' 5"	07h 08mn 14' 50"
19	Yves Cordier	FRA	00h 41mn 21' 06"	03h 30mn 10' 94"	02h 57mn 03' 3"	07h 08mn 35' 35"
20	Carl Macuiba	USA	01h 01mn 43' 04"	03h 47mn 20' 95"	02h 21mn 01' 6"	07h 10mn 05' 67"
21	Ivor Earl	GBR	01h 14mn 42' 00"	03h 34mn 47' 00"	02h 21mn 28' 1"	07h 10mn 57' 16"
22	Thomas Scheld	FRG	00h 48mn 01' 00"	03h 45mn 29' 00"	02h 37mn 29' 0"	07h 10mn 59' 08"
23	J. Claude Mosconi	FRA	00h 49mn 49' 05"	03h 47mn 16' 95"	02h 34mn 00' 1"	07h 11mn 06' 13"
24	Bill Leach	USA	00h 43mn 39' 08"	03h 27mn 53' 92"	03h 01mn 33' 5"	07h 13mn 06' 54"
25	Christopher Deplancke	FRA	00h 53mn 59' 06"	03h 37mn 18' 96"	02h 42mn 27' 2"	07h 13mn 45' 23"
26	J. Luc Capogna	FRA	00h 51mn 04' 00"	03h 32mn 55' 04"	02h 52mn 31' 8"	07h 16mn 30' 90"
27	Martin Dyer	GBR	00h 52mn 59' 00"	03h 39mn 40' 00"	02h 45mn 05' 0"	07h 17mn 44' 02"
28	Ingo Liebert	FRA	00h 46mn 13' 06"	03h 42mn 00' 98"	02h 49mn 47' 0"	07h 18mn 01' 06"
29	Georges Belaubre	FRA	00h 59mn 51' 00"	03h 37mn 14' 00"	02h 43mn 57' 5"	07h 21mn 02' 58"

#	Name					
30	Mugge Muller	SUI	00h 54mn 58' 00"	03h 49mn 59' 02"	02h 37mn 10' 8"	07h 22mn 07' 89"
31	Kevin O'Neil	GBR	01h 14mn 09' 02"	03h 48mn 37' 98"	02h 20mn 59' 6"	07h 23mn 45' 68"
32	Desmond McHenry	IRL	01h 03mn 54' 00"	03h 41mn 08' 00"	02h 39mn 11' 4"	07h 24mn 13' 43"
33	Jorg Ullman	FRG	00h 53mn 59' 00"	03h 50mn 43' 00"	02h 41mn 41' 2"	07h 26mn 23' 20"
34	Gordon Nowak	FRG	01h 01mn 13' 00"	03h 54mn 53' 00"	02h 30mn 17' 2"	07h 26mn 23' 20"
35	Gerd Uhren	FRG	01h 04mn 47' 00"	03h 51mn 20' 00"	02h 30mn 16' 2"	07h 26mn 23' 20"
36	Elain Alrutz	USA	00h 50mn 52' 09"	03h 46mn 13' 91"	02h 50mn 56' 1"	07h 28mn 02' 12"
37	David Petrie	USA	00h 56mn 03' 00"	03h 42mn 01' 00"	02h 50mn 19' 6"	07h 28mn 23' 60"
38	Frans Jansen	N.L.	00h 55mn 53' 00"	03h 49mn 10' 00"	02h 43mn 37' 4"	07h 28mn 40' 41"
39	Jann Girard	USA	00h 43mn 48' 02"	03h 46mn 33' 06"	02h 58mn 47' 5"	07h 29mn 08' 62"
40	Jean-Pierre Crohon	FRA	01h 12mn 56' 01"	03h 51mn 35' 99"	02h 25mn 48' 2"	07h 30mn 20' 27"
41	Colomby Michel	FRA	01h 13mn 37' 00"	03h 44mn 17' 00"	02h 32mn 37' 4"	07h 30mn 31' 44"
42	Jean-Pierre Desfaudes	FRA	01h 11mn 34' 09"	03h 57mn 56' 91"	02h 21mn 52' 7"	07h 31mn 23' 73"
43	Herve Cousty	FRA	01h 09mn 08' 02"	03h 48mn 47' 98"	02h 33mn 54' 9"	07h 31mn 50' 96"
44	Henri Boulanger	FRA	01h 01mn 53' 00"	03h 54mn 44' 00"	02h 35mn 38' 5"	07h 32mn 15' 51"
45	Denis Tassel	USA	01h 10mn 48' 00"	03h 40mn 59' 00"	02h 40mn 30' 3"	07h 32mn 17' 39"
46	Julie Olson	USA	00h 51mn 31' 08"	03h 55mn 02' 92"	02h 45mn 57' 1"	07h 32mn 31' 15"
47	Jim Edens	USA	01h 01mn 09' 00"	03h 55mn 25' 00"	02h 37mn 19' 6"	07h 33mn 53' 64"
48	Steve Griffith	USA	00h 52mn 48' 00"	03h 39mn 38' 00"	03h 03mn 27' 9"	07h 35mn 53' 92"
49	Goot Schep	N.L.	01h 18mn 15' 08"	03h 39mn 56' 92"	02h 38mn 18' 3"	07h 36mn 30' 34"
50	Sarah Springman	GBR	01h 02mn 07' 06"	03h 57mn 31' 94"	02h 37mn 23' 5"	07h 37mn 02' 59"

BRITISH & EUROPEAN TRIATHLON CHAMPIONSHIP
29 JULY 1984

Results

Position	Name	Overall Time	1m Swim Time	78m Cycle Time	17.5 Run Time
1	Klaus Klaeren	6–03–04	24m 25s	3–42–32	1–49–19
2	Martin Dyer	6–08–33	21m 36s	3–29–08	2–11–17
3	Ivor Earl	6–10–49	29m 39s	3–45–22	1–51–39
4	Mike Harris	6–12–25	23m 40s	3–49–39	1–56–33
5	Andy Priddis	6–21–27	22m 35s	3–54–34	2–02–04
6	Jim Wood	6–29–52	25m 41s	3–58–23	2–03–13
7	Mark Kleanthous	6–30–23	26m 24s	4–00–29	2–00–50
8	David Poulter	6–34–47	21m 49s	3–58–20	2–11–31
9	Daniel Guy	6–36–12	35m 09s	3–47–06	2–07–04
10	Bernie Shrosbree	6–37–31	24m 18s	4–01–44	2–05–58

BRITISH & EUROPEAN TRIATHLON CHAMPIONSHIP
29 JULY 1984

Swim 1 mile : Bike 78m : Run 17.5m

Women

			S	B	R
1	Sarah Springman	6.56.34	23.59	4.08.56	2.22.04
2	Fran Ashmole	7.00.32	27.48	4.14.04	2.11.40
3	Caron Groves	7.23.55	33.18	4.16.54	2.18.55
4	Josie May	7.39.18	24.07	4.22.35	2.52.32
5	Regina Schwarz	7.58.14	25.59	4.50.19	2.30.45

LONDON TRIATHLON 1984

Top Ten Men and Women

1	02:46:10	Glenn Cook	03:09:17	F. Ashmole
2	02:47:13	Peter Moysey	03:14:34	Ms Kirk
3	02:51:19	Mark Kleanthous	03:17:41	Caron Groves
4	02:52:44	John Groves	03:20:24	Penny deMoss
5	02:53:28	Steve Trew	03:24:57	Ms Cavanagh
6	02:54:14	Vernon Sharples	03:34:22	Ms Penney
7	02:55:18	Colin Bateman	03:34:39	Kathy Walsh
8	02:56:26	Mr McMenamin	03:37:48	Cathy Bow
9	02:56:37	Alan Bell	03:40:32	Ms Richardson
10	02:57:11	Malcolm Kelvie	03:43:08	Ms Roberts

Select Bibliography

Costill, David C., *A Scientific Approach to Distance Running*.
Counsilman, James, *The Science of Swimming*
Cooper, Kenneth, *Aerobics*
Fixx, James F., *The Complete Book of Running*
Fixx, James F., *Jim Fixx's Second Book of Running*
Madsen L. & Wilke K., *Das Training des jungendlichen Schwimmers*
Sisson, Mark, *Runner's World Triathlon Training Book*
Sheehan, George, *Running and Being*
Steffney, Manfred, *Lauf' mit!*
Temple, Cliff, *The Challenge of the Marathon*
Wilson, Niel et al., *The Marathon Book*
Smith, Nathan, J. M. D., *Food for Sport*
The AAA Runners Guide
Edwards, Sally, *Triathlon: A triple fitness sport*
Steffans, Thomas and Dr. Günter Lachmann. *Triathlon: Die Kröne der Ausdauer*

Magazines

Tri-Athlete, 1983, 1984
Midwest Triathlete, 1983, 1984
The Runner, 1983, 1984
Marathon and Long Distance Runner, 1983
Runner's World, 1982, 1983, 1984
Running, 1983
Spiridon: Laufmagazin, 1982, 1983, 1984
Winning, 1983, 1984
Bicycling, 1983, 1984
Sports Illustrated, 1979, 1983

Biography Index

Index

Index